OFFICIAL REPORT

OF THE

TWENTY - THIRD INTERNATIONAL

CHRISTIAN ENDEAVOR CONVENTION

HELD IN

TENT WILLISTON AND OTHER AUDITORIUMS

AND CHURCHES

SEATTLE, WASH., JULY 10-15, 1907.

First Fruits Press
Wilmore, Kentucky
c2015

First Fruits Press
The Academic Open Press of Asbury Theological Seminary
204 N. Lexington Ave., Wilmore, KY 40390
859-858-2236
first.fruits@asburyseminary.edu
asbury.to/firstfruits

Rev. W. A. Spalding, D. D.   Rev. M. A. Mathews, D. D.   John Schram   Homer L. Bull   Carl H. Reeves
Frank L. Horsfall, M. D.   F. Edgar Barth   George A. Virtue

THE SEATTLE CONVENTION COMMITTE.

The Story
Of the
Seattle Convention

THE OFFICIAL REPORT
— OF —
THE TWENTY-THIRD INTERNATIONAL
Christian Endeavor Convention

HELD IN
TENT WILLISTON
AND OTHER AUDITORIUMS AND CHURCHES

Seattle, Wash., July 10 - 15, 1907

Copyright, 1907, by the U. S. C. E.

UNITED SOCIETY OF CHRISTIAN ENDEAVOR
BOSTON, MASS.

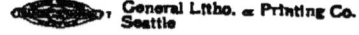
General Litho. & Printing Co.
Seattle

CONTENTS

		Page.
Committee of 1907		5
Foreword		7
Chapter.		
I.	On to Seattle	9
II.	The Opening Session—Tent Williston	13
III.	The Opening Session—First Presbyterian Church	24
IV.	Training for the Church of the Future	32
V.	The Junior Rally	42
VI.	Union Workers' Rally	46
VII.	The Complete Christian	50
VIII.	Christian Endeavor a Federation	57
IX.	Reaching Out	64
X.	The Denominational Rallies	74
XI.	Thy Kingdom Come	80
XII.	Training in Citizenship	91
XIII.	The "Messiah" and the Camp Fire	102
XIV.	The Men's Mass-Meeting	105
XV.	The Women's Meeting	110
XVI.	The Boys and Girls' Meeting	113
XVII.	The Japanese National Rally	115
XVIII.	International Peace and Arbitration	118
XIX.	Fatherhood and Brotherhood	120
XX.	Two Enemies of Our Civilization	124
XXI.	Two Present Day Problems	127
XXII.	Training for Missionary Service	131
XXIII.	Christian Endeavor's Opportunity	136
XXIV.	The School of Methods	140
XXV.	The Noon Evangelistic Meetings	146
XXVI.	The Purpose Meetings	148
XXVII.	Gleanings by the Wayside	154
XXVIII.	Greetings from Many Lands	158
Officers and Trustees of the United Society		163
Index		165

LIST OF ILLUSTRATIONS

The Seattle Convention Committee		Frontispiece
Views of Seattle	opposite page	9
Delegates Boarding the Street Car	"	13
Arriving Delegates	"	13
Tents Williston and Endeavor	"	17
President Francis E. Clark, D.D. LL.D.	"	21
Some Seattle Notables	"	25
General Secretary William Shaw	"	29
Arriving Delegates	"	33
The Junior Rally	"	41
The "Messiah" Chorus and Orchestra	"	49
Building the Bridge at the Junior Rally	"	49
Crossing the Bridge at the Junior Rally	"	49
Interior of Tent Williston	"	57
Convention Speakers	"	65
The Reception Committee at the Union Station	"	73
The Japanese Rally	"	73
Vice President Fairbanks and Committee	"	81
Convention Speakers	"	89
United Society Officers and Convention Speakers	'	97
The Canadian Delegates	"	105
Convention Speakers	"	113
Tent Williston at Night	"	121
Convention Speakers	"	129
Miss J. Kajiro in Japanese Costume	'	137
One of Seattle's Reception Committee	"	137
Rev. John Pollock	"	145
Four Racial Representatives	"	145
Sunday Service in Jail	"	153
The Automobile Ride	"	161
The Boys' Band from the State Industrial School	"	161

COMMITTEE OF 1907.

EXECUTIVE OFFICERS.

CHAIRMAN	F. EDGAR BARTH
FIRST VICE CHAIRMAN	JAMES A. MOORE
SECOND VICE CHAIRMAN	REV. M. A. MATTHEWS, D. D.
SECRETARY	CARL H. REEVES
TREASURER	GEORGE E. COMBS

Chairmen Sub-Committees.

FINANCE	JOHN SCHRAM
ENTERTAINMENT	THOMAS W. LOUGH
RECEPTION	FRANK L. HORSFALL, M. D.
HALLS	HOMER L. BULL
MUSIC	C. C. ENGELHARD
PRINTING	JOSEPH E. THOMAS
USHERS	E. G. CROSSETT
REGISTRATION	J. W. HERBERT DOIG
DECORATIONS	THOMAS S. SEMPLE
PRESS AND PUBLICITY	GEORGE A. VIRTUE
PULPIT SUPPLY	REV. B. H. LINGENFELTER
EVANGELISTIC	REV. W. A. SPALDING, D. D.
EXCURSIONS	JOSEPH A. CAMPBELL
INFORMATION	FRANK H. CAMPBELL

HONORARY	MISS MINNIE A. GIBBONS, State Secretary
ORGANISTS	C. C. ENGELHARD, MRS. WILLIAM B. JUDAH

FOREWORD.

In previous years, the Convention Report has been published in Boston at the United Society's printing plant, after the return of the delegates to their homes. This enabled the United Society officers to give more thought and care to its preparation than would be possible were it issued earlier. On the other hand, it has often been thought that much of the helpfulness and influence of the Report were lost by reason of the long time that elapsed between the Convention and the publication of its proceedings. This year, therefore, the plan was inaugurated of compiling the Report day by day during the progress of the Convention.

When one considers the number of meetings that are held during an International Convention—in the present instance, one hundred and eighty-three meetings, with more than one hundred different speakers—and the additional fact that many of these meetings were held simultaneously, the compilation of a Report that will do justice to all is no easy task. The compiler takes pleasure in acknowledging the services of Prof. Amos. R. Wells, Rev. Wm. T. McElveen, D. D., Rev. W. J. Twort, Rev. Ira Landrith, D. D., Rev. J. M. Lowden, D. D., Rev. James A. Francis, Rev.. Chas. Stelzle, Rev. Alexander Francis, D. D., Rev. Floyd W. Tomkins, S. T. D., Mr. Von Ogden Vogt, Rev. W. I. Chamberlain, Ph. D., Rev. John Pollock, Mrs. H. N. Lathrop, and of many leaders of meetings and conferences whose helpfulness in reporting various sessions of the convention has made the early publication of this Report possible.

With the prayer that the reading of it may be spiritually uplifting to thousands of young people and may give them many suggestions for the betterment of their work in the Master's cause, this account of the proceedings of the Twenty-third International Christian Endeavor Convention is sent forth.

George B. Graff,
Publication Manager U. S. C. E.

Seattle, July 16, 1907.

A SECTION OF SEATTLE'S WATER-FRONT.

A VIEW FROM THE FIRST HILL.

PUGET SOUND AND THE OLYMPIC RANGE.

CHAPTER I.

ON TO SEATTLE!

A Great Trip Across the Continent—Majestic Scenery—Inspiring Meetings—Characteristic Incidents.

ONE OF THE BLESSINGS that come to Endeavorers attending an International Christian Endeavor Convention is the education afforded by travel. This is especially true, when, as in the present instance, the convention is held on the extreme border of the country. A trip across the continent cannot help but impress the one that takes it with the grandeur and beauty of our land.

The route taken by many of the eastern delegations to Seattle was via the Canadian Pacific Railroad; the line of matchless wonders, of rolling prairies and snow-clad mountain peaks; of roaring canyons and silvery cascades. Here, amid scenery the like of which is found nowhere else upon this continent, the delegations from Massachusetts, New Hampshire, Vermont, New York, New Jersey, Pennsylvania, Ohio, Indiana, Illinois, Wisconsin, Minnesota and many other states, frequently came together with the invariable result that a Christian Endeavor prayer meeting or miniature convention was soon in progress.

Banff, so delightfully situated in the heart of the Canadian Rockies, seemed to be the Mecca to which all the delegations journeyed for their Sunday's day of rest.

Whoever has not seen the Bow valley from the great hotel at Banff or from some of the nearby observation points has not seen the fairest and at the same time one of the grandest views on earth. The superb mountains, serrated and snow-clad, the swift green river, the tumultuous cataracts, the verdant valley and the crowded spruces, and the wide sweep of that amphitheatre of glories, made the Sabbath at Banff an experience to be remembered even among the happy hills of heaven.

Seldom, if ever, have the churches of Banff seen such audiences as gathered that Sunday morning. A goodly company crowded the Presbyterian church, organized by Ralph Connor, reaching the church at ten thirty, only to find that the service did not begin until eleven. The Endeavorers began singing on the church steps, but the house was soon opened and they were most cordially invited to continue their service of song on the inside, which they did most zealously until the arrival of the minister. Dr. Clark was invited to conduct the opening exercises, and then, after an admirable sermon on "The Good Shepherd," by Rev. Mr. McIver, Dr. Smith Baker gave a rousing talk on "Endeavorism."

In the afternoon the delegates enjoyed one of the most inspiring Christian Endeavor meetings ever held, even in our long history of inspiring meetings. It could hardly be otherwise, in that magnificent presence. Endeavor meetings have been held in many wonderful places, but surely never before in the midst of a panorama so majestically lovely as that which spread before us as we stood on the terrace at the Banff Hotel.

Dr. Clark, who led the meeting, first had us repeat the Traveler's Psalm. Then we sang "Blest Be the Tie," and many Bible verses were repeated—the grand mountain verses of Holy Writ.

A large portion of the service was in memory of our beloved field secretary, Rev. Clarence E. Eberman ("C. E." Eberman,), who died there at Banff in the midst of a Christian Endeavor journey after two years of splendid service as field secretary, preceded by grand work as president of the Pennsylvania Union—and he was known as "the president in the saddle," so thoroughly did he give himself to the work. Dr. Clark refused to allow this part of the service to be gloomy. "There was nothing gloomy about Eberman," he declared.

Dr. Bannen, Mr. Eberman's successor in the Pennsylvania presidency, offered prayer. Then Dr. Tomkins, trustee from Pennsylvania, spoke of Mr. Eberman's humility, geniality, brotherhood, executive ability and high intellectual and spiritual power. Dr. Hill gave a reminiscence showing how, though Mr. Eberman always met men upon the same level, yet instinctively they looked up to him as a superior. Secretary Shaw, the "little brother" to Eberman's "big brother," praised his splendid "fighting loyalty" to Christian Endeavor. Secretary Wells spoke of Mr. Eberman as a typical Moravian, typical in his missionary spirit of joyful and devoted service. He read one of Mr. Eberman's favorite hymns, Zinzendorf's "Jesus, Still Lead On," and we sang another favorite hymn of his, Matheson's "O, Love That Wilt Not Let Me Go." Dr. Lowden spoke of the strong impression made upon him by Mr. Eberman, the immediateness and completeness of his response to the call of duty. It was indeed a loving and sincere series of tributes to our departed comrade, and we whose lives have been blessed by knowing him felt that we had met his spirit once again in that glorious scene which was his entrance door to the unending service of heaven.

A pleasant example of the Endeavor spirit very fittingly closed the meeting. It was announced that one of the delegates to the convention—a young lady from Massachusetts—had been stricken on the train with peritonitis and was then lying dangerously ill at the Banff Sanitarium. In less than five minutes the Endeavorers most eagerly contributed more than $130 to meet the unexpected expenses of the delegate. Thus the Endeavorers proved their faith by their works and illustrated by blessed deeds the blessed tie of which they had been singing.

Daylight lingered astonishingly long in that northern valley, and as the trains were not to leave till midnight or later, the station platform at Banff resounded with gospel songs for three hours at least. The enthusiastic Ohio delegation seemed to be leaders here, and Dr. Clark, on his return from the hotel, was received with such a serenade as even he has seldom heard.

And Banff is only at the beginning of the Canadian Rockies. Each hour, from that marvelous portal, was crowded with deepening wonder and delight.

Scores of us walked up the two and a half miles from Laggan to Lake Louise, along a singing mountain stream, with the constant comradeship of mighty hills. Others made precarious ventures on the back of a broncho or crowded the carriages.

Arrived on high we found a lake of superb green, clear and sparkling, a mile and a half wide, but dwarfed to the eye by the stone giants that stood solemnly around it. Was ever snow so brilliant as the dazzling snow-fields that hung on those stupendous crags, or crushed themselves, on the bosom of the mountain, into miles of viscid ice?

The Illecillewaet glacier was in some ways the climax of the journey. For hundreds of Endeavorers it was their first contact with a lake and river of ice, that unique fancy of Mother Nature. The walk thither was a long anthem of towering spruces, rushing glacial torrents, and glimpses through green vistas of Sir Donald and other cathedral summits.

One of the delegates, Rev. James A. Francis of New York, was so impressed with the sight that he dropped into poetry, and here is the poem just as he wrote it:

THE RIVER OF ICE.

We stood by the mouth of the river of ice
As it came from its home in the clouds,
When the shadows dark wrap the mountain sides
Like so many mighty shrouds.

'Twas a silent stream, that river of ice,
  As silent and massive as stone,
But from under it issued a stream so clear,
  Like the river from 'neath the throne.

'Twas a changeless stream, that river of ice,
  The natives might pass away,
But it kept its course from age to age,
  Like God's eternal day.

We lifted our thoughts to the Maker's hand,
  So silent and changeless, too,
Whose resistless might on the side of right
  Remains forever true.

And we went our way with humble hearts
  And a deeper faith in God,
And the whole world seemed like a temple grand
  Where angels' feet had trod.

Who can forget the song and prayer service on the platform of Glacier Station, led by President Straughn? We sang "America," and "God Save the King," also, in honor of our Canadian audience, and on that soil that no American will call foreign, from many states and countries, we felt ourselves drawn mightily to one another as our thoughts turned toward the Father of us all. These prayer services along the way, as they are among the most characteristic features of our Christian Endeavor excursions, are also among the happiest.

A beautiful incident was the passing of Mt. Stephen, which seemed to rise out of the green hill behind until it stood forth revealed in all its majestic grandeur. "Ah," said one, "how like the revelation of God to the soul; when surrounded by the mountains of trials and temptations, God suddenly reveals himself in the midst."

Who can ever forget the fellowships, the vast prairies and prosperous farms, the buffaloes, the bears, the Indians, the mighty canyons and rushing rivers! And yet through it all, our mind seemed to be keeping time with the clatter of the wheels on the track: On to Seattle! On to Seattle!

DELEGATES BOARDING THE STREET CARS NEAR THE DEPOT.

ARRIVING DELEGATES.

CHAPTER II.

THE OPENING SESSION.

Wednesday Evening, July 10.

C. E. Attle is the new way to spell the name of the hustling, bustling city of the Northwest. With propriety Seattle might change its name to Endeavor, for a busier city does not exist on the American continent. The Seattleites are alive with the consciousness of coming days. Their boat is buoyed to a rising tide. Their city is already a great city, but it is going to be a much greater city. Two decades will see two million people dwelling within its borders. Seattle is soon to be the great Pacific Coast American city. It is growing by leaps and bounds. The entire city is being transformed. The hills are being leveled at tremendous cost. Old buildings are being discarded and mammoth and beautiful buildings are being erected. The New Yorker, being accustomed to torn-up streets in the great Atlantic municipality, feels thoroughly at home in Seattle. Seattle isn't finished—it has only begun to be. It is in the process of becoming. All is toil and turmoil, but out of the travail is to come a fair, municipal gem. Splendid railroads and an ideal harbor (a harbor which is to be augmented by digging a canal from Puget Sound to Lake Washington), together with the nearness to Japan and Alaska conspire to give Seattle a very great advantage over other cities.

But Seattle's greatest asset is the spirit of its citizens. They are proud of their city and prouder of its possibilities. They are determined to make these possibilities actualities. Nothing can discourage them. They possess the true "endeavor" spirit—the spirit that prompts one to something better.

And what a welcome they gave us! Though the city had a thousand and one things to do, they took time to tastily decorate their streets, squares, houses and stores. Green and white are Seattle's colors, and they were everywhere in evidence.

When the Boston train rolled into the King street depot, Seattle, it was greeted by a uniformed band playing "Onward, Christian Soldiers!" and by a hurrahing welcome from the efficient reception committee. The New Englanders responded with their rub-a-dub-dub slogan and committed themselves without hesitancy to the cordial Seattleites.

In a very few moments, some by automobiles and others by trolley cars, the tired but glad company were on their way toward their hotels and temporary homes.

The green and white were mingled with the red, white and blue upon almost every street corner, and the buildings were adorned with the Christian Endeavor flag. Seattle had evidently attacked the great problem of entertaining an international convention with real Western enterprise.

Over 8,000 people faced Dr. Clark on Wednesday evening when he arose to announce the opening hymn in Tent Williston. For a moment all was pandemonium. Handkerchiefs fluttered, flags waved, hands were clapped and voices raised to express the love of the assembled throng for our beloved leader. But, with characteristic modesty, Dr. Clark attributed the applause to the movement of which he is the founder, rather than to himself personally.

After a reverent prayer, by which the audience was made to feel the very presence of God, Dr. Clark said: "The great, dominant word of this convention is the word "train." The Christian Endeavor Society is a training school. To train is more than to teach. Teaching addresses itself to the mind; training addresses itself to the individual in his entirety. Teaching gives knowledge; training gives skill, shapes habits, develops character, and prepares for service."

Wednesday evening was good citizenship night, as well as good fellowship night. Piety and patriotism so intermingled as to be almost identical.

The Honorable Albert E. Mead, governor of the State of Washington, welcomed the Endeavorers in behalf of the million people of that splendid Northwest commonwealth. He said:

"I take great pride in the responsibility of inviting you to hold this great gathering in this city. I am certain that Seattle and the entire state will profit immeasurably from your visit. This convention counts for more than you may think in the development of this city and state, because it will encourage the perfecting of citizenship and the advancement of the highest governmental ideals.

It has been the privilege and the honor of the state of Washington that it has entertained two great national conventions this year, the Baptist Young People's Union at Spokane, and the Christian Endeavorers at Seattle. This, I believe, is the first time that conventions of this broad character have been held in our state, conventions in which all the states of the American Union are represented, conventions that bring together the representatives of every part of this great continent.

Your presence and your deliberations here necessarily will have a marked effect in extending the cause for which you are organized, and also promoting that cordial feeling that should exist among the various states and localities of our common country. Godliness and

patriotism go hand in hand in our Christian land, and it is an essential to true patriotism that it should not be bounded by sectional lines nor insular prejudices. And the surest way in which to obliterate those lines and prejudices is through such gatherings as this.
It is my sincere hope that you may always think well of the Pacific Northwest. I wish you a hearty 'God-Bless-You.'"

The Honorable William H. Moore, mayor of Seattle, was unable to be present because of the sickness of his father, but his place was ably taken by City Engineer R. H. Thomson. Mr. Thomson's speech betrayed him. He talked like a man who either had been an Endeavorer, or who had Endeavorers in his home. He told the Endeavorers graphically with what great desire the young people of Seattle wanted to have them see their city. Like all other Seattleites, he rejoiced that he was a "citizen of no mean city." He gloried in its cleanliness, material and moral. He told of its remarkable growth and expressed his faith that the one great thing, the one imperial thing, necessary to make the city of Seattle the city it ought to be, is the saving grace of Jesus Christ.

Mr. F. Edgar Barth, in a few well chosen words and felicitous phrases, spoke for the 1907 Christian Endeavor Committee:

"It is my happy privilege to extend to you the welcome on behalf of the committee of 1907. We have been preparing and looking forward with eager anticipation for many months to this eventful day.

And as we have labored amid joys and discouragements, we have had for our sympathetic friends these grand old mountains—sentinels of our city, we call them, as they have stood ever encouraging and beckoning us on—on to this day of all days, when you, the Redeemed of the Lord, should gather in this beautiful city, that is set on hills, and lift up your voices, in praise and adoration to the Father, for His wonderful goodness to the children of men.

We welcome you because of the mighty impetus you have given the movement for international peace, hastening the day of universal brotherhood among mankind."

The applause had hardly died away before Dr. Clark presented the tall, handsome, magnetic, clear-voiced, bushy-haired pastor of the First Presbyterian Church, Dr. M. A. Matthews, who expressed the welcome of the churches of the city. He bid the Endeavorers not only welcome, but he urged them to stay and make Seattle their home. "If you have good judgment," he cried, "don't go back." But he was not content in expressing a word of welcome. He told the vast audience what "Christian Endeavor" stood for, and what "Christian Endeavor" denounced.

"We welcome you because of your Christian worth, your Christian character, your intelligence and your perseverance as soldiers of the Cross.

We plead with you to speak as never before for the purity of the home. The licentious hand of the divorce court is reaching out to touch, stain and damn the homes of this country. Demand the purity of the home, the sacredness of the marriage vow, and the abolition of the divorce court.

Let us have your assistance in exterminating the saloon.

Our two great crimes are the open saloon and Sabbath desecration. The day has come for some section of this country to write the emancipation declaration and give the youth of this land freedom from the infamous saloon. I believe as the North wrote the declaration and freed the negro, God has intrusted to the South the greater honor, blessing and opportunity of writing the declaration which will mean the death of the saloon and the freedom of the children of America from the accursed liquor traffic.

Our Sabbath desecration is making of this an immoral and criminal nation, and, unless we stop, repent and properly observe God's day, we will have to suffer an awful national judgment.

As the wave of civic righteousness has rolled from the Atlantic to the Pacific, and from the Pacific back to the Atlantic, let this convention speak as never before on the question of good citizenship."

The convention was exceedingly fortunate in having almost every speaker announced in attendance. But the Rev. John Pollock, president of the European Christian Endeavor Union, and pastor of St. Enoch's Presbyterian Church, Belfast, Ireland, missed some railroad connection, and was therefore unable to thank the representatives of the state and the city and the committee and the churches for their cordial words of welcome. However, we saw the genial face and heard the gladsome voice of Dr. Pollock many times in the other sessions of the convention.

Mr. Hiram N. Lathrop, the new treasurer of the United Society, at this time read the following greeting from President Theodore Roosevelt, and hearty applause punctuated the message of the nation's chief executive:

"The White House,
  Washington.   June 2, 1907.

"My Dear Mr. Shaw: I thank you for your letter. Thru you I wish to extend to the International Christian Endeavor my heartiest good wishes for the admirable work they are doing. Let me in particular express my earnest hope that you will emphasize as one of the features of your convention the need that the Endeavorers should take a first rank in good citizenship. I am glad you are to endeavor to bring this subject so prominently before this meeting.

It will be a pleasure to accept honorary membership in your Christian Endeavor Patriots' League, for I am sure that with the general purpose and efforts of that League I shall have the heartiest sympathy, tho of course I could not commit myself in advance to agree with all of their views without knowing them.

I wish you God-speed in your work, because the Christian Endeavorers are working for the things that are vital to the soul, and

TENTS WILLISTON AND ENDEAVOR.

I believe that they can do much that is of the very greatest value to the cause of good citizenship; for in the last analysis the fundamental requisite of good citizenship from the standpoint of the country is that a man should have the very qualities which make him of real value in the home, in the church, in all the higher relationships of life.

Faithfully yours,

THEODORE ROOSEVELT.

Mr. William Shaw,
General Secretary, United Society of Christian Endeavor.

But the convention was not simply a national gathering: it was international in membership, and so Dr. Clark requested the audience to sing one verse of "America," one verse of "God Save the King," and then one verse of "Two Empires by the Sea." This the audience did with evident enjoyment.

A unique and enjoyable exercise followed. Dr. Clark explained that it was an apparent impossibility for everybody in the great tent to shake everybody else's hand, and so he suggested that they follow the Chinese fashion and each one shake his or her own hand. This was done amid laughter and applause.

After the singing of a hymn there came the simple but solemn service of inaugurating the three new officers. With a voice throbbing with emotion, Dr. Clark presented Mr. William Shaw, general secretary, Mr. Hiram N. Lathrop, treasurer, and Prof. Amos R. Wells, editorial secretary. Dr. Floyd Tomkins of the Holy Trinity Church of Philadelphia offered the installing prayer. A solemn hush pervaded the great tent. Dr. Tomkins' words fell upon the ears of the people as if they were quotations of God's own mind. All felt as if the spirit of God was anointing with His own grace and power this splendid trio for holy service, and when they came to speak their brief but tender words it was evident that they were as able as they were consecrated.

Mr. Shaw, with almost a sob in his voice, testified to the influence that Dr. Clark had wielded over his life; how he had imparted to him of his holy inspiration and divine ideas; how he helped him to discover that there was something better than things. Wonderful, indeed, is the friendship between these two leaders. Charles Kingsley was once asked the secret of his noble life, and he answered: "I had a friend." So Mr. Shaw testified that the spirit of Dr. Clark had in a large measure dwelt in him and made him what he was.

Mr. Lathrop spoke feelingly of the love and loyalty which characterized the relations of the leaders of the Endeavor movement. He referred to the immense amount of unpaid services which not only the leaders but the rank and file of the Endeavor host rendered.

"If Dr. Clark had received the salary of a life insurance president, or if Mr. Shaw were the recipient of the income of a Pierpont Morgan, they could not have done more or better work," said Mr. Lathrop.

Prof. Wells was reminded of the old doggerel that "children should be seen and not heard," which he revised to "Editors should be neither seen nor heard." Moreover, he explained that he could not write prose while riding to the beautiful state of Washington, so he clothed his thoughts of self-dedication in the following poem:

THE CHRISTIAN ENDEAVOR PEN.
By Amos R. Wells.

The prophet's lamp of ancient days,
  By heavenly favor fed,
Maintained its clear and steady rays
  When other lights were dead.

The eager oil in constant flow
  From olive trees above
Poured in the flaming lamp below
  Full streams of power and love.

Today, O God of life and light,
  Thy truth is flashed to men
By lines of black on paper white,
  Thy prophet's torch the pen.

But still the reservoir is small,
  And still the words run dry
'Till fed and filled by sources tall,
  As God's eternal sky.

Unseal Thy holy influence, then,
  O Spirit! Deign to be
The Fount of every fountain pen
  That moves for men and Thee!

When fancy flags and vigor fails
  From out the barren page,
When courage sinks and fear bewails
  And zeal is faint with age,

O Spirit of the written Word,
  In that expectant hour
Fill Thou the pen with language heard
  In heaven's courts of power!

For times may change and customs grow,
  But still the wise confess
Who speaks for God must ever know
  His own sad feebleness.

And men may speak in many ways,
  By tongue or deed or pen;
But there's no skill, nor power, nor praise,
  Save when God speaks through men.

After singing, Dr. Clark gave his annual address, "A World-Wide Training School in Expression, in Service, and in Fellowship." Because of the lateness of the hour he abbreviated somewhat his most excellent setting forth of the basic principles of the Endeavor movement. He insisted that the Christian Endeavor Society was more a doing society than a talking society. No impression without expression; no stirring of the emotions without translating those emotions into altruistic service. Religion is not simply feeling good: it is being and doing good.

DR CLARK'S ADDRESS.

The key-word of Christian Endeavor is Training, training in expression, training in service, training in living, training of the heart, training of the mind, training of the tongue; training of the boy and girl, training of the young man and woman; training to make men and women, training to make citizens, training to make effective Christians; training in the church, training for the church, training by the church.

This great convention from beginning to end is an exposition, a practical exhibit, so to speak, of the idea for which we stand. This convention would have been impossible, were it not for the trained myriads of Christian Endeavorers who for a quarter of a century have been exemplifying the broad idea of training for the service of the kingdom of God.

This, I think we may say, was the great thought which the Christian Endeavor movement introduced into the church life of the day, or at least the great undeveloped thought which it emphasized twenty-five years ago, and which it has continued to emphasize ever since. It is the training-school of the church as the Sunday-school is the teaching-school of the church.

The successes of Christian Endeavor have come in proportion as this thought has been developed; its failures have resulted from ignoring this principle.

I have just returned from a long and arduous pioneering journey in the "Neglected Continent," neglected to the last by Christian Endeavor as well as by other Protestant forces; but I have found that there, among the Andes and on the pampas, in the busy cities of this Continent of Opportunity, a far better name for South America, as well as where Christian Endeavor has been known and prized the longest, there as well as here and everywhere else, I say, the supreme work of the Society is training the church of the future.

The Three Great Departments of Christian Endeavor.

Consider for a few moments what may be called the three great departments of Christian Endeavor: the Weekly Meeting; the Committees; the Unions; each of them indispensable to the movement, and each of them, wherever established, so many training-schools for the church, the nation, the world of the future.

The Prayer Meetings are training-schools in Expression.

The Committees are training-schools in Service.

The Unions are training-schools in Fellowship and United Action.

First, consider the Weekly Christian Endeavor Prayer Meeting. There is something sublimely inspiring in the thought of what it has become. Nearly 70,000 meetings held every week in the year. Multiply 70,000 by 50 and you have approximately the number of Endeavor prayer meetings held every twelve months. If my arithmetic does not fail me, that means three million five hundred thousand meetings every year.

Each one of these meetings may be unimpressive to the cool and cynical man of the world; the aggregate must inspire even him with some respect for the cause which year after year can sustain them.

What does this tremendous fact signify? It means that Christian Endeavor is a great world training-class in the expression of the religious life. It means also that there is a distinct need felt in the hearts of young Christians for such expression of the religious life. As the bird must sing, and the flower must bloom, and the lover must express his affection by gentle word as well as deed, so the young Christian must express his love if any love for God is in his heart; and the Endeavor meeting gives him his opportunity.

Right here we see the importance, yes, the necessity, of a Christian Endeavor pledge to the best and largest results. It had come about especially in Anglo-Saxon lands that Christians, particularly young Christians, had become tongue-tied and dumb in the expression of their love for Christ. Conventionality, timidity, bashfulness, the tradition of the elders, who relegated the young people to a back seat, had practically sealed the lips of the young Protestant Christians of the world; and they were growing up without the inestimable privilege of expressing their love for Christ, an expression which is of itself an education.

The pledge, always voluntarily taken, came to the rescue to unseal their lips, to touch dumb tongues as with a coal from the altar of God; and our sons and our daughters began to prophesy as in the days of Pentecost. While we do not insist on the use of this formula or any other special form of words, I venture to say that the little phrase, "I will take some part aside from singing in every prayer meeting," has done more to restore the idea of the healthy expression of the religious life to its normal place in the church of Christ than any other twelve words that have been uttered or written, simply because they have brought into this training-class of expression so many millions of conscientious scholars.

Training in Service.

But, again, the Society from the beginning has trained its members in service quite as much as in expression. It has been far more a doing society than a talking society. If we were amazed at the number of meetings held each week throughout the world when we came to reckon them up, what shall we say about the working committees which are equally essential to Christian Endeavor?

Multiply the 70,000 societies by five, the average number of committees, and that by five again, the average number of members on each committee, and you will approximate the number of workers, who are also scholars, in this school of applied Christianity, the number who are being trained every week in actual, practical, definite work for Christ and the church; and, as these committees frequently are changed, twice this number, probably, in the course of the year go to this training-school of service.

Innumerable Activities.

But such figures are cold and tame compared with the glowing, human, Christlike work for which they stand. The uplifting meetings planned for, the souls won, the music that thrills, the sanctuaries that are beautified, the poor who are relieved, the sick who are visited,

DR. FRANCIS E. CLARK, D. D., L. L. D.
President World's Christian Endeavor Union. President United Society of Christian Endeavor.

the prisons that are entered, the children who are made happy, the sailors who are cheered, the money that is secured for philanthropies, the pastors who are encouraged, the missionaries who are supported— all these things are being accomplished, while at the same time the doers are being trained for still larger service in this practical school of activity, a school that is never closed, that takes no vacations, that goes on in spring and summer and autumn and winter in every corner of every continent, quietly, unostentatiously training its scholars for the larger service of the days to come.

The innumerable forms of active Christian Endeavor for the prisoner and the soldier and the sailor; for the inmate of the hospital or the sick-room; for the children of the Fresh-Air Camps; the Comrades of the Quiet Hour, the Tenth Legionaries, the Macedonian Phalanx, the Good-Citizenship clubs,—are all outgrowths of this twin idea that Christian Endeavor is a training-school in action as well as expression, in doing as well as speaking for Christ.

A Word of Caution.

But because Christian Endeavor aims to be such a comprehensive training-school let me urge my older friends not to put all the burdens of church and mission upon the shoulders of the young people, and lay all sins of omission at their door, as some are inclined to do. There are older people as well as younger in the church. There are fathers and mothers as well as sons and daughters. If the congregations fall off, if the Sunday-school is diminished, if the week-night prayer meeting drags, if the missionary collection is smaller, I have known some ministers and churches and missionary secretaries to charge all deficiencies on the Endeavor society, forgetting that primarily the society is a training-school, and that they do not expect scholars while they are at school to do all the work of trained graduates. As well might you expect the boys in the grammar school to be the chief breadwinners for the home and leading citizens of the state.

However, we will accept the challenge made by even these unreasonable demands, and so far as in us lies we will, even while we are at school in Christian Endeavor, do the work of today, which is the best training for the larger work of that of tomorrow.

Training in Fellowship.

Once more, the Christian Endeavor movement is a great worldwide training-school in fellowship. One would think that Christian fellowship would be spontaneous, as in the early days of the apostolic church, and need no training; but sectarianism has been rampant and unrestrained so long that we need special training to get back to the first principles of Christianity. In the providence of God Christian Endeavor interdenominational unions have become established in every land. Today here in Seattle our international union of the United States and Canada begins its convention, every session of which will be a training-class in Christian brotherhood.

The biennial session of this school will last but five days; but during this short time Baptists and Presbyterians, Methodists and Lutherans, Disciples of Christ and Congregationalists, will learn many a lesson of fraternity and good will. Not only this, but Washington and Maine, California and Massachusetts, Ontario and New York, Mexico and Alaska, and all the nations, States, and Provinces in North America will go to this school of fraternal good will.

Three Thousand Schools of Brotherhood.

Is it for nothing that God has established in all the world those three thousand schools of Christian brotherhood, otherwise called Christian Endeavor unions? I cannot believe it. In His infinite wisdom He saw that the time was ripe for a new union of the forces of evangelical Christendom. Sectarians have fought against His plan, for sectarianism dies hard. Rival societies have been started to destroy this brotherhood, and in some places they have succeeded for a time; but on the whole, through our national, international, state, and local unions, every one of which is a training-school in interdenominational and international fellowship, the cause of Christian fraternity has gone steadily forward; and the outlook for its final triumph among the torn and rent divisions of Protestantism was never so bright as now.

But we cannot rest on our oars. The battle is only half won. The nations are still building ironclads. Some denominations are still fighting against the brotherly spirit of the times, which is the spirit of unity in Christ.

The Hague Conference of the Denominations.

But The Hague Conference is in session and more conferences will be held, I believe, until at last men beat their spears into pruninghooks and nations learn war no more. Thousands of Christian Endeavor conferences have been held, each one a training-school in denominational comity, and they will continue to be held until sects, though still loyal to their own tenets, together wage war for the conquest of the world to Christ. Christian Endeavor is The Hague of the denominational world, and every convention is a conference of The Hague, where Christians of many denominations can look one another in the face, grasp one another by the hand, and swear allegiance to the common Lord and Master of us all.

Already the signs of a blessed unity which the world never knew before appear on the horizon. In Canada, in Australia, in the United States, in Great Britain, the first steps are being taken toward a federation of the churches, while each may hold in peace and love its own views of doctrine and polity, for the thousands of Christian Endeavor training-classes in brotherhood have not been held in vain.

A Larger Mission Still.

And do we not feel, as, year by year, our ranks are enlarged and strengthened, the impetus to still greater and more definite work along social lines; standing together for true patriotism, the enforcement of law, for justice between man and man, rich and poor alike, not as fussy, carping critics, but in a generous constructive spirit? Through the "Patriots' League" and the "International C. E. Brotherhood," of which you will hear more, great things, with the Divine blessing, may be accomplished.

What, then, is the conclusion of the whole matter? Take courage and press on, Endeavorers; "see clearly; think straight; and act."

Plainly our mission is to furnish for the evangelical Christian world these training-schools in expression, in service, in brotherhood. The history of these years proves it. God has marked out our path. Keep on, then, in His way.

Glory in your prayer meeting. It is your God-ordained school of expression. Shrink from no vow, from no effort, which will make it more stimulating, helpful, and effective.

Glory in your committees; they are all classes in our training-school of service; and they develop workers for every form of philanthropy, good citizenship, and practical Christianity.

Glory in your fellowship, and let no ruthless sectarian hand snatch it from you; for it is a training-school for the universal Christian brotherhood, which one of these days, please God, will fulfil our Lord's last prayer that "they all may be one, as thou, Father, art in me and I in Thee, that they also may be one in us."

The Christ of the Andes.

On the border-line between the republics of Chile and Argentina, on the crest of the Andes, where the only pass over the mountain is more than twelve thousand feet nearer the stars, stands a gigautic figure of our Lord Christ holding His cross and with His upraised finger pointing every traveler to the skies. It was erected to celebrate the conclusion of the boundary dispute between the two republics which long threatened a disastrous war. On the base of the statue are symbolic figures of the two republics in bas-relief representing Argentina and Chile clasping hands, and underneath is the motto, "He is our peace, who hath made both one."

This may well be our motto, too. He, the Lord Jesus Christ, is our peace; and He hath made us all one;—all denominations, all nations, one in Endeavor for Him.

He is our peace, who hath made us all one.

You have often asked me for a motto for each new year of service. This year let me give you a brief prayer which long ago the Apostle Paul taught us, a prayer which I trust Endeavorers in all the world may offer day by day for all other Endeavorers: "The Lord make you to increase and abound in love one toward another and toward all men."

The immense company tarried for a moment to have its "picture took," and then united fervently in the Mizpah salutation, and Dr. Matthews brought the first great session of the convention to a close.

CHAPTER III.

THE OPENING SESSION IN THE FIRST PRESBYTERIAN CHURCH.

In order to accommodate the large number of delegates, it was necessary to hold two sessions the opening night. The first one was held in Tent Williston and the other in the First Presbyterian Church. In the latter place, that versatile member of our Board of Trustees, Rev. James L. Hill, presided. The speakers were for the most part the same as in Tent Williston, the Governor, Hon. A. E. Mead and Seattle's Chief Engineer, Mr. R. H. Thomson, coming from the tent to address this meeting. The welcome from the churches was voiced by the Rev. H. C. Moore, D.D., pastor of the University Congregational Church, who gave a short address in keeping with the Seattle spirit, inviting the guests of the city to inspect the resources of the Northwest, because "they might take a fancy to the country and decide to remain here to enjoy its benefits and assist the Christian Endeavor work."

Mr. Carl H. Reeves, Secretary of the Convention Committee, then extended the welcome of the committee. He said:

Mr. Chairman, Brothers and Sisters:

The course of life may bring to us many experiences, fraught with joy and sorrow. Most of our joys, as well as our sorrows, are dependent upon our own actions.

Many months of preparation have preceded this convention. From all over this fair land hearts have been in preparation for this great gathering, with its untold blessings. The general committee, surrounded by all of the beauty of God's handiwork, has been working for the success of this convention. And might I say here to you, God's elect, that no convention can ever be a success until every member of the committee in charge learns the blessedness of drudgery for Christ's sake?

The state is yours, friends. Make this old city tremble to its very foundations; fill our churches with your laughter and songs, and consider the general committee your servants indeed and in very fact.

On behalf of the committee of 1907, I welcome you all, the world's finest and best, to this, the Queen City of Puget Sound. "For Christ and the Church," we greet you.

Welcome, every one of you; aye, thrice welcome. Be with us. Stay with us. And may our lives all unite in praise to God for His wonderful blessings to the children of men.

The response to these addresses of welcome was voiced by the Rev. George M. Ward, D. D., LL. D., now president of Wells College, in Aurora, N. Y., but who, as all Christian En-

deavorers know, was one of the first General Secretaries of the movement. Mr. Ward said:

In the life of every individual there are occasions when he realizes his utter dependence upon God. It is not in time of great danger, nor yet of great joy, that this is made most clear to him. It is when he views the accomplishment of others; realizes the success which has followed their endeavor. He turns to his own quiet, uneventful life and wonders if, when his occasion for service comes, he will be found worthy. Then it is that he realizes the truth of Scripture: "Not by power, nor by might, but by my Spirit," saith the Lord of Hosts.

How well I remember that first visit, and your city as I then saw it; its rough, ungraded streets, with the tree stumps so frequently in evidence. Your curiously staked out harbor lots, which, in my earlier ignorance, I laughed at. I wish some one had taught me sense at the time. I'd have come to this meeting in a private car. I remember your hopes and your ambitions along railroad lines. Alaska was nothing to you in those days—not even a neighbor. Tacoma was an acknowledged rival. Your plans were largely on paper. And now, this beautiful, prosperous and dignified metropolis—one of the first cities of the United States.

Great as is the change in things secular, how much greater is the change in things religious. I spoke, if I remember rightly, in an opera house, and the subject was comparatively a new one. I was asked again and again, What is Christian Endeavor? Can you imagine a child of tender years asking such a question today? Sitting on one of the Sound boats en route to Victoria the next day, a stranger, seeing an account of our meeting in a local paper, said to me: "Do you know what that is all about?" I tried to explain, and, summing it all up, said: "It is an effort to give to God's service the same careful training that is given to all other worthy efforts. It is a training school in the church." I can see his amused face as he laughingly answered: "Does a man need a training to know how to walk down the church aisle on Sunday and take his seat in the pew?" Crude, wasn't it? But do you know I gained a dim impression during my first visit that the Pacific slope's ideas of Christian worship twenty years ago were a little crude? You remember the old adage about leaving our religion at the Missouri River. I have tried for twenty years to make the Eastern man see that the reproach in that story was up to him; no man was Western until he got beyond the Missouri. When he laid down his religion he was an Easterner, a tenderfoot, and incidentally a mighty mean one. The man who carried his religion with him, who kept it with him, was the real Westerner, who built up this region, and recognized that the land of his adoption, and not the land he had left, was God's country, and must for him always be, in time and eternity.

I heartily appreciate the privilege of being allowed to answer these addresses of welcome. This whole incident is proof that the world is growing better. The world is broader than it was, and even that portion of it which does not make Christian profession, recognizes that the Christ Standards are the best—the only ones consistent with true progress.

We are greeted tonight as honored guests by state, by municipality and by the representatives of the trades and the professions. We acknowledge with pleasure the courtesies extended us. We come in the name of Jehovah, visiting this promised land of the West, not to drive out a hostile people, but to rest awhile at this beautiful spot, and to spend with you to whom we are joined by ties of blood, of nationality, and of religious belief, those restful hours in earnest contemplation of the things of God.

From you, sir, the Governor of this broad land, we accept the hospitality of the State. We view with wonder its fertile field, its virgin forests, its mountains of precious minerals, its limitless possibilities of commerce. It is to us, sir, a type of that most glorious country to which lands are tributary, whose riches are unnumbered, whose inhabitants need neither light of sun or star, since the Lord God giveth them light, and they shall reign forever and ever.

From you, sir, the representative of the Mayor of this wondrous new city, this proof of the possibilities of the untrammeled strength of a free and intelligent people, we accept the freedom of your city, praying that one day you and those you represent may walk with us the streets of the city beautiful, and meet with loving greeting Him who rules therein.

From you who represent the Church of God on this Western outpost we accept the brotherly greetings of fellow laborers, who have borne and are bearing the heat and burden of the day in our Master's Kingdom. From you whose trained voices have joined in our welcome in song, we accept your music as the earthly echo of the hallelujahs of Heaven we shall all sometime join. And to you who en masse have furnished the sinews of war, the necessary enthusiasm and the busy work of detail, to one and all we extend the greetings of Christ and the Church.

Twenty years ago, in the City of Chicago, I welcomed the first great Western Convention of Christian Endeavor ever held, by the quotation of that old thought, that the nearer we came to each other, the nearer we came to God, like the line of a circle, the nearer we approach the center the nearer we approach each other.

May it be true of this meeting. In ever lessening circles we have come from the East and West, from the North and South, and I pray that here at this beautiful center we shall all tighten our grip on the hand of Almighty God.

After the singing of an anthem by the choir, General Secretary Shaw made his annual report. Mr. Shaw was received with enthusiastic applause, showing the grip which he has already secured in the hearts of the Christian Endeavorers.

SECRETARY SHAW'S ANNUAL REPORT.

In presenting this, my first report as General Secretary of the United Society of Christian Endeavor, I cannot help contrasting the present mighty movement of more than sixty-nine thousand societies and nearly three and a half million members, in more than sixty evangelical denominations, on every continent, its literature printed in eighty languages, its manifold activities touching every department of life—business, social, civic, intellectual, moral and spiritual—wth the little group of forty-eight struggling societies that were in existence when I joined the ranks of Christian Endeavor.

I rejoice that I have lived to see Christian Endeavor enter upon its second quarter of a century larger in numbers, stronger in organization, broader in its range of practical activities, and deeper in spirit than ever before in its history.

Some Figures.

I shall not trouble you with a statement of the thousands of miles traveled by your secretary, the tens of thousands of patient hearers addressed, the scores of thousands of letters and circulars mailed, and the millions of pages of printed matter circulated since our last convention.

My loved and honored predecessor as General Secretary, Mr. Von Ogden Vogt, reported at the Baltimore convention 66,772 societies in all the world. It is my privilege to report the present net enrollment of 69,138 societies, a net gain of 2,366 societies. Of these, 47,761 are Young People's, 2,365 are Intermediates, 18,947 are Juniors, and the rest are Floating societies and other classes, with a total membership of 3,456,969.

From reports received from the societies in this country, we learn that 167,508 members have united with the churches during the past year. A reasonable estimate for all the societies for the two years would be 446,688, or an average of 223,344 for each year.

The gifts for missions and other benevolences, largely local church work, aggregate $4,378,920 for the two years since the last report, or an average of $2,189,460 for each year.

A long list of Junior and Intermediate societies report gifts of over $100 each, and a still longer list of Young People's societies report contributions ranging from $150 to $1,050 each.

If I am to judge from the reports, many churches use their Christian Endeavor society as a convenient agency for raising money for local needs. I am convinced that a much larger proportion of the money given by the children and young people should be used for missionary purposes in extending the Kingdom in the regions beyond.

What Endeavorers Are Doing.

Christian Endeavor is a department of the church for the training of young people in Christian life and service. This training should be as broad as the work of the church, and as deep as the needs of the human heart. We believe that religion is a natural experience in the life of young people, and that it has natural modes of expression in life and service.

The reason why religion seems so unnatural to many young people is because of the strained and utterly unnatural type of religion that they see in so many older Christians. We believe in the expression of the religious life through the service of the life and the declaration of the lips—not either, but both. By their works and by their words shall the followers of Christ be known.

More than anything else today the church needs Christians who are not ashamed to "say so," men and women who can give a reason for the faith that is in them. It will be a sad day for our churches if the lecture by the pastor supplants the social service by the people, and the pulpit expresses all the religious experience and life of the church.

Out of a spirit of loyalty to our own church and the development of the individual, there has naturally come the spirit of fellowship with others which is so marked a characteristic of Christian Endeavor. The work of our unions has never before been so vital and successful as during the past two years. This has been illustrated in work for Christian Citizenship, which includes campaigns in the interest of temperance, Sabbath-observance and other moral reforms.

Missions have had right of way, and normal classes have been held by our unions for training leaders of mission-study classes, and thousands of these classes have been organized in our individual societies.

Plans for promoting systematic and proportionate giving have been presented, and the Tenth Legion, an enrolment of those who give not less than one-tenth of their income for God's service, now numbers 23,718 members.

Evangelism has gripped the hearts of our young people as never before. In many societies and unions training-classes for personal workers have been organized. Leading evangelists bear glad testimony to the intelligent and hearty co-operation of Christian Endeavorers with them in their meetings. Rev. J. Wilbur Chapman reports: "The Christian Endeavorers have been most helpful in my work." Rev. R. A. Torrey writes: "I do not know of any society in the churches in which there is more of the evangelistic spirit. I haven't a doubt that their training as Christian Endeavorers has made them more effective as soul-winners." Rev. James A. Francis says: "I find the Endeavorers in many churches the readiest of all to help. The training they have had in taking part in public services enables them to help with a freedom from self-consciousness and an intelligence above others." Rev. Arthur J. Smith says: "We cannot conduct a campaign with any degree of success without the co-operation of the young people who have been trained in Christian Endeavor and kindred societies." Time and space will not admit of even a mention of the varied forms of work of an evangelistic nature undertaken by Christian Endeavorers.

Advance Steps.

The past year has been fruitful in advance steps in Christian Endeavor. One of the most notable is the appointment of Pastoral Counsellors for the city, county and district unions. When completed, this plan will give the United Society a body of more than one thousand representative pastors to counsel and advise regarding the development and spread of the movement. Christian Endeavor can achieve its largest success only when it has the sympathetic co-operation of the pastors. This is just as true of the union work as of the individual society.

Unions Unified.

Another important advance step is the plan for the unification of our unions, and the publication of our new monthly magazine, Union Work, which will be devoted exclusively to the plans and methods for local, county, district and state unions. Three numbers have been issued, and they have been enthusiastically received by our workers. A careful study of the whole field is being made, which will result in a forward movement all along the line. Special attention will be given to the different departments and committees, and to the extension of Floating and Prison Endeavor.

Juniors and Intermediates.

One of the most hopeful advance steps is the increased attention given to Junior and Intermediate work, and the publication of the new monthly magazine for Junior and Intermediate superintendents, Junior Work. The first number was issued in June, and it starts off with a good list of subscribers. It will provide just the helps needed for Junior and Intermediate superintendents, and will make it impossible for any bright young man or woman to say: "I should be glad to take up the work, but I don't know what to do." Junior Work will tell what to do and how to do it, and will equip for intelligent service.

WILLIAM SHAW
General Secretary United Society of Christian Endeavor.

Summer Schools and Assemblies.

The Christian Endeavor Summer School or Assembly idea has had a marked development during the past two years, and is spreading in all sections of the country. The Maine Summer School was the pioneer, and each year it has made a new high record. New York, New Jersey, Maryland, California, Illinois, Michigan, Rhode Island and other states have done something along this line, either in the way of a Summer School or Workers' Institute at some other season of the year.

The most permanent and general enterprise in the country is the Sagamore Beach Assembly, in which the United Society is represented. A beautiful location has been secured on Cape Cod Bay, sixteen miles below Plymouth. A Christian Endeavor summer colony has been established, with private cottages, two hotels, assembly hall, recreation grounds, and many helpful features. Four conferences will be held there this summer, closing with a Christian Endeavor Assembly the last ten days in August.

Such gatherings are of great educational value in our work, and there is scarcely a state union that could not successfully arrange for such an assembly.

In Foreign Fields.

Every foreign country without exception reports encouraging progress in Christian Endeavor work. One of the most notable events is the organization of the European Christian Endeavor Union, whose president, Rev. John Pollock, we are delighted to welcome at this convention. The organization of this union will mean much for the advancement of Christian Endeavor on the continent of Europe. There, more perhaps than anywhere else, the evangelistic fervor, the practical methods and the interdenominational and international fellowship of Christian Endeavor are needed.

Another event of great significance and far-reaching importance is the enlargement of Christian Endeavor activities in South America through the visit of President Clark, who has just returned from a four months' campaign in the "Neglected Continent." I must let him tell the story of his journeyings, which I am sure will move our hearts, and prompt us to do something to send Christian Endeavor to our brothers and sisters in our sister continent.

Our International Building.

The past two years have witnessed the inauguration of plans for the erection in Boston of an International Headquarters Building, as a memorial of the first quarter century of Christian Endeavor service. This movement ought to meet with the enthusiastic and generous co-operation of every Endeavorer and every friend of Christian Endeavor.

Here is a great world movement, whose whole plan and method tend to the development of workers for the local church and the wider work of the Kingdom. It asks nothing for itself but the privilege of service. Its trained workers early leave its ranks to take up the work for which they have been trained. Its members have contributed millions of dollars to missions and other philanthropies, while the United Society has earned by its business department every dollar that has been expended in its far-reaching work.

All that its friends ask for it now is the equipment that a building will supply for the world-wide work. The rental saved and the additional space provided will enable the United Society to more than double its present work.

With Christian people erecting, by their generous gifts, quarter-million-dollar and half-million-dollar Y. M. C. A. buildings in every leading city, surely it is not unreasonable to ask the Endeavorers and their friends for one building for all the world, for the movement in whose ranks are being trained the members of the church of the future, and those who are to be the leaders and workers in all our great religious organizations.

Nearly fifty thousand dollars has already been contributed to this object, largely in small amounts, by our loyal Endeavorers. We ought to have ten times this amount.

I hope that before this convention adjourns, Seattle, 1907, will be made memorable in the history of our great conventions by the inauguration of a movement that will speedily secure the half-million dollars needed, and start Christian Endeavor on its second quarter-century fully equipped for the mighty work that God in His providence has for it to accomplish.

Next Steps.

We have every reason to face the future with high hopes and undaunted courage. Our God has been good to us, and has marvelously multiplied the little "mustard seed" of His own planting until today, after but twenty-six years, it has become a great tree, rooted in every land and bearing fruit suited to every clime. Let us move forward along the lines of loyalty, service and fellowship.

Loyalty to Christian Endeavor.

Let us stand by Christian Endeavor, not as a form of words or a prescribed method, but as a great movement possessed and energized by the living Spirit, with unlimited possibilities for growth and development.

Let us emphasize the fact that anything any pastor wants to do for his young people may be done through Christian Endeavor. Forms of expression and methods of service may change, but the fundamental principles and high ideals of Christian Endeavor include intelligent faith in Christ, outspoken allegiance to Christ, faithful service for Christ, and fellowship with Christ's other disciples—and these will abide forever.

Service of Christian Endeavor.

Salvation for service, not for selfish satisfaction, is the keynote of religious thought today. As a department of the church, let us magnify the service side of Christian Endeavor. This will mean securing a larger membership in all our societies, and new societies in all our unions. We must reach and touch the young people before we can help them.

It will require better work from all our officers and committees. Old methods must be revived and revised, and new methods devised to meet the ever-changing needs. Our test should be, Does it work? If not, find a method, or make one, that will work.

It will demand more generous giving. We must cultivate this grace also. For the sake of the church of the future, we must train the young people in systematic and proportionate giving.

New and helpful forms of definite, practical service will be opened up to us through the Christian Endeavor Patriots' League and the World's Brotherhood, about which you will hear at a later session.

Fellowship in Christian Endeavor.

Let us stand by our fellowship, interdenominational, international and interracial, blest of God and blessing men.

One of the grandest tributes ever paid to Christian Endeavor is that given by those who are opposed to any union of the churches, even of the broken fragments of the same denomination, when they say that Christian Endeavor is responsible for the present spirit of union so manifest in many quarters. We accept the responsibility, and thank God that we have been counted worthy to help on the glorious consummation of that day of which the lamented Dr. Dickinson sang:

"O golden day, so long desired,
   Born of a darksome night,
The waiting earth at last is fired
   By thy resplendent light.
And hark! like Memmon's morning chord
   Is heard from sea to sea
This song: One Master, Christ the Lord;
   And brethren all are we.

"The noises of the night shall cease,
   The storms no longer roar;
The factious foes of God's own peace
   Shall vex His church no more.
A thousand thousand voices sing
   The surging harmony,
One Master, Christ; one Saviour-King;
   And brethren all are we.

"Sing on, ye chorus of the morn,
   Your grand Endeavor strain,
Till Christian hearts, estranged and torn,
   Blend in the glad refrain;
And all the church, with all its powers,
   In loving loyalty,
Shall sing, One Master, Christ, is ours;
   And brethren all are we.

"O golden day, the age's crown,
   Alight with heavenly love,
Rare day in prophecy renown.
   On to thy zenith move.
When all the world with one accord
   In full-voiced unity
Shall sing, One Master, Christ our Lord;
   And brethren all are we."

Let us work and pray that the time may soon come when Christian Endeavor shall unite the young people of all denominations, and when, in loyalty to our own church and in fellowship with others, we shall win and train for Christ and His church the young people of the whole wide world.

CHAPTER IV.

TRAINING FOR THE CHURCH OF THE FUTURE.

Thursday Morning, July 11.

The topic for both meetings on the morning of the second day of the convention was devoted to "The Church of the Future," or especially to the children, juniors and intermediates. As Dr. Clark most justly said, "This is not at all too much time to devote to this great theme." In Tent Williston the first address was by the Rev. P. T. Pockman, D.D., pastor of the First Reformed Church, New Brunswick, Nova Scotia. His subject was

THE NEED OF THE DAY—TRAINED CHRISTIANS.

"The church of the future will be made up of the material now in hand. The plastic young mind and heart of today moulded in the best form of Christian service will see the church of twenty years hence stronger and more efficient than now. The church of the present is of a far different type than it would have been if Father Endeavor Clark had not inaugurated the Christian Endeavor movement a quarter of a century ago.

The training required is toward an ideal. That ideal is distinctly outlined in Ephesians 5:25-27.

Christ loved the church, and sacrificed Himself for it—with what intent? That He might sanctify it, and that He might present it to himself (eventually) a glorious church; a holy and unblemished church. Such a church we have never seen, except through a spiritual telescope. Faith alone can make it real to our longing eyes. But our heads and hands should unite in giving substantiality to the vision. The pattern we have, let us set it upon earth. The call is for trained Christians to do this. Old methods do not suffice. Modern builders of character, like modern builders of houses, tunnels, bridges, railroads and aqueducts, use improved systems.

We must have expert leaders. Worldly corporations tell us it is far more economic and effective to have the best possible superintendents, and their practical wisdom should guide the church in her conduct of the affairs of the Kingdom of Christ. Give us men bred in the open for leaders; men trained under the open sunlight of heaven. Not such as love darkness and dampness—the abode of owls, bats and ghouls. These are not the class of leaders for these strenuous times. With expert leaders and competent followers, what may we not accomplish?

Paul always trained his associates for effective service. Jesus held the twelve close about him, bearing with their infirmities, until each decided his own fate. The rank and file should be trained for usefulness by educating them in the truth, by inspiring them with sympathy for their fallen fellow mortals, and then by giving them a finishing course in two directions: 1. An open-vision course, wherein

ARRIVAL OF THE NEW YORK AND PENNSYLVANIA DELEGATIONS.

ARRIVING DELEGATES.

they are taught to see the world as Christ sees it, and also to see the unblemished church as the dear Lord sees it; and, 2. A bended-knee course, wherein they close their eyes to all material considerations and just commune with the Head of the Church until they find themselves wrapped up in His arms and plans, and count nothing too great a sacrifice to hasten their fulfillment."

"When a man introduces his own wife, she is sure to have the last word," was the happy way in which Dr. Clark introduced Mrs. Clark to the convention. Mrs. Clark's theme was "Training the Children," and she treated it in the wise and witty way that is so characteristic of her. She told the story of the Scottish mother who was talking about the fine qualities of her prospective son-in-law. He was rich, industrious, moral. "There's only one thing," she remarked, "the lassa canna abide him. But that's aye something." Thus, Mrs. Clark said, we are liable to teach our children everything except the one most important thing, that never should be taken for granted, their religion. And she outlined in a most attractive fashion the simple but effective plan by which this religious training is accomplished in the Junior Society.

"Training the Youth" was the topic assigned for the Intermediate Christian Endeavorers. It was treated by Rev. R. G. Bannen, D.D., President of the Pennsylvania Christian Endeavor Union. He said:

"Some time ago a great church historian, as he looked out over the sea of Endeavorers' faces in a meeting in New York, said: "This is a new chapter in the history of the church which has never been written, and I have wondered who but the Recording Angel could write the story of Christian Endeavor, or who can measure its power on the present or estimate its influence on the generations that shall come." The church is the hope of the future, and as a Christian she teaches that she is the hope of the world. Have you ever asked yourself the question, What will the church of the future be if it is trained in Christian Endeavor? Briefly, let me say it will be a church of larger gifts because of the Tenth Legion. It will be a church of world-wide activity because of the Macedonian Phalanx. It will be a church that will furnish men of honor for the high places in our civilization. Sitting at a table for early breakfast some months ago, a business man by my side was speaking of the life insurance companies and the railroad companies, and then he added that the day is not far distant when a man to be regarded as a business success must be clean, straight and honest, and I have wondered what place Christian Endeavor, with its good citizenship work, will have in bringing this about.

From the second Christian Endeavor society that was organized in the great State of Pennsylvania, five young men have gone into the Christian ministry. The church of the future will be a church of larger faith because of the quiet hour and the study of the Word of God.

One of the leaders of the Salvation Army, as he spoke to me about his work in New York City, took down a little book from a pigeonhole in his desk and said, as he pointed to a question on the first page: "This question is here to save me from discouragement." The question was: "Is anything too hard for God."

If the church of the future is to measure up to this high ideal, then she must care for the boy and the girl of the Intermediate Society—that most critical period in every life—when the little fellow is too old to be a child, yet too young to be a man; that period in life when the Sunday school and the church is suffering her heaviest losses. Should I care to take your time I could bring you facts and figures in abundance to prove that this is the period at which more people give their hearts to Christ than any other. From 776 graduates of the Drew Theological Seminary, the average age of conversion was 16.4 years, and from 527 Y. M. C. A. officers it was 16.5 years; and whether in bringing the young to accept the Christ or in training them for service after they have accepted him, the Intermediate Society has a large and important place.

You have doubtless heard the story from one of the wars of the old world when a number of men were convicted as spies and were sentenced to be shot. Among them was a little fellow of 14 (an intermediate). The men were lined up, and when the volley was fired everyone fell except the little fellow at the end of the row. He stayed there with a great gash torn through his shoulder by the deadly bullet. An officer said: "Let's pardon him now,' but the little fellow rolled back the lapel of his coat and said: "Ain't better men than me. Here's my heart—it's beating for the King." So may our hearts beat true to the King of Kings, though it may even cost our life."

After Dr. Bannen's inspiring message, Dr. Clark spoke of the new hymn which had been written for the convention by our Publication Manager, Mr. George B. Graff, to Dr. Dickinson's words, "We Battle for the King of Kings," and asked the congregation to join heartily in singing it, which they did with a will.

"How the Parents Can Help" was a very practical theme discussed in a most helpful way by Rev. W. H. Barraclough, B. A., pastor of the Queen's Avenue Methodist Church, New Westminster, B. C. He said:

"Back behind the training of the church of the future is the bringing of the children to Christ. There will be no church of the future unless we are steadily winning new recruits to its ranks.

But how is this to be done? How are the children to be influenced to enlist in the service of the King?

There is no more powerful influence than that of example, and in the work for the children, the example of the home. It is not enough simply to exhort the children to love and follow Christ. We must first set them an example of faithfulness and devotion to Christ if we would win them for Him.

If the parents would help train the church of the future, let them take an active interest in the church of the present. Make the children to feel the importance of the services of the church by your regular and faithful attendance. Make them to realize the importance of all Christian and philanthropic effort by your deep interest in the success of such effort. Let the church be first in your plans, and it is not likely to take a second place in the thought of your children.

We need a revival of family religion, of the family altar and the family pew, and their influence in the developing of character if the church of the future is to keep up the long record of unselfish devotion.

The parents can help in training the church of the future by giving the children a broad outlook upon life. Their eyes have opened upon a different world than ours, and they will have to undertake larger tasks than were ever allotted to us, and face problems which we have never been called upon to face. Let us help them to build upon the rock. Give them a reason for the hope which has sustained their fathers and enabled them to press through the waves of doubt and difficulty. Train them to think clearly and rightly and righteously. Give time to their education on moral and spiritual lines. It is not waste time. If you do not want a harvest of tears, instill into their hearts a hatred of sin in all its forms, which will lead them to joyfully step into the ranks, when you fall out, and take up the battle with renewed vigor.

Teach them respect for authority. In these days of national unrest, when anarchial sentiments are being pressed openly, we cannot too strongly enforce this. Never permit a word derogatory to President, or Governor, or minister, or teacher to pass unrebuked. You may have your opinions, but if you value the souls of your children do not express them.

Teach them the sacred use of money. In this age of prosperity, of greed of gold, of luxury breeding selfishness, impress upon the coming church that life was not made for mere getting or mere sensual gratification, but for service. Teach them that it is better to die poor and unknown than to grow rich at the price of human suffering and misery. Set an example of generous liberality. Educate them from earliest childhood to contribute to all the schemes of the church and to contribute systematically of what they receive or what they earn. Follow this method, and the church of the future will be an enthusiastically devoted, broad-minded and large-hearted church."

After prayer by President Harpster, of Ohio, Secretary Shaw conducted a lively open parliament on the problems confronting the Junior and Intermediate Society workers.

Emphasizing the point that the Junior Society must work with the material given it, and no other, Mr. Shaw told the story of the disgruntled farmer who complained of his incubator: "The miserable thing hasn't laid an egg yet."

Questions came thick and fast. "How teach the Juniors to pray?" Get them on their knees and let them say just what is in their hearts. Get them to understand that when they speak to their Heavenly Father they can speak as simply as to their mother and father in their home. Let the children in their home prayers at night talk to God about the events of the day.

"To what extent is it wise to have organization in the Junior Society?" One of the crying needs in the church today is to have more business in our Christianity, and that means organization, provided it is alive.

"What to do with the older children who say that there are too many babies in the Junior Society, and so remain outside?" Remind them that they themselves were babies once. Make the Junior meetings such that the older young people will feel the work there to be worthy of them.

Dr. Smith Baker, who closed this exhilarating session, was introduced, and rightly, as "the youngest Endeavorer of us all." It was his part to tell of "The Pastor's Part in the Training Process." He spoke from wide experience and practice when he said:

"The pastor must be in the society and let the society be in him. The personal consecration of the pastor by the society decides his influence over it and his power to use it. I have noticed that when boys do not enjoy staying at home evenings, it is generally because the parents do not make that home what it ought to be, and when the Endeavor Society does not find the young people closer to the church it is because the pastor neglects the young people. When the Endeavor Society seems to separate the young people from the older, the pastor and deacons are to blame.

The pastor is not to be a pope, or dictator, or find fault or scold, but one with his young people, advising, leading, instructing. Then the young people will follow and surround him with loyalty. Talk about finding fault. It never does any good, at home or in the church, or anywhere else. It always drives people from us. The pastor should use the young people. That's his business. That's what the Endeavor Society was formed for, as a means, an instrument to help the pastor in his spiritual work with the young people.

The pastor should give the young people something to do in church work. Let them be responsible for the singing in the regular church prayer meeting. Ask the Endeavor Society to take charge of the church prayer meeting once a month. Give them the missionary concert once in a while to work up. Send the young members to call on the old people. Give them a share in the church offices. Such is the way it is done in the original society at Williston Church, and as a result the young people are as loyal to the church and all its work as are the older people, and the pastor can depend upon them as truly as upon the church officers. When the pastor neglects the Endeavor Society he must expect the Endeavor Society to neglect the church.

An ideal family is not where there is an aged couple of 80, and no one else, or where there is a middle-aged man and his wife, or where there is a young married couple and no one else, or where there is an old bachelor in his room alone, or an unappropriated blessing in her room alone, or where there are only two young children; but the ideal family is where there is grandfather and grandmother, and the middle-aged people and young people, and lads and girls and little children. Thus they educate and help each other. The ideal church and the ideal prayer meeting is not one of all old people, or all middle-aged people, or all boys and girls, but where there are old people of 80 and young people and boys and girls of 8. Thus they help each other. Thus the pastors work to mix the people like a large family, and thus the old people give wisdom to the young people, and the young people give life to the old people.

The pastor makes a sad, inexcuseless mistake who does not use the Endeavor Society for all it is worth in bringing the young and old together."

First Presbyterian Church—Thursday Morning.

In the First Presbyterian Church, Dr. Hill again presided, and introduced as the speaker of the morning that staunch friend of Christian Endeavorers, the Rev. E. R. Dille, D.D., pastor of the First Methodist Episcopal Church in Oakland, Cal. His topic was "Training in Expression":

TRAINING IN EXPRESSION.

"Up to twenty-five years ago, edification, instruction, was the fetich of Christian work. The Sunday morning service, the Sunday evening service and the Sunday school were for instruction. The prayer meeting was for edification, and therefore no one must speak or pray who could not do so to edification, which generally meant the minister and deacons over 60. When Dwight L. Moody spoke for the first time in prayer meeting, he was asked if he was not ashamed of himself to speak when he could not speak to edification. "Yes," he said, "I am ashamed of myself, but I am not ashamed of my Master."

The Christian Endeavor Society was organized not for teaching but for training; not for preaching but for practice. It is a drill ground where we learn to marshal all our powers and make them render their best service; where we not only give ourselves but ourselves raised to the highest power. In short, the Christian Endeavor Society is the West Point of the Army of the Lord.

Does it reduce a soldier to a mere cipher that he is put under dicipline—that he is required to march and wheel and lift each foot and set every muscle at the word of command? Does it take a man's liberty away and make him a milksop, a mere broth of a man, to put him under dicipline? That's what men sometimes say of the renunciation and obedience to the Christian life. No! This discipline and drill invigorates every manly quality, and it is the only way soldiers and heroes can be made.

Why are fifty boys of your Washington National Guard more than a match for a mob of a thousand? Discipline and drill make all the difference.

Expression is, in the nature of the case, an essential part of the school of the Christian soldier. It is profoundly significant that when the Holy Ghost came on the Day of Pentecost its symbol was not a sword, nor a sceptre, nor a pen, nor a book, but a tongue—a tongue of fire, which sat not only on the heads of the twelve, but on the head of each member of the church, and when the tongue of fire touched them they began to speak as the Spirit gave them utterance.

The secret of the rapid spread of the Gospel of the First Century was a band of disciples, everyone of whom were witnesses. Even in the age of persecution the church spread with redoubled rapidity, for in the hour of martyrdom the most timid of the disciples broke into impassioned speech as they were touched at the stake, as at Pentecost, with the tongue of fire.'

Christian Endeavor says to the young Christian what Paul said to Timothy: "Neglect not the gift that is in thee." You have precious powers unsuspected, undeveloped, unused, which Christian Endeavor is just adapted to call into action. I know the trouble with some of you. You are so afraid that you won't speak tactfully, gracefully and creditably that you will not speak at all. That is a subtle form of spiritual pride that is not willing to fail or break down, if need be, for Christ.

How may you learn to speak for the Master? If down in our hearts we feel that we have truth necessary to our brother's salvation, that there is no other name given under Heaven or among men whereby we can be saved; if, as Cardinal Manning said of the Salvation Army: "We have a passion for sinners," we will find a way to talk to people, and if we cannot find a way we will make one.

From the Christian Endeavor, the West Point of the Lord's army, and not from the awkward squad, are to come the best of our best, who shall carry the flag and bear the ark into the noon of the Twentieth century."

"Training in Prayer—Public and Private" was the subject of the Rev. H. W. Frazer, D.D., pastor of the First Presbyterian Church, Vancouver, B. C. Dr. Frazer seemed to be filled with the importance of his subject, and filled all his hearers likewise.

"Need I say that this is one of the most important subjects—only too often relegated to an unimportant place, or overlooked altogether? There are at least three reasons why it should be otherwise.

First, because of its nature. It is a solemn interview with Diety; and surely, if anywhere, it becomes us to make due preparation when we are about to enter into the presence of Him, before whom, angels who have not sinned, in adoration veil their faces.

A second reason is found in our purpose. We are suppliants. In our approaches to earthly tribunals, we do so in a respectful attitude and in fitting terms we ought not to do less when we make known our desires to God. It is to be with thanks, and it is only as we do so that the peace of God comes to fill heart and life.

But a third reason why we should prepare—training ourselves in prayer is found in the fact that it is after all an act involving the understanding, the emotions, and the will. As such it makes no small demand upon the whole man.

How, then, shall we train ourselves in prayer?

1. By the cultivation of the prayer spirit. Thus David explains in one of the Psalms the source of his inspiration. The river of devotion will never overflow its banks until fed by the secret springs.

2. Let us cultivate the art of prayer; for prayer is an art. We sometimes speak of it as a gift. It may indeed be so, but it is also an art. It has an order of development as well as definiteness of purpose. When the disciples asked: 'Lord, teach us to pray,' Jesus said after this manner, 'pray ye," and then gave to them that matchless prayer which for all time will be known as the model prayer. Set it in contrast with the ejaculations known as sentence prayers; set it over against the average prayer, and the necessity for the cultivation of the art of prayer becomes at once evident. It at least is reverent, direct, comprehensive, and humble.

3. Cultivate the habit of prayer. Cultivate it in the seclusion of your closet; cultivate it in the Quiet Hour, in the prayer meeting. Like every other habit its use leads to ease in expression, and becomes a settled part of our daily life. Fluency may never mean fervor and

words, no matter how many or how well strung together, may not be prayer, but if we would in any sense become intercessors with God for our fellows, it will be true that in order to do so, we must train ourselves in the spirit of prayer, in the art of expression in prayer, in the habit of praying. Then we will be like the men of old who by faith and prayer worked wonders."

"Training in Giving" was the subject assigned to the Christian Endeavorers' long-time friend, the Rev. J. M. Lowden, pastor of the First Free Baptist Church of Providence, R. I. His address was an able presentation of the claims of the Tenth Legion.

"The Tenth Legion is an enrollment of Christians whose practice it is to give to God for His work not less than one-tenth of their income.

We are urged to this practice by the following considerations:

A man's use of money is the truest exponent of himself. The Christian spirit is sacrificial, therefore a man's use of money must manifest this Christian characteristic. Hence God's special appreciation of it. "God loveth a cheerful giver"; and this because our beneficence manifests His spirit in us.

Beneficence is also a stimulant of all Christian graces: a condition of their fullest growth and development. It therefore touches the whole question of Christian growth and attainment.

Even prayer is determined and limited by the spirit of giving. Prayer is of the heart, and when the heart is not right true prayer is impossible. If we are withholding from the Lord that which is His, we cannot in sincerity offer the prayer: "Thy kingdom come."

Further, money rightly used is power utilized, according to the purpose of God for the good of men. Money is a necessary factor in extending the Kingdom of God. Money hoarded is power unused; money selfishly used is power wasted; money rightly used, given to God for His work, is power utilized and directed to meet the world's need.

Money rightly used is also a supreme expresssion of devotion to Christ.

The Christian motive in beneficence can never be impulse. Such motive is not sufficiently strong, neither has it the grace of continuance. The only true motive is the sacrificial spirit of Christ. Not sacrifice in imitation of Christ, but self-sacrifice the result of being in Christ.

The guide in this beneficence is reason enlightened by the Spirit, not impulse. We must not waste the Lord's goods. We must give wisely if we give Christianly.

The spirit of this beneficence is the spirit of joy. Our giving, our tithing, is in the spirit of gladness: it is privilege, it is Christian altruism—not duty. We feel that every Christian should give at least a tenth of his income to Him who has given us all.

Further, tithing has this great merit; it is systematic and proportionate; two essentials of the grace of beneficence.

Fellow Endeavorers, the Lord is sitting over against the treasury today, as in the olden time, for here, as not elsewhere, we reveal what we are; here He sees us as we are. May it be true of us that the Christ-like spirit of beneficence shall be in us to the world's good and our Master's glory."

The Publication Manager of the United Society, Mr. George B. Graff, spoke on the topic, "The Right Use of Helps." He quoted President Tucker's words, voiced several years ago: "What we are is God's gift to us; what we make of ourselves is our gift to God." He then said: "It is not so much the talents that count as it is the use that we make of the talents. While consecration, character, goodness, piety are all most excellent, if we would have our lives count for the utmost, these characteristics should be augmented by material aids to give us greater knowledge." He illustrated the ignorance displayed by some people by quoting some of the absurd questions that are frequently sent to the United Society office, and then gave a practical talk on some of the helps that are published to assist the different officers, committees and members of the Society. He closed with an earnest plea to Christian Endeavorers to make the most of their lives by gaining knowledge from others, reading good books, studying Christian Endeavor helps. "It is the increase of our lives that Jesus wants, as that is our gift to God."

Following the address came an open parliament, conducted by Mr. Guy M. Withers of Kansas City, Mo. It was a most interesting and attractive fifteen minutes. Questions came thick and fast. There was not a dull moment, and not a foolish question was asked or answered.

The closing speaker of the session was the Rev. John Pollock, President of the European Christian Endeavor Union and pastor of St. Enoch's Presbyterian Church, Belfast, Ireland. Dr. Pollock wore his badge of office, a golden linked chain, around his neck, from which hung a large golden C. E. monogram. This was Mr. Pollock's first appearance before the convention, and he was accorded a splendid ovation. He caught the attention of the audience in his opening remarks by saying that he was now facing the greatest problem of his life, and that was how he was going to begin his address "twenty minutes ago," as it was already twenty minutes past the closing hour. However, so interesting was Mr. Pollock's address that he held the closest attention of the audience until he had finished. His subject was "Training in Service."

Whatever might be the case on this side of the ocean, it was undeniable that on the other side there was a prejudice in the public mind against committees. And not altogether without reason. There was a suspicion that committees existed chiefly for the purpose of shelving awkward business. At the best the term committee was generally regarded as a synonym for delay. Too often it meant theory without practice, talk rather than work. Perhaps Spurgeon was right when he said that if the work had been left to a committee the ark would never have been built. Now, it might be said that Christian Endeavor had come to change all this, in our churches, at all events.

THE JUNIOR RALLY.

Has it done so? What said the speaker, about your society, your own committee, yourself?

It seemed to him that Christian Endeavor committees had three main purposes. A committee that was worthy of its appointment must exist, of course, for the prosecution of a particular work. It was there that the work might be done, and be well done. Christian endeavor had a profound belief in prayer; but it did not live in the clouds. It recognized the need for the use of means. But strange as it might seem to say so, the doing of work was by no means the chief end of a Christian Endeavor committee. Its primary object was training. Christian Endeavor recognized this important fact, that you cannot train for service except in service.

There was, in relation to each of the committees, and especially to the executive committee, training for the whole membership of the society, in the demand which was made upon them to respect the findings of their representatives. That was a discipline much needed in the present day when the too prevalent spirit of individualism was showing a tendency to assert itself more aggressively within the church itself.

Training was needed in methods of Christian work, in devising and operating an effective organization, in the transaction of business, in tactful visitation, in the art of hand-shaking. This principle ought to be kept in view by the nomination committee. They ought to put some of the brightest members on the social committee, that the work might be well done; but that was just where some of the other sort ought to be put for their training. Committees existed for training in such business virtues as courtesy, method, and punctuality. Above all there was needed training in faithfulness. If only Christian Endeavorers were faithful to their solemn vows, the word "committee" would be redeemed from much of the contempt in which it is justly held. If he were asked how long they could best commend this best of movements to the best of men, he would say by being faithful. Let them keep their vows.

He would remind them also that Christian Endeavor did not exist for itself. It was the devoted handmaid of the church. Training in their committees was not to be regarded as a training for Christian Endeavor, but in order that they might be good church workers; for to the church alone had come the commission to go into the streets and lanes, into the highways and hedges, into all the world. Christian Endeavor sought simply to assist the church in the doing of the church's work, and all their training for service meant training for the service of Christ through the church.

CHAPTER V.

THE JUNIOR RALLY.

Tent Williston Thronged with an Enthusiastic Audience.

The Junior Rally of late years has come to be the great, picturesque feature of the Christian Endeavor conventions. It is always a most attractive feature, for who is not interested in the children. The Junior Rally at the Seattle convention was no exception to the general rule. Long before the hour of opening Tent Williston was packed with an audience that filled every nook and corner of the immense canvas. About 700 Junior Endeavorers of Seattle sat upon the platform and took part in the exercises. The great feature of the program was the exercise entitled "Building the Bridge." Two hundred children, under the direction of Mrs. W. B. Judah, took part in it, and it was given from beginning to end without an error, and received praise and applause on every hand. The girls, dressed in pure white, and crowned with floral wreaths, presented a picture that was at once inspiring and attractive. They were assisted by surpliced choir boys, who were a pleasing feature of the service. Many times the enthusiasm of the audience gave vent to applause. Little Miss Marion Ohnick, daughter of a Japanese business man of Seattle, was accorded an ovation at the close of a recitation by her in the bridge construction feature.

A special feature of the program was the rendition of the hymn "Pass It On," by Paul Feirendo, a little six-year-old lad of Seattle, who mounted the bridge, and bravely facing the great gathering sang in his small voice (nothing less melodious for its lack of volume) the sacred song.

The services began with a song by the children, and prayer was offered by Rev. John Pollock, of Belfast, Ireland. Rev. Wm. T. McElveen of Boston was introduced and held the closest attention of the audience, even to the smallest and most mischievous of the children during his entire address. His subject was: "What can boys and girls do for Christ and the Church?" He said:

"Boys and girls can be Christians. Size, weight and age have nothing to do with being a Christian. A little apple tree is just as much an apple tree as a big apple tree. And a little boy or girl may be just as much a Christian as a big man or woman. What makes an apple tree an apple tree? Not its size; not its age. A tree is an apple tree when a certain kind of vegetable life courses through its trunk and branches. And a boy or girl is a Christian when a certain kind of life enters into and energizes them: It is apple life in the tree that makes it an apple tree. It is Christ life in the boy or girl that makes them a Christian boy or girl. There are many different kinds of apple trees. There are Baldwins, etc.; and there are many different kinds of Christians—Episcopalian, Methodist, Presbyterian, Congregationalist. But an apple is an apple whatever the kind and a Christian is a Christian whatever the denomination. You boys are not half men, and you girls are not quarter women. You are little men and women. You are made of the very same kind of material as men and women, only in you there is not so much of it. Here are two books—a big one and a little one. The same number of chapters, verses and words are in the little book as are in the big book. Both books are Bibles—one is a pulpit Bible, the other is a pocket edition of the Bible. So you boys and girls are pocket editions of men and women. And you can be little Christians. In the Old Testament there is a story about a boy Christian. His name was Samuel. His mother, Hannah, made him a little coat that was exactly like the prophet Eli's coat. Eli had his ephod and Samuel had his little ephod. The one was a big minister, the other was a little minister. Samuel had something to do in the tabernacle. The Bible says a number of times that Samuel did minister before the Lord. Samuel, the boy prophet, was a duplicate in small of the man prophet Eli. God spoke to Eli and He spoke to Samuel. And Eli spoke to God and Samuel spoke to God. And though Samuel did not know as much and did not do as much as Eli, religion was in the boy as well as in the man. Remember what we said about the little and the big apple trees. An apple tree a few years old will not yield as many apples as an apple tree twenty-five years old, but it is just as much an apple tree. And it is not to be expected that a boy or girl Christian would be able to do as much as a man or woman Christian, but a child Christian is as much a Christian as a grown-up Christian. A circle an inch in diameter is as much a circle as a circle a mile in diameter. The words little and big describe quantity. But Christianity has to do with quality. It is not how many inches tall you are, or how many pounds you weigh, or how many years you have existed; it is the sort of a person you are, the kind of life you are living, that makes you a Christian. Christ took children in his arms. We do not read of Socrates or Plato or Aristotle doing that. And Jesus said "of such is the kingdom of heaven." None of the great Greek and Roman thinkers and teachers ever said anything like that. They made men and women teachers of children, but Jesus also made children the teachers of men and women. He told the grown-ups "except ye become as little children ye shall in no wise enter into the kingdom of heaven." Jesus did not mean by this that all children are naturally Christians, but He does mean by these statements that there are in all children certain qualities that make it easy for them to become Christians.

Childhood is the proper time to become a Christian. At no other time can you become a Christian so easily. When should a child begin to walk? "Just as soon as he can," you answer. But suppose you boys and girls were kept in your cradles until you were 20 or 30 years old, or until you were 50 or 60 years old, until your bones and muscles were stiff and your limbs were like sticks. Do you not think you would make very funny work of trying to learn to walk then? It is just that kind of work that a full grown man makes of beginning to be a Christian. He shambles around and he falls often. We have an old proverb that says "You can't teach an old dog new tricks." If you begin when the dog is a puppy you can train him to do a hundred and one tricks. And it is just so with boys and girls. If there is a man or woman here today who is 50 or 60 years old and not a Christian, it is not probable they ever will be one. That is a sad thing to say, but it is true. He has got so stiff in his way of thinking and acting that it is next to impossible for him to be anything else than he is.

After the address the children began the building of the Christian Endeavor bridge. The foundation stones and the piers of the bridge were laid by boys dressed in white surplices. The keystone of the arch bore the word "Jesus." The chorus sang fitting hymns while the other parts of the bridge were put in place, and when the bridge was about completed little white-robed maidens came forward bearing lighted torches. The boys hung up banners, and all united in singing "Onward, Christian Soldiers." The outline of the exercise was as follows:

   Exercise: "Building the Christian Endeavor Bridge."
     Steps of Childhood.
"I Think, When I Read That Sweet Story"....................Chorus
    Foundation Stones.
  Recitation: "Faith."
  Recitation: "Hope."
    Piers, Stones of Service.
Prayer Meeting............................"Sweet Hour of Prayer"
Lookout......................................"Always on the Lookout"
Missionary..."Speed Away"
Sunshine ...."Looking Upward"
Temperance ...."The Temperance Rally"
Social ...."Social Committee Song"
Music.."Music Committee Song"
Whatsoever..........................."Scatter Seeds of Kindness"
Pastor's Aid.................................."We're a Junior Band"
Flower ...."Beautiful Flowers"
    Arch, Stones of Power.
   Christlikeness   Endurance
   Holiness   Neighborliness
   Regeneration   Devotion
   Inspiration   Enthusiasm
   Sacrifice   Ardor
   Thankfulness   Vigilance
   Integrity   Obedience
   Alms   Unity
   Nobility   Reverence, Prayer
     Keystone.
"TAKE THE NAME OF JESUS WITH YOU"..................Chorus
    Spandrels.
"FOR CHRIST AND THE CHURCH".......................Chorus
    Capstones.

Recitation: "FIDELITY."
Recitation: "FELLOWSHIP."
        Panels, Pledged Purpose.
"TRUSTING JESUS, THAT IS ALL"..........................Chorus
       Pledge Hymn (or Junior Christian Endeavor Pledge).
              Center Capstone.
              Capstone.
"GOD IS LOVE"..Chorus
              Pathway.
Recitation: "WAY OF HOLINESS."
              Lamps of Truth.
Recitation: "PASS IT ON."
Recitation: "BEATITUDES."
              Lights of Life.
Recitation: JUNIOR.
        Flags of International Fellowship.
"FLING OUT THE BANNER"...............................Chorus
              Steps of Service.
"OUR LIVES TO CHRIST WE DEDICATE"..................Chorus
              Recessional.
"ONWARD, CHRISTIAN SOLDIERS"........................Chorus

Take it all in all, the Seattle Junior Rally was perhaps the most successful of any of those heretofore given at an International convention.

Hon. James R. Garfield, Secretary of the Interior, arrived too late to address the entire audience, but spoke informally to those present when he arrived. "You recognize only one Master," he said, "and your work is one of cooperation. The aim of Christian Endeavor is not for its members to live as selfish individuals, but to ease the burdens of the less fortunate, to work for one another, and thus work out the Golden Rule."

CHAPTER VI.

UNION WORKERS' RALLY.

A New Feature in Christian Endeavor Conventions.

A new feature was introduced into the program of the Seattle convention this year, and that was a Rally of all officers, superintendents of departments and chairmen or members of committees in local, county, district, city or state unions. The Rally was held at the same hour as the Junior Rally, the latter being, as is well known, one of the most largely attended meetings during a Christian Endeavor convention.

The large number which filled the First Presbyterian Church, therefore, where the Union Rally was held, was a surprise and delight to the hundreds of workers in attendance. The meeting was conducted by Secretary Shaw in his usual happy vein. He kept all good-natured, and at the same time enforced the truths presented by the speakers as only he can do. Two points were emphasized in the meeting. First, that union work must be made attractive if it is to appeal to young people; second, that executive and administrative ability must be brought to bear in the management of the unions, and that the work of the unions should be arranged to deal with the live topics of good citizenship as well as with church affairs.

In his introduction General Secretary Shaw spoke of things to be done and to be left undone. He said: 'In the first place, we must be united in our efforts. Let us be earnest —not on the gathering of statistics, but on the promotion and improvement of the work. Many union officers seem to be more interested to find out what societies are doing than in getting them to do things. Start in on new lines. Do new things. Do business that is worth while, and the young people will back you up. Get new blood into your societies. Go out and get the young men and young women who do not care to he Christian Endeavorers. To do this make the society attractive. Make it efficient.''

Our old-time friend Mr. Von Ogden Vogt, Secretary of the World's Christian Endeavor, and now Young People's Secretary of the Presbyterian Board of Home Missions, spoke upon the topic ''Shall Our Unions Be Christian Endeavor or

General?" "I desire to say five things," said he, "about Christian Endeavor, and in order that they may not be lost, put them down not only in your heads, but in your note-books. What is Christian Endeavor for? First, it is a clearing-house of information. Second, it should see that no phase of work is neglected in any society. Third, it should look after all the functions of the society, such as organizing new societies. Fourth, it should help union meetings and conferences. Fifth, it should do good things for your city, joining with others in like efforts for the upbuilding of your community. It is not fair for certain societies in a city to say 'We want a new federation in which we will be included.' They should be willing to come into a Christian Endeavor Society and become part of it in its work. Christian Endeavor is a federation itself. I look for the day when Christian Endeavor shall be a power that will teach us to move against the great evils of the world and conquer them. It is not fair for one or two denominations to dictate to the other denominations as to the abandonment of their methods of work and the name which they prefer. It would be as if Oklahoma should say, 'We should like to join the union of states, but we will not come, in unless you drop the Declaration of Independence and change the name of the United States to Columbia."

This important topic was discussed with fullness and fairness by the workers present, and it was the general feeling that the Christian Endeavor movement cannot be efficient unless in its unions it is entirely free to push its ideals and methods, and untrammeled by societies that do not endorse all the Christian Endeavor principals.

The well known secretary of Ohio's forces, Rev. C. H. Hubbell, spoke on the financial side of the work, his topic being "Union Finances—How to Get the Money." He said: "Believe in the work you are doing—it is a worthy cause. The man who asks for money is not a beggar but a benefactor; he is not a pauper, but a philanthropist. The way to get money is to go and ask for it. There are four things you must do—Pray, Plan, Push, and Praise—then you will get money. If a man does well, say so. Always remember to say please and thank you. 'Motion' will get more money than emotion or commotion. Go out and work."

President Tarring, of the District of Columbia Union, spoke on "Union Departments and Committees—How to Work Them." The Washington Union is one of the very best organized Unions in the country.

Mr. Tarring gave some idea of the work that his Union is doing. He said: "Our Union in the District of Columbia is organized into different departments. We have a press department, a Citizenship department, and a Junior department. We advertise. We have found that this pays. It is like the boy who wrote upon the schoolroom blackboard, 'Johnnie Jones can hug the girls better than any boy in school.' The teacher came in a few minutes later, and when she saw the writing on the blackboard she said: 'Johnnie, did you write that?' Johnnie assented, and the teacher then informed him he was to remain after school. When Johnnie came out of school, a crowd of boys asked him in one breath, 'Did you get a licking? Did she scold? What did she do to you?' Johnnie answered 'No' to all of this, but finally remarked, 'Well, it pays to advertise.' Develop the originality of your committee chairmen by throwing them on their own responsibility. Require frequent reports, thereby showing that definite results are expected."

Mr. J. H. Mansfield, of the Connecticut C. E. Union, spoke on the subject of "Union Conferences—Their Value and Helpfulness." He had just come from a remarkable series of conferences, and he spoke of them, illustrating their value, and urged upon his hearers the larger use of conferences by unions in their work. "These conferences," said Mr. Mansfield, get hold of individual workers and develop new ones as no meetings can. They are organized by the state or local union, and a series of them deal with practical matters and solid sense for Christian Endeavorers."

"Union Programs—How To Prepare Them," was the topic of Editorial Secretary Amos R. Wells. "In building a Christian Endeavor program," he said, "we should construct as we construct anything else. The Christian Endeavor meetings are only to build up the Christian Endeavor work. Therefore, when you build a program, make it a Christian Endeavor program. See to it that Endeavorers themselves are largely utilized in the program. Be sure that the local pastors are given a chance to discuss practical Christian Endeavor themes. Exercise ingenuity in seeing that the program is diversified and that novelties are introduced as often as possible."

Mr. Walter K. Ceperly, ex-President of the Chicago Union, spoke of "Practical Plans For Unions To Do." He suggested the systematic study of missions, evangelistic work in hospitals (109 of the conversions came as a result of one month's work of a Christian Endeavor evangelist in the Cook County Hospital), civic study, outdoor missionary meetings, work for sailors, prison work, work for the poor, co-operation in the world wide work of the United Society, and gave many other most excellent suggestions.

Field Secretary Edds, of the New York Union, spoke about "Country and Rural Societies," showing how rural societies

THE "MESSIAH" CHORUS AND ORCHESTRA.
BUILDING THE BRIDGE AT THE JUNIOR RALLY. CROSSING THE BRIDGE AT THE JUNIOR RALLY.

could fill the religious needs of country places and bless them mentally, socially and spiritually. He stated further that you cannot have as fine churches in the country as in the city, but you can have just as fine prayer meetings and do just as good work in proportion to your environment.

The climax of the Union rally was reached when General Secretary Shaw (characterizing "Willie) and Secretary Wells ("Willie's Papa") conducted a dialogue on the memorial building. We shall not attempt a description of it here. It was mirth provoking throughout, but sane, common sense ran all through it. As a result, it is believed and expected that the building fund will be largely increased. The rally closed with an open parliament on union work, conducted by Mr. Lathrop. The themes principally discussed were union work and the memorial building. And the rapid manner in which the questions were presented showed that the workers were intensely interested in both subjects.

Union rallies will hereafter be a feature of all convention programs as it was proven one of the most helpful features of the Seattle convention.

CHAPTER VII.

The Complete Christian.

THURSDAY EVENING'S SESSION.

It was a tent-inflating audience, filled with enthusiasm in the sacred literal meaning of that oft-misused word, that enjoyed the great Thursday night program on "The Complete Christian." The singing was good because it was both hearty and unanimous. From the first it was plain that the opening prayer by Rev. Charles Stelzle for the continuous presence of the Spirit in the meeting, had been answered. It was an ideal Christian Endeavor Convention audience; and it got what it came for—spiritual and intellectual food and refreshment, delightfully provided, with just enough and not too much appetising humor.

A welcome surprise came early in the meeting when the presiding officer, Dr. Ira Landrith, pleasantly introduced Rev. John Pollock, president of the European Christian Endeavor Union, who spoke briefly but thrillingly a message of fraternal love from European Endeavorers in general and from British Endeavorers in particular. The audience cheered and cheered, and then got on its feet and cheered some more, when Dr. Pollock declared, "We British Endeavorers love you and we are never more at home than when standing with you in such meetings as this, the Stars and Stripes above us both. When I reached America on Independence Day I enjoyed your fireworks very much, and it did not dawn upon me for some time that every squib sent up towards the heavens meant that you had licked the Britishers. Personal feeling has almost completely passed away between the two countries, and the Briton's heart is warming towards America every day."

"When Dr. McElveen speaks on 'Training the Body' he manifestly practices what he preaches," was the way the physically powerful and in all other ways equally strong Rev. W. T. McElveen, Ph.D., of Boston, was introduced. Dr. McElveen not only occupied, he completely filled, the speaker's stand, and the audience testified by repeated applause its acknowledgement of the masterfulness of the orator in the stand. "Some there are who, like the chairman, think they are spiritual when they are only spirituelle!" was the clearer way the speaker got even with the equally robust presiding officer. Dr. McElveen thought:

"With the idea of Christ being the savior of our souls we are very familiar. But Ephesians, 5:23 declares that Christ is the savior of the body. Christ saves all of man; his redemption has to do with the body as well as the soul. If he is really saved he must be wholly saved. The physical is an inalienable part of our being. A soul without a body is not a man any more than a body without a soul is a man. We are never to be disembodied spirits. We are always to live in some sort of a body. Each kind of life has its own body. There is one kind of body for man, another for beasts, another for fishes and another for birds. Each being has a body suited to its state and environment. So there is a kind of body in which we live when on earth and a kind in which we shall live in the future heaven. "There is a natural body and there is a spiritual body." As man now bears the image of the earthly so by and by he shall bear the image of the heavenly. When, what we call death, brings to an end this present rudimentary form of embodiment, the apostle suggests that our spirits will have another fairer, finer embodiment. There is no part of our complicate being that Christ's vitalizing energy does not effect. Every part of man's varied and composite being receives enlargement and enrichment when His quickening life enters into a man. The entire man is blessed. Christ is the savior of the body and Christianity is the sanctification of the whole man.

God's grace is not like a scanty brook, but like an overflowing river. We are to grow up into the measure of the stature of the fullness of Christ. Now this redeeming effluence that we call grace is so rich, so abundant, so full that it flows with the plentitude of a flood, not only into the faculties of the soul and mind, but into the powers of the body. The soul with all its capacity cannot contain it. It overflows with its refreshing and renewing energy into the mind and the body. Its fallowing influence is felt in the basement as well as in the upper room of our human house.

There are people who confound being spiritual with being spirituelle. They think that to be spiritual they must be anaemic. They believe that they feed their souls by starving their bodies. They imagine that they develop their spiritual power by impoverishing their physical powers. They act as if they would like to be pure spirits— disembodied souls without any encumbering bodies. They seem to chafe at the limitations that their bodies create and long to be rid of them.

Now that heresy, that the price of the soul's redemption is the crucifixion of the body, dies hard. Charles Kingsley found it in the minds of the Englishmen of the middle and latter part of the last century. Physical beauty was counted a snare. Our great grandmothers in Old England—and in New England, too,—were compelled to hide their loveliness by wearing unbecoming gowns. Ugliness was a virtue and sickliness a sign of sanctity."

Dean Herbert L. Willett, of Chicago, delivered a classic and very able address on "Training the Mind." Said he:

"President Nicholas Murray Butler well insists that the child is entitled to the full measure of his inheritance from the past, and that such an inheritance includes all that he can appropriate of science, literature, aesthetics, institutions and religion.

Of all the creatures man is the only one who looks upward, and that which gives him the upward look is his mental life. It is the training of this characteristic of human nature which is the great permanent enterprise of the race wherever it reaches the level of civilization.

The phrase "training the mind" implies that we are dealing with an active, eager part of the life of youth, which, if it is not trained, goes on with the same unavoidable activity, only its growth is not directed and the result is likely to be dangerous to society. The proper direction and discipline of mind is education.

The intellect can only be trained in contact with the world about it. Therefore the facts of all the sciences and arts are its instruments.

But the facts should be not mere random ingathering of information, but selected in relation to their value, and then mastered. Whether it is a historical date, or a conjugation, or a poem, or a chemical reaction, or the habits of a bird in protecting its young, the fact ought to be mastered. Only so can it serve its purpose in mental training.

But education is more than the drawing of facts. Encyclopaedic information is not intellectual discipline. That is the process of putting together the few facts one has mastered, and making them the basis for the interpretation of such other knowledge as may be acquired. The value of studying Latin, or Higher Mathematics does not consist in the larger field of knowledge so gained, but in the power which results from such discipline.

But the mind is more than intellect. If this were all, the beauty of life would be gone. In every nature there are capacities for imagination, emotion, artistic enjoyment which require culture. Every child is in some sense an artist, a being of the imagination. To keep something of this divine gift, and train it to serviceable ends is the task of education.

Nor is it for art's sake, but for life's sake that these elements of beauty must be given a place in character. For the moral nature is a work of art, and he alone who is an artist at heart will persevere and covet the charm of humanity, courtesy, courage, calmness, enthusiasm, cheerfulness and the other arts of life whose lack or whose marring leaves a blot upon character. To be lacking in these virtues is not only wrong but inartistic, uncultured, vulgar.

And once again, the training of the mind involves the culture of the will. The course of any life is a weak invertibrate will which takes refuge in declarations of inability at the approach of duty. "I cannot help it," is the coward's retreat from responsibility.

And the purpose of the prepared and cultured mind, intellect, emotion and will, is the performance of a helpful part in the social order, which is also the kingdom of God.

Only in seeking enrichment of mind—not for self, but for service, can the high honor of our royal age be attained."

Following an anthem by the Convention Chorus the audience was permitted to "hear the conclusion of the whole matter" when the Rev. Floyd W. Tomkins, S. D. T., rector of Holy Trinity Church, Philadelphia, spoke out of the richness of his own consecrated life on 'Training the Soul." Said Dr. Tomkins, among other things:

"I agree with all that has been said concerning the training of the body and the mind. Yet you must recognize that in speaking of the soul we are treading on holy ground. The soul is given by God—it is God in man, and is to rule body and mind. Therefore before we go further let us kneel and pray for grace to learn aright how to train this priceless heritage. (Here prayer was offered).

We must remember that God alone can train the soul. Yet He has given us means to use through which His help flows. We cannot be good of ourselves alone. God cannot make us good, unless we do as He asks. But we become good—our souls are trained, when we trust God and use the means He has provided.

These means are prayer, Bible, worship and service. A man who uses these with faith and constancy cannot fail to grow in grace.

We must be sincere in our obedience to God's will. We cannot play with life. Only as we are true and loyal in all things and banish wrong can we please God.

A trained soul keeps us from error in doctrine. The world is full of heresies and queer teachings because men have not followed the divine culture.

A trained soul is strong and courageous. Bravery for the right and against the wrong can only come through religion.

A trained soul gains the victory and even when seemingly defeated makes glorious the work of God. Like the forty wrestlers through death the Christian man gives llife to others.

Oh, the blessedness of this training! The body becomes holy and is mastered. The mind becomes holy and is guided, and the full man is made like the Son of God."

FIRST PRESBYTERIAN CHURCH.

The meeting at the First Presbyterian Church Thursday evening considered the same three topics as were treated in Tent Williston, but by different pastors. The church was completely filled with an audience that gave undivided attention to each speaker.

Prayer was offered by Rev. O. L. Smith, of Oklahoma.

"Training the Body" was the subject of the address of Rev. Hugh K. Walker, D. D., pastor of the Immanuel Presbyterian Church, Los Angeles, Cal. We regret that we cannot give all of Dr. Walker's excellent address. He said in part:

"The church is slowly awakening to the fact that the training of the body is as essential as the training of the mind. If we are to perpetuate an active Christianity we must give our young people good strong bodies. It is true that our Y. M. C. A. and Y. W. C. A. are training our young people to some advantage. But we need more than this, we need to train all of our young men and women so that their bodies shall be strong and ready to do God's work in the world. Paul would have enjoyed a baseball game, I think, if He were on earth. As to a football game, I do not know. It should be, body, mind and soul, I believe. We must have strong men. Jesus Christ took the image of man when he came to earth, and we should remember this."

It was a great pleasure to the delegates as well as to the officers of the United Society of Christian Endeavor to have present at this convention one who may really be considered the first Secretary of the United Society, Rev. Geo. M. Ward, D. D., LL. D., now President of Wells College in Aurora, N. Y.

Dr. Ward was received with hearty enthusiasm, and spoke upon the subject for which he is most excellently fitted, "Training the Mind." He said:

"The character of this gathering decides for us our model, Jesus of Nazareth, the founder of civilization, the perfect Man, the only complete Christian. There is a vast difference between a model and an ideal. An ideal we strive toward but never expect to attain; a model is capable of imitation. There is no sacrilege in calling Christ a model. The more completely we model our lives on His, the greater honor we pay Him.

As we review history, we find that the world, like the individual, has passed through two distinct stages, the physical and the mental. For years Christ imitation was the imitation of one incident in Christ's life, His sacrifice. The world was dominated by the physical. Today we are under the second standard, the reign of brain. War, business, society, religion, are all under its sway. I believe that today marks the high tide of the second period.

As the change from the physical to the mental was a gradual and an over-lapping one, so there is in the world today a comingling of the mental and a third factor we call the spiritual, for lack of a better term, a factor that is not in accord with either muscle or brain. When we reach the land where time is only an incident, and adopt the standards of God, we shall find what an important part this third factor has played in world development. The survival of the fittest is a relative truth. Under the physical it was a law of brain, the survival of the brightest. Under the spiritual it will be the law of God, the survival of the soul.

Mind is the linking factor between the animal and the spiritual, the earthly and the Divine. Training the mind is broader than mere learning. There is a vast difference between an intelligent person and a merely learned one. Learning is the acquisition of facts. Intelligence is the broadening of self. The training of today is teaching men that dishonesty is illogical. No principle that tells you to get as much of your neighbor's possessions as you can for as small amount of your own as you can force him to take, is either honest or logical. It has been dearly brought home to the public mind that no man has a right to any possession either in amount or character which injures or restrains his fellowman in the honest pursuit of the needs and decencies of life.

We are training men to realize that there is no excuse for the errors of ignorance. If you are ignorant, you are ignorant by choice. If your lack of knowledge causes your neighbour harm or renders you incapable of performing your legitimate function in society, you must pay the price. You had no business to be ignorant.

We are training men to realize that it's logical to be truthful in matters of real moment. If your ambition is to shine in society as you find it, or to be a multi-millionaire, the above is not true. When they are dead, we honor men like Agassiz, who are so busy with worthier aims that they "haven't time to make money." We unanimously rank them amongst the greatest Americans and write their names in the Hall of Fame.

Mental training has re-organized society. Her call is especially clear to the young women. They carry a nation's morals in their hands. For society is the ruling aristocracy of the world. It is only aristocracy that does rule. In society woman dominates. Mental training has rung the death-knell of the hypocrite. There is no place for him in human economy; there never has been in the Divine. Today's training has raised the level of the average intellect. Heretofore one had to have all the talents in the Almighty's gift to get anywhere near the top. This is the day of the average intellect, but the average is much higher than it ever was before. Mental training today takes Christ for its model. Christ wasn't a genius. He was a perfect man, and that means an average man. A genius is an imperfect man, oftentimes a freak.

There is plenty of room on top, the real top, for the average man. The old idea of prominence at the expense of others was a transparent falsehood. There used to be room for only one on that kind of a top. Each aspirant could retain his footing only by pushing his predecessor off into space and destruction. But in the great high tide level of God's plans for all His children, there's no lack of opportunity. America is broad enough and big enough to give every one a field for all the work he is capable of. America is a republic, and a republic is the imitation on earth of Christ's plan of a self-respecting place for everybody."

After Dr. Ward's address the congregation united in singing the new hymn entitled, "Endeavor," the words of which were written by Rev. Charles A. Dickinson and the music by our publication manager, Mr. George B. Graff.

Dr. Clark requested Mr. Graff to lead the singing and the audience responded with hearty good will ringing out the words:
"We battle for the King of Kings,
Around the world our watchword rings—
Endeavor, still Endeavor."

Dr. Frank G. Smith, pastor of the Warren Avenue Congregational Church of Chicago, spoke on "Training the Soul." In a few pleasant words he gained immediate sympathetic control of his audience and then went straight to his theme. He recognized the great importance of training the body and the mind; of having a magnificent temple for the soul's dwelling place and a splendid mentality through which the soul can partially express itself to other human being, but after all, it is the soul itself, the spiritual being, that is eternal and abiding.

"No matter how well the body be trained, it will crumble at last to a handful of ashes; and no matter how well the mind be trained, most thinking men today realize that mind lies only on the surface of our real being. That slumbering beneath the physical being and the mental as well, there is the Spiritual, the real self, and that when this is separated from the body it will not be dependent upon our slow mental processes for its knowledge. Towering above everything else, there is the importance of training the soul.
What is life? Whence does it come? Whither is it tending?

What is this indefinable, inexpressible something within that throbs and pulsates; this something that we are so conscious of and yet cannot understand, this something that defies chemical analysis and scientific research; that will not be classified; this something that we can never fully express or understand, and yet that we know enough about to know that it is more than the body and vastly more than mere mentality?

Science seems to have the center of the stage in our age; but science has absolutely no answer to give. Art gives us many beautiful and helpful lessons in interpreting life, but can give no answer to the question asked. Turning to the realm of literature; surely somewhere in the record of the world's history, its human experience, its philosophy, its theology, its poetry or its prose, we shall find answer to our question. Nowhere, however, in the whole realm of literature can an answer be found to the question asked. There is only one place in all the world where the question is answered, and that is in the Bible. There we are told simply, sweetly, trustfully, that life is the gift of God. That back of all the manifested glory of nature we see about us there is a Great, Supreme, Spiritual Personality, Our Father, God, Whose law is truth, whose motive is love, whose essence is goodness and whose atmosphere is peace and good will to men. He gave us life. We are all thoughts from the Eternal Mind, all sparks from the Divine Flame, all stamped with the Divine Image, all have with us the embryo of Divine Possibilities to be unfolded according to a Divine plan. Now our question in training the soul is to know that plan and to carry it out absolutely. I never look into the face of a great American Beauty rose but what I think of the buried magnificence that rested one day in the quiet clasp of a little black seed somewhere, and I never hold an acorn in my hand and look up into the giant tree from which it fell but what I think of the buried majesty that rests in the quiet clasp of that little shell. Now, no short process had ever been devised by man whereby the clasp of the seed or the shell could be broken and the buried, hidden majesty and beauty be revealed. They must unfold according to a Divine plan inwrought in their very nature by the Divine Creator. So it is with man; within the closely folded links of his physical being and his mental being there lie Divine possibilities. These never come to their perfect beauty their supremest loveliness, their most sublime majesty until they unfold according to the Divine plan inwrought in the life of man and revealed to him day by day in that "Inner light that lighteth every man that cometh into the world."

Dr. Smith closed his address with one or two gems of poetry and an illustration that gave a touch of life and vitality to all he had said and made every one in the large audience feel that he must give himself more definitely and purposely to the training of the soul; to the development of its untold possibilities for the glory of God and for the service of man.

INTERIOR OF TENT WILLISTON.

CHAPTER VIII.

CHRISTIAN ENDEAVOR A FEDERATION.

Interdenominational, International, Inter-racial.—Tent Williston
Friday Morning, July 12th.

The chair was occupied by the Rev. W. T. Johnson, D. D., of Richmond, Va., one of the trustees of the society. In a few well chosen words, he expressed the earnest hope that all present would get an uplift and receive inspiration from the addresses that were to be delivered that morning. After praise and prayer, the chairman introduced Rev. James L. Hill, D. D., of Salem, Mass., who immediately arrested the attention of the large audience by asking, apparently apropos of nothing, but really with direct reference to his subject and his speech: "Is Marriage a Failure?"

"I say yes, when a man persists in arguing over a matter on which on account of a temperamental difference he and his wife never think quite alike, and never have thought quite alike and on this matter never will think quite alike, and it is not at all important that they should think alike. I abominate a woman who, when asked what she thinks has only to say, "I think just what my husband thinks." Now, here is the matter of religion. What do you think about it? "I think just what my husband thinks." What do you think about music? "I think just what my husband thinks." What do you think about art or about this convention? "I think just what my husband thinks." That is not harmony. It is stupidity. There is no conversation, only monologue. When a person wants harmony and goes to the keyboard of a piano he does not keep striking one key. That is monotony. It is tedium. It is weariness. Real harmony comes from striking the different notes in an octave.

In a great burst of sympathy, in our immense conventions I have seen the flags of the different nations entwined amid great enthusiasm, and with an outbreaking demonstration of approval. Each flag stood for a different type of political government, for a different people, with a different national temperament. The nations were an ocean apart, but striking the religious note they sound in complete harmony. Any society that becomes only denominational can never have the spirit, the responsiveness, the great effects, the popular favor of our great interdenominational, international, inter-racial— I had almost added, interplanatary conventions. The transcendent advantage of an interdenominational society is the harmony like that of music, which comes from striking different notes. In the last conference that I attended, held under Christian Endeavor auspices, the man I admired most was a Baptist. He was what, in a religious way, I desire to become. He had what I desire to acquire. Our contact was an inspiration. The pleasure we had in each other was greater by reason of the fact that we were from different states, different families, different denominations, yet completely blended and lost in perfect unison of feeling touching redemption, the great doctrines of grace and all the things of the cross. Let it be distinctly noted that our theme is not the advantages of an undenominational society. We would not if we could divest ourselves of the strong ideas that the several denominations contribute. We are better for them. I have just met a physician practicing in Hartford, wearing a Christian Endeavor pin, who told me that having been trained from his boyhood in a Christian Endeavor Society, where in local unions and great conventions he had met Christians of all denominations, he did not know anything about the inharmonies of religion or about the antipathies of sects, except by hearsay. He had only learned about them as he had read the reminiscences of the church. Practically he had only seen the harmonies of our common faith and his wonder was that any one was disposed to go back and dig up the old contentions. An interdominational society has the effect upon its members of leveling them to the best there is in any church or denomination or believer. As the Apollo Belvidere and the Venus De Medici are more perfect than any single human being made up by assembling the graces and perfections of parts in the best human forms, so an interdenominational society is better than any single human organization could possibly become. It assembles the best things, the highest perfections, that any of the societies have attained."

Dr. Hill spoke with his usual nerve, and as he sat down enthusiastic applause marked the approval of his earnest plea for the widest and most comprehensive union.

The chairman then introduced the Rev. B. B. Tyler, D. D., pastor of the South Broadway Christian Church, Denver, Colo., who immediately won the hearts of the audience by the simple narrative of the journey he had undertaken in order to be present at that meeting, he having made a direct and uninterrupted journey from Rome, over the European continent, Great Britain, the ocean, and the American continent to Seattle. Dr. Tyler is by no means amongst the youngest in years of the delegates to the convention but the vigor with which his speech was delivered, in spite of the long and fatiguing journey, illustrated at once his enthusiasm for the cause of Christian unity through Christian Endeavor and, also, the youthful heart of the venerable teacher and preacher.

Dr. Tyler frequently took the audience into his confidence and with simplicity, naturalness and sincerity he, at the outset, explained that while he had many hobby horses which he delighted to ride, his favorite and the one he most often mounted was that of Christian unity, as from the first it appealed to and mastered him because of the promise that it gave of leading all nations, denominations and races into the oneness for which Christ prayed; that when he was still a boy at school he had the ambition to be a preacher of the everlasting word, and in those days, accordingly daring, he wrote a sermon whose theme was "Church Union"; that he then started out and struck a note which he has continued to sound during his strife of fifty years; that unity is fundamental, and, until it is realized, Christ has unrealized His desires and aims. He further stated that the origins of denominations has always had a fascination for him, and the more deeply and carefully he studies these, the clearer does it become to him that each denomination came into existence by the will of man and not by the will of God. Wesleyanism, for example, was called a denomination in spite of Wesley's persistent declaration that he was of the Church of England, and in it would remain; Luther also said: "Call no church Luther." Other denominations also had been similarly established. He further said that it was the will of God that different aspects of divine truth might be presented to the world, and that different kinds of souls might find their proper environment; yet denominationalism represented merely a transition period. The church is now as God meant that it should be now, yet it is not what God intends that the church shall be. It is our part at the present time to nurture a growing spirit of unity, and then God in his own time will make his church visibly as well as essentially one.

Dr. Tyler then proceeded to ask and answer the question as to how Christian Endeavor could promote this consummation most devoutly to be wished. He stated that it could be done and was being done by bringing together the people of different nations and denominations in conventions such as this one at Seattle.

"The more I know people," continued the speaker, "and especially the more I know bad people, the better I like them. I can discover why they are and what they are, and 'To know all is to forgive all'—'Pity is akin to love.' And thus as I know different denominations, I discover in many of them practices that are not mine; beliefs that differ from mine and loyalties which are other than mine; yet in them all I discover a fine loyalty to Christ, and that discovery makes me realize that they and I are one. Secondly, working together brings men together, making them realize their common need, and in the sense of common weakness rather than in the sense of common strength are the hearts of men knit to each other."

Dr. Tyler then described the Sunday School convention at Rome, from which he had just come, at which convention there were represented 40 countries and 46 denominations, and yet no man knew or cared to know to which particular denomination any man at the convention belonged. This at Rome was a significant fact, for Rome with her splendid and worldwide organization, producing a semblance of unity, says that Protestantism is divided. And there in Rome itself Protestantism gave its reply to "the bachelor in St. Peter's Church," and its reply was: "Look and see that unity is with us. One body we." That in producing this, Christian Endeavor had been and was destined still to be a tremendous factor; and that, therefore, heart, soul and body he was by God's grace and would so remain, an Endeavorer.

Dr. Tyler was immediately followed by the Rev. W. I. Chamberlain, Ph. D., ex-president of the United Society of Christian Endeavor for India, Burmah and Ceylon.

Dr. Chamberlain spoke quietly and concisively with the precision of the scholar, and yet with the fire and force of an Endeavorer whose heart is aflame with the desire for union in Christian service of all denominations, in all parts of the world and particularly on the mission field. Treating his subject in the form of a syllogism, he said:

Christian Endeavor and Church Union on Mission Fields.

Church Union a matter of Christian Principle. Not only an ideal sentiment, a clear, logical deduction from admitted premises.

I.—Premises: Teachings of Christ authoritative and universal in application. Christ the Sovereign Lord and Master of Life. Final Authority over Life Not in the Christian Church, nor in the Bible —nor yet in Christian consciousness. God in Christ—final authority.

Christ's commands have projected themselves through nineteen centuries and live today as potent and authoritative as when first heard.

Christ came into the world as a great authority and lives in the world today as a great authority. He was so true, so correct, so completely what He represented Himself to be that He carried in Himself a conscious sense of his right to lead men and to direct men.

II.—Christ's Teachings were Universal in their application. Their wide acceptance a proof of their capacity to reach the minds and hearts of every race and every tribe.

Christianity the only religion that is represented in every part of the world. Thus in striking contrast to Hinduism—only in India! Buddhism—only in Asia; Mohammedanism—not in Europe or America. No bounds—physical, climatic or racial—to duty. A religion not from man, but God. It is continually sharing in increasing measure the universal character of its divine founder and of the higher life of mankind.

If therefore the Teachings of Christ are authoritative and universal in their application, should not the Church unite in making them known?

The feebleness and the grandeur of the Church is that it excludes nothing that belongs to man. The universal is feeble as the special. As a center of religious tradition the Church received from all parts a crowd of local beliefs. She presented herself to the world as the world made her. She appeared before it in the parti-colored robe of history. Like the mighty ocean she received whilst she cleansed the impurities of the world.

Freer from this historical association and religious tradition than the Church in Europe and America, the Church of Asia has made more rapid progress in approaching a realization of the principles of federation and union before non-Christian faiths.

In China: Eleven Presbyterian bodies have united and definite plans are being made to unite all Protestant bodies.
In India: Seven Presbyterian bodies have united and definite overtures have been made to the Congregationalists and Methodists.
In Japan: All Presbyterian bodies have united and overtures have been made to Congregationalists.
In Korea: The Presbyterians have united and plans are forming to unite all Protestant bodies.

The Part of Christian Endeavor.

Great as has already been the contribution of Christian Endeavor to the spiritual life and religious activity of the youth of the world, even greater, perhaps, is its growing contribution toward the consummation of that unity among His disciples for which Christ prayed. For Christian Endeavor, while not neglecting denominational ties, magnifies and exalts and illuminates the essential unity of all Christians. It leads to the exchange of near-sighted, parochial views for far-sighted visions of the kingdom. Many leaders in the Church owe their present catholic and Kingdom-wide interest to this factor. This is particularly true of the mission fields. While the movements toward union began many years ago, it is a significant fact that they have been consummated within the last ten years, since Christian Endeavor has entered the mission fields. It is also significant that those who are now leaders in Church Union on the mission fields are also the leaders in Christian Endeavor. This is more than a mere coincidence.

The cruel and selfish motto of the Roman Empire was:
"Divide and Rule."
The nobler watchword of the Christian Church should be:
"Combine and Conquer."

After prayer for unity in spirit and service, in which the congregation was led by the Rev. Floyd W. Tomkins, S. T. D., of Philadelphia, Pa., President Clark spoke on "Christian Endeavor a World Organization—The International Brotherhood of the World's Christian Endeavor Union." He said:

Every organization must study its capabilities and its possibilities and thus determine the particular mission which God has marked out for it.

If any one thing is plain it is the providential purpose to make of Christian Endeavor a world-wide movement to strengthen the bonds of international, interdenominational Christian Brotherhood.

We shall be derelict to the direct plain leadings of Providence unless we do the work of a world-wide organization for which we were designed of God to bring the evangelical forces of the world together in a closer, more effective fellowship.

Moreover it is not too much to say that the Christian Endeavor movement is the only one to which this especial mission has been intrusted. The Y. M. C. A., glorious as its work is, is undenominational, not interdenominational, and it touches but a fraction of the

Christian young people reached by Christian Endeavor. The Salvation Army, too, is undenominational and works for a special class and not for all classes, as does Christian Endeavor. It does not pretend to bring the denominations together in full.

The Sunday School is more nearly analogous to Christian Endeavor than any other organization, but it has never emphasized the fellowship of its members, and indeed the rank and file of Sunday School scholars are too young to appreciate the importance of this phase of the Christian life.

Read the inspiring list of countries where the society exists and in most of which it is strong. The very list is an eloquent one:

United States	Formosa	Madagascar
Canada	France	Madeira Islands
Africa	Germany	Marshall Islands
Austria	Gibraltar	Mauritius
Australia	Gilbert Islands	Mexico
Barbados	Great Britain and	Newfoundland
Belgium	Ireland	Norway
Bermuda	Grenada	Palestine
Brazil	Guatemala	Panama
British Guinea	Haiti	Persia
Bulgaria	Hawaiian Islands	Philippine Islands
Caroline Islands	Holland	Porto Rico
Chile	Hungary	Portugal
China	Iceland	Russia
Colombia	India	Samoa
Costa Rica	Italy	Siam
Crete	Jamaica	Spain
Cuba	Japan	Sweden
Denmark	Korea	Switzerland
Egypt	Labrador	Syria
Ellice Islands	Laos	Tokelau Island
Fiji Islands	Lapland	Trinidad
Finland	Loyalty Islands	Turkey

The list of services undertaken is no less striking than the countries where the society is formed. Prayer meetings, conventions, evangelistic meetings, sailors' mission, prison work, hospital visitation, soldiers' societies, fresh air camps, church building, denominational missions, patriotic demonstrations, flowers for the Church and fruit for the sick, Christian Endeavor chorus, Quiet Hour propaganda, proportionate and systematic giving, temperance, social purity and good citizenship in all its multifarious forms.

It is safe to say that every need of mankind can be touched by Christian Endeavorers, and few forms of philanthropy or Christian service have not been attempted by these militant hosts of young disciples.

Thus the adaptability of the movement to every need of young Christians in every land indicates its world-wide scope.

WHAT THE WORLD'S CHRISTIAN ENDEAVOR UNION CAN DO FOR INTERNATIONAL BROTHERHOOD.

I.

It can weld into one compact and effective band many of those whose efforts for peace and good will would not otherwise be effective.

II.

It can voice the sentiments of all its members on the subject of international and interdenominational comity through the press and on the platform.

III.

It can secure the publication of much valuable educational material concerning peace and unity in the political and religious world.

IV.

In a word, it can and will do its utmost not only to spread Christian Endeavor throughout the world, but to promote in every church and every land the democratic Christian Spirit of Universal Brotherhood, to unite people of every race and creed that accepts the principles of Christian Endeavor in an active propaganda for a larger fellowship of nations and churches and for the fulfilment of the Lord's last prayer that they all may be one.

At the close of Dr. Clark's address a memorial service was held "in loving remembrance of Rev. Charles A. Dickinson, D. D., Bishop Arnett, D. D., and Rev. Teunis S. Hamlin, D. D."

Dr. Hill, Dr. Lowden and Dr. Clark spoke in appropriate terms of the services of these three faithful Endeavorers, who, as trustees and in other capacities, with humility, patience, fidelity, faith and prayer had given of their best to promote the cause which lay very near to their hearts.

This memorial service, which was quite solemn and impressive throughout, was fittingly concluded by prayer of thanksgiving and of consecration, offered by the Rev. Floyd W. Tomkins, of whom Dr. Lowden said, "He always knew the way to God."

CHAPTER IX.

REACHING OUT.

First Presbyterian Church—Friday Morning.

Dr. Hugh K. Walker of Los Angeles presided and President Hartman of West Virginia conducted the devotions.

President Hall of the Minnesota Union spoke first on "The Democracy of Christian Endeavor."

He quoted the sentence of John Bright: "The nation dwells in the cottage," as he urged that no institution can grow without the spirit of democracy.

It is the altruistic spirit that forgets self in an outlook toward all. This is the Christian Endeavor spirit. We must tell every new society that it does not exist for itself, but for all the world.

We shall see this democratic spirit manifested in several ways.

First, by closer co-operation among the members themselves.

Second, by a closer drawing together of the society and the Church itself, a sympathetic guidance on the part of older church leaders.

Third, by going outside the church to bring in all that need.

The next speaker was Secretary Von Ogden Vogt of the World's Union. He talked about "Affiliated Groups, Clubs and Classes."

What are the elements of Christian nurture? The answer would help clear up the subject before us. The most important elements are the teaching of religious truth and a chance for expressing the same in some form of service.

The average church uses the Sunday School for one of these purposes and the Endeavor Society for the other. But most large churches are not so logical. They have several kinds of societies or clubs among the young.

The objections to this varied situation are many. It is haphazard, often unhappily competitive. There are several ways for an Endeavor Society to adjust its forms to solve the difficulty.

An affiliated membership—placed between the active and associate —would win many in some churches.

A group society with several departments, each organized with its own officers, but all working in harmony, has been successful in some churches.

The federation plan is worth trying. This would mean the forming of a central cabinet representing all societies or clubs for the young of a church—and calling the whole federation the Christian Endeavor Society.

Where the men and women of a church are well organized, it might be well to try the boys and girls in separate Endeavor Societies.

MR. WM. PHILLIPS HALL
NEW YORK, N.Y.

REV. FLOYD W. TOMKINS

REV. GEO. M. WARD
D.D. L.L.D.
AURORA
N.Y.

HON. OLIVER W. STEWART
CHICAGO, ILL.

REV. SMITH BAKER D.D.
PORTLAND, ME.

IRA LANDRITH, D.D. LL.D.
NASHVILLE, TENN.

Lastly, the society anywhere should be enriched by more educational emphasis. Studies in mission and church affairs or even ethics will win the co-operation of many thoughtful young people.

And for the less thoughtful youths there are wonderful possibilities in glee clubs, tramping clubs and what not, organized directly by the Endeavor Society and leading up to it.

President Straughn of West Lafayette College, Ohio, then spoke to the topic: "Christian Endeavor: Spirit, Not Letter."

Spiritual things are spiritually discerned and may not be revealed in the form of letter. They are therefore not understood by many and open to criticism.

Christian Endeavor is an idea, not a machine; a green twig, not a ripened branch. As an idea, it is to take form according to the need of the organization of the church of which it is a part. Every society should be somewhat distinct and peculiar. It should fit the needs of each church. It is not the pledge, nor the United Society, but the idea for your church.

It finds expression in the pledge as a medium of exchange. This pledge may be adapted. There are four pledges recommended by the United Society.

The chief objections to the pledge are by those afraid of any sort of obligation. It really imposes only Bible reading, prayer and church loyalty. How can one be a Christian without such developing obligations?

The pledge has the elements. Its hardness helps to cultivate power. We have not always kept the spirit of the pledge when we have read the Bible daily nor always broken it when we have not done so. Its helpfulness, its urging of work is a spiritualizing agency. Its hopefulness is the Christian Endeavor disposition."

Mr. William Phillips Hall of New York plead powerfully for the evangelistic spirit in Christian Endeavor. He said:

Every Christian an Evangelist. Some one has said: "The trumpet call of the new kingdom is, 'Every Christian an evangelist.' Wherever this becomes the watchword, the triumph of God's Kingdom will be near." When the Spirit of God came mightily upon the prophet Joel, and, through him, spake in thrilling words of the great evangelistic age to come, He said: "And it shall come to pass, in the last days, saith God, I will pour out My Spirit upon all flesh ,and your sons and your daughters shall prophesy, and your young men shall see visions, and your old men shall dream dreams. * * * And it shall come to pass that whosoever shall call upon the name of the Lord shall be saved." Acts 2:17, 21.

On Pentecost's glorious day a foretaste of fulfillment of the great promise was realized, when one hundred and twenty young people in the upper room were "all filled with the Holy Ghost, and spake with other tongues, as the Spirit gave them utterance, of the wonderful works of God." But that was only an earnest, a beginning of fulfillment of a divine promise that was and is in later days to find its highest level in a universal outpouring upon all flesh, and especially upon the "sons and daughters"—the Christian Endeavorers—of the Church of God.

Divine Preparation. A careful student of the Word of God cannot fail to be impressed with the invariable preparedness that precedes all of God's great works. Unknown ages were consumed in laying the foundations of the world, but each step taken prepared the way for the next. In like manner, from the day of the fall of Adam to the day of our Lord and Saviour Jesus Christ in the flesh, may we behold the ever-broadening purpose of the perfectly prepared redemptive work of God.

May we not in these great facts discern the operation of a divine principle and purpose which, if by us recognized, appropriated and applied, may swing the mighty Christian Endeavor hosts into line as the divinely owned and used leaders in the greatest evangelistic advance that this world has ever known?

Christian Endeavor an Evangelistic Army. Who dares question the presence of the hand of God in founding this wonderful movement through the instrumentality of our beloved leader, Dr. Francis E. Clark? And what true follower of our Lord Jesus Christ for one moment ventures to question or limit the evangelistic possibilities of the Christian Endeavor Societies, under the mighty hand of God? It was indeed a marvelous thing that God should have condescended to so wonderfully revive His people in the little principality of Wales, that in a few brief weeks over one hundred and twenty thousand of persons were converted and swept into the spiritual kingdom of His dear Son! But more marvelous and significant still was the fact that the revival—the most Pentecostal revival since Pentecost—was inaugurated and carried on, under God, almost entirely through and by young people, many of whom were members of the Society of Christian Endeavor! Is there not a lesson in this for Christian Endeavorers throughout the world? Are the spiritual and evangelistic possibilities of Christian Endeavor any less throughout the world than in little Wales?

Christian Endeavor Can Lead World Revival. Let us remember that it was, primarily, through the willing and fearless instrumentality of one young girl in a Christian Endeavor meeting that God set all Wales on fire with the Holy Spirit! And let us also remember the old and true saying that "history repeats herself"—and that which God did through the willing instrumentality of one young girl in Wales, He can and may do yet again through one girl or boy, young man or maiden in every city, town and village of our old world!

A clean heart and a right life, a working knowledge of the Word of God, and, above all else, the baptism of the Holy Ghost, are all essential in the service of our King. With this equipment we may go forth into our Lord's great spiritual harvest field, being well assured that we shall have good success in the greatest work in the world—the winning of our fellows back to God! Pardon a few words of personal testimony: I had an unsatisfactory religious experience for several years after I gave my heart to God, and, finally, I was brought face to face with the fact that there must be something more in Christianity than I had experienced, or else religion was a very unsatisfactory thing. My condition of mind at that time reminded me of the colored brother who, when asked how he was getting along in the Christian life, said: "It seems to me dat de furder I go in dish yer way de worser it gets." That describes my state of mind exactly! I felt that something must happen in my religious life before my service for God could be efficient. In reading the blessed Book of God one day I read: "Where the Spirit of the Lord is, there is liberty." And that was just what I wanted—liberty and power to live and work for my Master, and to win souls to Him. I went out into the hay-loft of an old barn on the place where I was boarding, down in an old New England town, one Sunday afternoon, and knelt there for over two hours praying that God would grant me the baptism of the Holy Spirit. I expected some sort of an electrical sensation, but I didn't get it. It was probably fortunate for me that I did not. God doesn't deal with all men alike. Paul's experience belonged to Paul, and God evidently intended that my experience should belong to me. I finally got up from my knees. I felt no different, and I said: "There is nothing in this." After supper I went to my room, and this promise came to my mind: "What things soever ye desire when ye pray, believe that ye receive them, and ye shall have them." And yet again came the promise: "Ask and ye shall receive. Seek and ye shall find. Knock and it shall be opened unto you." I said: "Oh, my God, though Thou slay me, yet will I trust Thee. I will rest wholly on Thy word." I went down the street with a strange, confident feeling in my soul that God was about to fully make good His word to me. I went into a meeting of young people. As I entered that place it seemed as if the windows of heaven were opened upon my soul, and there came an overwhelming desire to witness to those young people of the fact of my salvation, and I went down to the front and said: "May I speak?" And the minister said: "Certainly." And the power of the Most High came down upon me, and upon that audience, and when I gave the invitation over twenty of those young people yielded to Christ! That's what we have all got to come to if we are ever going to be largely used of God to win souls to His dear Son.

Some people call me the business men's evangelist. That's a misnomer. I am a business-man evangelist. And I believe that every Christian business man ought to be an evangelist, and I believe that every professional man ought to be an evangelist, and every father, every mother, every sister, every brother—that every daughter and every son in all the Church of God ought to be an evangelist. Years ago the evangelistic call came to me—as it came to Peter and James and John and Paul—and as it always has come and always will come, sooner or later, to those who seek to know the will of God and to do it. Years ago there came to my heart a conviction that the whole world lay in wickedness, and sin, and that God had given it to me, an humble instrument in His hands, to do my part in the great work of winning souls from the evil one to God. I then went forth into the great spiritual harvest field. In this glorious service I have spent hundreds of Sundays and week days, God by His good providence enabling me to do this "without money and without price." In this service I have found the most supreme satisfaction. In this glorious work I have found the most delightful enjoyment, and in this most blessed partnership with Jesus Christ I have more fully realized the right and power of the Holy Ghost in my poor heart and life, and I most ardently prize a similar experience for each and every Christian Endeavorer throughout the world! When a lad, some fifteen years of age, after listening to a sermon by a dear man of God, the invitation was given to those who wanted to seek Christ to go down to the front. I went down the aisle with a heart burdened for the lost. I saw a handsome fellow sobbing as if his heart would break. I put my hand upon his shoulder, and said to him: "Will you go forward?" "No, I do not care to go now," he said. "Why not?" "I promised mother some years ago that I would be a Christian, yet I felt that when I took that step I would have to give all my time to Christian work." "My friend," I said, "you ought to heed that conviction." We got down upon our knees, and at last he grasped our blessed Jesus, and then he turned to me and said: "What shall I do? I have got to go to work for God."

That man was Alfred M. Ingham. He became Secretary of the Young Men's Christian Association of Brattleboro, Vt., and labored there for some time with success and blessing. After a time his health broke down. He went South and then to California, and one day he stepped from the golden sands of California to the golden streets of Heaven.

Alfred Ingham had gone home. One day, years afterwards, my dear friend, Rev. Dr. Arthur J. Smith, one of our leading Christian Endeavor evangelists, came into my office and said: "Didn't you lead Alfred M. Ingham to Christ?" I said: "I did, when I was a boy about fifteen years of age." "Well," said Doctor Smith, "Alfred Ingham led me to Christ; and I believe that makes you my spiritual grandfather."

Oh, how my heart welled up with joy! Most wonderfully has God used Doctor Smith in winning thousands to Christ! Now, fellow Christian Endeavorers, if God can use a fifteen year old boy to win souls for Him, He can use everyone of us. May we all go and do likewise!"

The session closed with many helpful ideas by Mr. Amos R. Wells, as he discussed

THE IDEAL SOCIETY.

"If you want to know all about anything, ask three questions:
"What is it to do?"
"Who are to do it?"
"How is it to be done?"

Here are some men, some boards and some bricks. What is to be done? A house is to be built. Who are to do it? The architect, diggers, masons, carpenters, and the man with the pocketbook. How is it to be done? By digging, sawing, hammering, plastering, according to a plan.

Here is a college. What is to be done? Minds are to be trained. Who are to do it? Students and faculty. How is it to be done? By lecturing and listening, reading, writing, thinking and speaking, according to a curriculum.

Here is a young people's religious society. Let us ask those three questions about that thing.

In the first place, what is it to do?

It is to give the young people religious training. Not secular training, but religious training. Not musical training, but religious training. Not literary training, but religious training. Not athletic training, but religious training. The ideal young people's religious society must be predominatingly religious.

Christian Endeavor is that. It is too religious, some folks think.

The substitutes for Christian Endeavor are always less religious. They are clubs for the study of Browning or of art, or they are social clubs, or musical clubs, or athletic clubs, and only incidentally are they religious. Christian Endeavor is fundamentally religious.

Christian Endeavor believes in literary study, and it fosters it wherever it is needed; but generally the school gives enough of it, and the church makes a tactical blunder when it duplicates the work of the school.

Christian Endeavor believes in athletics and fosters that wherever it is needed; but generally the young have enough athletic interests, and the church makes a tactical blunder when it duplicates interests.

Christian Endeavor believes in music, and fosters it; but usually the young have many musical and social interests, and the church makes a tactical blunder when it duplicates them.

But Christian Endeavor believes that the young people need religious training. Here is something the school, the college, athletics and society are not giving them. There's no danger of duplicating here.

Let other agencies train the body. Christian Endeavor will, if they do not. But Christian Endeavor's great work is to persuade the young to use their bodily strength for Christ.

Let other agencies train the mind. Christian Endeavor will, if they do not. Christian Endeavor's great work is to arouse the mind to study missions, the Bible, the needs of our country and the world.

The substitutes for Christian Endeavor have feared to be too religious. They have envied the world its power over young hearts, and they have sought to gain that power by worldly means.

Christian Endeavor believes that nothing more attracts the young than the religion of the young man Jesus. That is why Christian Endeavor succeeds, because it is predominatingly religious. That is why the substitutes for it fail, because they are less religious. The first question about the ideal religious society for young people was, "What is it to do?" And I know you agree in the answer. "It is to make the young people religious—grandly, efficiently, powerfully religious."

The second question is, "Who are to do it?" My answer is, "Principally the young people."

A young people's society must be by and for and of the young people. Christian Endeavor has succeeded because it remembers that. The substitutes for Christian Endeavor have failed because they are pastor's societies or denominational societies and not young people's societies. They are pastor's societies. They reflect his hobby. They study his specialty. They listen to his lectures. It is all very delightful, and the society flourishes until he gets tired or moves away. Then it collapses, because it has been the pastor's society and not the young people's. Or they are denominational societies, forced on the young people from without, according to a denominational formula and prescription. They are not the growth of the young people from within. The young people have little enthusiasm for them, and they fail as soon as denominational authority is relaxed.

But Christian Endeavor trusts the young people, and in that trust it is strong. It throws responsibility upon them. It does not prescribe methods, but sets the young people to inventing them. It does not prescribe undertakings, but bids the young people do Christ's will and they take up countless activities for themselves.

That is why Christian Endeavor is so hard to kill, because it is a life and not a formula. That is why Christian Endeavor is self-propagating. Do you suppose that Dr. Clark and his half-dozen helpers could ever have planted 70,000 societies all over the world? The young people have made the society their own, and they have seen to its growth, and they will see to its perpetuation.

That is why Christian Endeavor turns out so many church workers, self-reliant church workers that go ahead and do things without being pushed and prodded. It is because they have been trusted to do things. The greatest need of the church is for workers that do not need the spur. Christian Endeavor trains such workers because it throws the young people on their own resources.

Of course, I do not mean that our society does not need the pastor and the denomination. Just because it sets the young to doing original, self-directing work, it needs the pastor and the denomination all the more. A society of the machine type may be left to run itself until the fuel gives out; but the more you throw young people on their own responsibility, the more carefully and lovingly you need to watch them and guard them.

The Christian Endeavor prayer meeting needs the pastor far more than the older prayer meeting, the socials need his presence far more than the older socials, the committee work needs his help far more than the older church committees. The pastor would far more wisely and safely leave mature Christians to condust the church without him than leave the young to do their work without him. They are being trained, and they need a trainer. Only, they are being trained in self-reliance, and they need a trainer who will keep in the background and develop their initiative, leading them to become leaders, and rather spurring their wills than harnessing their energies. The society does not need the pastor as a boss; it sorely needs him as a friend. It is unjust to expect an ideal young people's society unless you also expect an ideal young people's pastor.

And, though the ideal young people's society is of and for and by the young people, it is also a church society. No danger that the churches will plan too much for the young; they do not plan enough.

Every church should know what its young people are doing. It should be familiar with their methods. It should know what products their society produces. It should incorporate those products in the older church work as soon as they are produced.

But how many churches do this? How many churches are so close to the young that they know the results of their work, and utilize them?

Is the atmosphere of the church prayer meeting such that the Endeavor graduate can step into it, feel at home, and easily continue his prayer meeting activities? Are the church committees so numerous and varied as to take up and use the Endeavor graduates? Or is the average church both letting its young people train themselves and forcing them after they are trained to make a place for themselves in the older church work by a skill and persistence that not one mature Christian in a thousand would possess?

The ideal young people's prayer meeting has contributions from all the young Christians present. Is the church seeking such conditions in the older church prayer meeting?

The ideal young people's society has committee work for all kinds of ability and degree of development, with every one at work along some line. Is the church pressing such an ideal upon the older church members?

Let the church expect an ideal young people's society, but let it desire as zealously an ideal church to receive the products of the ideal young people's society. Christian Endeavor wants the fullest pastoral oversight, the fullest oversight of the church and the denomination. The young people's society does not need drivers, but there is nothing that it so much needs as leaders.

Now I have asked the first question, "What is the ideal young people's religious society to do?" and the answer has been, "It is to give a religious training."

And I have asked the second question, "Who are to do it?" and the answer has been, "The young people themselves, led—not driven—by their pastors and churches and denominations.

Now let us ask the third question, "How is it to be done?" And my answer is, "By setting up a standard and holding to it."

What do I mean by setting up a standard? I mean saying what you propose to do. No organization on earth that amounts to anything can avoid saying what it proposes to do. It is glad to set up a standard. It is proud of its standard, and tries to rally everyone to it.

Every college sets up a standard. The students may choose electives freely, yet they must bind themselves to definite undertakings, and they must accomplish a prescribed amount and kind of work, or else they must leave.

Every well-managed home has a definite program for the servants, and definite tasks for the children.

Every prosperous store sets up standards for its salesmen, that they be prompt, courteous, accurate, convincing. If they fall short of those standards, they leave the store.

Every successful worker settles what he will do. Most failures in life are caused by the lack of definite aims, persistently pursued. They are caused by the failure to set up a standard and hold one's self to it.

Our Christian Endeavor pledge is such a standard, and that is all it is. It is our program of religious education. It is our platform. It is our declaration of purpose. Call it by any of those names, if you like. No one has ever insisted on the word "pledge."

And no one prescribes, either, just what you shall set up for a standard. The United Society now has four different forms of active member's pledge, among which pastors and societies may choose; or if they can find nothing to fit their needs and desires, they may write their own. From the beginning it has been felt that goals chosen by the worker are more likely to be attained than goals chosen for him.

What are the United Society standards suggested for your adoption? They include, in the fullest and latest form of the pledge, these ten things, and see if you think any one of them should be left out of a scheme of religious training: Bible-reading, prayer, witness-bearing, practical service, church-attendance, church-support, liberal giving, soul-winning, Christian patriotism, Christian brotherhood—all of these according to the measure of Christ's will, as an enlightened conscience may disclose it to us.

But the United Society forces its standards upon no pastor or society. It merely urges that standards be set up, and that they be worthy standards. It merely says, "You call yourself a Christian Endeavor society? Then what are you endeavoring to do for Christ, and in His strength?" A statement of that endeavor will be a Christian Endeavor pledge. A society that is making no endeavor, or is so ashamed of it or afraid of it, or ignorant of it, that it cannot or will not state it, can hardly be called a Christian Endeavor society.

That third question was, "How is it to be done?" And now you see why my answer is, "By setting up a standard of purpose and effort." But it is not enough to set up a standard; we must hold to it.

Christian Endeavor has three principal ways of maintaining adherence to its standards. These are the consecration meeting, the lookout committee and the union work.

The consecration meeting is to remind us of our standards, and perhaps to set up new ones. It is a meeting for the renewal of purpose and the strengthening of will.

Don't stumble over the name, "consecration meeting." That is not essential. Call it a purpose meeting, a review meeting, an experience meeting, a reminder meeting—call it what you please.

And don't stumble over the question of frequency. If you think once a month is too often, hold it once in two months, or once in three—as often as proves most profitable.

Don't stumble over methods of conducting consecration meetings. The formal roll-call is only one way among dozens that are in use.

Make what changes you please in the non-essentials, but note the essential, a definite, regular time for a review of purpose and progress, and the forming of fresh resolves. Every successful undertaking requires this. The ship's captain must daily find accurately his position on the chart. The merchant must periodically balance his books. The scholar must regularly pass examinations. The soldier must systematically undergo inspection. The house must be swept once a week, and thoroughly cleaned twice a year. There is no department of ordered life that can get along without the equivalent of the consecration meeting.

The second Christian Endeavor means of maintaining adherence to its standards is through the work of the lookout committee. You are your brother's keeper. When you fully realize that truth, you are beginning to be a useful Christian. Our lookout committees are training brothers' keepers.

If I were a minister, I should count the work of the Christian Endeavor lookout committee among the most valuable in my church, because just so far as it succeeds, it is training the most useful kind of church members—those that set others at work, and keep them at it.

See what faithful lookout committee work requires: It requires tact, courage, wisdom, patience, perseverence. It bids the Endeavorer stimulate the sluggish, spur the unfaithful, sober the careless, encourage the timid, direct the awkward. Could there be a better drill for the most difficult church work than service on a lookout committee Could a pastor spend time more gainfully than in guiding such committee work?

The third of these principal ways of maintaining adherence to Christian Endeavor standards is our union work.

By our unions, the few Endeavor leaders in any one church are buttressed by the many leaders in all the other churches. By our unions, the wise plans of one society become the property of all the societies. Our unions create an atmosphere of zeal and of achievement. Rightly conducted, they give the societies a matchless stimulus and a constant, practical aid. The standards are set up higher because of them, and maintained with far greater firmness.

A few denominations, because of their bigness, have thought them selves sufficient to themselves, and have isolated their young people from contact with other denominations. Those churches are not only withholding from the smaller and weaker denominations the inspiration which they, with their greater number ought to give, but they themselves, however large they may be, are losing immensely because of this very isolation. There is no denomination in the world so large that it has not much to learn from the Friends, the Moravians, and many other smaller denominations. In our Christian Endeavor unions the very diversity of views and differences of methods are immensely stimulating, and they keep us gloriously out of the ruts.

And I might put this upon much higher ground. I might speak of the blessed tendency of the age toward the union—the reunion, rather —of all of Christ's followers. Christian Endeavor has been the greatest single force tending to bring together the sundered portions of Christ's one body, the Church. Christian Endeavor has done more than any other force to answer Christ's repeated prayer, "That they all may be one." The 168 sects into which American Christianity is weakly and pitifully separated, have been introduced to one another by Christian Endeavor, and are coming, through its fellowship, into that heart unity which is the necessary precursor of unity in action. In its union work, Chistian Endeavor moves along the irresistible current of Providence, and the future, coming slowly but surely, is all its own.

THE RECEPTION COMMITTEE AT THE UNION STATION.

THE JAPANESE RALLY.

And now let me not give the impression that I am blind to the failures of these three ways of maintaining adherence to Christian Endeavor standards. I see them very clearly. I know that the pledge may be broken. I know that consecration meetings may become farces. I know that the lookout committee may degenerate into a mere name. I know that the union work may grow mechanical and profitless. I am not claiming any automatic perfection for these three devices of the consecration meeting, the lookout committee, and the union work. If any one can invent a better or a surer way of accomplishing these ends, it will be adopted with eager gratitude. Christian Endeavor wants the best. But, so far as I know, these are the best ways yet discovered of maintaining fidelity to the standards set up in our societies. The essence of them is, a regular time and occasion for reviews of progress and renewals of purpose; a mutual oversight and encouragement, both within the individual societies and among the societies of the churches. That is the Christian Endeavor way, and that is the answer to the third question I set out to answer.

I have been talking about the ideal society. Let us never be satisfied with less than that. The religious education of the young must never stop short of the best. Christian Endeavor is proud of its past, but it is not bound to it. Christian Endeavor cannot be superseded by any improvement, because it is eager and ready to incorporate all improvements. It knows but one desire: The best for the young, that the young may give their best for Jesus Christ. And if our Christian youth, led by their pastors and upheld by their churches, and bound together in the phalanx of a universal brotherhood, but once determine to do the will of Christ, His entire and blessed will, then the kingdoms of the world will become the kingdoms of our Lord, and He will reign forever and ever.

CHAPTER X.

THE DENOMINATIONAL RALLIES.

The Denominational Rallies at an International Christian Endeavor convention are looked forward to with eager interest by thousands of Christian Endeavorers. To many these Rallies afford about the only opportunity that the young people have of coming into close contact with their denominational leaders and of taking part in discussions affecting their own particular branch of the Lord's kingdom.

The Rallies at Seattle were without exception well attended, many of them being, in fact, small conventions fraught with great possibilities for the larger development of church work.

Particular interest was given to the Methodist Rally by the presence of the Vice President of the United States, Hon. Charles W. Fairbanks, who took a prominent part in the meeting. The Baptist, Presbyterian and Congregational Rallies were very enthusiastic meetings. We wish that we had the space to give a full account of the proceedings at all of the fifteen rallies, but can only give a brief synopsis.

The Baptists.

For the first time the Free Baptists joined with the—well, the so-called "regular" Baptists in their Rally this year, and the heartiness of their welcome was typified by the cordial embrace given to Rev. J. M. Lowden, the trustee representing the Free Baptists, by the chairman, Treasurer Lathrop, when he introduced him. No heresy was discovered in his doctrine or in that of Rev. W. J. Twart, of Lawrence, Mass., another Free Baptist, as they unfolded "What Baptists Owe to Other Denominations."

The colored Baptists were ably represented by another couple, Dr. W. T. Johnson of Richmond, Va., and Rev. Walter H. Brooks of Washington, D. C., the one a present and the other a former member of the Board of Trustees. Mr. Brooks, noting the small attendance of his race at the meeting, had written the following beautiful poem, which was enthusiastically approved by his audience:

> I see the lambs of the fold,
>   You've sought and striven to keep,
> But, brother, tell me where
>   Is the Master's lost black sheep?
>
> The Shepherd gave His life,
>   'Mid sorrows dark and deep,
> To bring again to the fold,
>   And home, His lost black sheep.

Go, as He bids you, then,
And glory you shall reap—
Go, bring to Him his own;
He loves His lost black sheep.

Think not the fleece's hue
Can ever render cheap
What, in His sight, hath worth
Like the blood-bought lost black sheep.

But the gem of the meeting was the witty, pungent, masterly address of Rev. James A. Francis of New York, who pithily summed up the distinguishing characteristic of the Baptist denomination as the twin truth of "the sufficiency of the God-head man-ward and the sufficiency of the soul of man God-ward."

The deadness of the issues that divide many of the denominations now-a-days was aptly shown by the call from Mr. Francis for all those who could give a clear and accurate statement of the reasons for the separation of the Baptist hosts to raise their hands. Of all the large audience, only two ladies had the hardihood to do so, although thirty-five clergymen were present. But all rose unanimously to express approval of an organic union of the two bodies.

The Christian Disciples.

Claud E. Hill of Mobile, Ala., presided. Guy E. Withers of Kansas City led the devotional service. Rev. A. L. Chapman of Seattle delivered the address of welcome. A response by Rev. O. L. Smith of El Reno, Oklahoma, proved to be inspiring by the wit and humor that came out of the address.

Dr. B. B. Tyler of Denver, "the young man of sixty-seven years," spoke eloquently and with great spiritual import on "The Present Era of Young People. It was an optimistic address. The Doctor closed by saying that he never expected to die, but just to be changed.

Rev. W. A. Moore of Tacoma, Wash., next spoke on the religious spirit of the twentieth century, and the plea of the Disciples. The speaker presented with forceful unction the thought that the spirit of this great convention and the pleas of the Disciples were in exact accord.

Rev. W. A. Warren of Pittsburg, Penn., next discussed the centennial of the Disciples, which occurs in 1909. He complimented Christian Endeavor by declaring that what was needed was to carry out its principles. The Disciples needed the Tenth Legion and missionary zeal. The Endeavorers were to furnish the greatly needed recruits in the ministry, and on the mission fields. Christian Endeavorers seem to pass on to be the leaders of the church.

Rev. A. W. Kokendoffer of Mexico, Mo., made an earnest plea for the next National Convention of the Disciples, and Dean H. L. Willett of Chicago closed the meeting with prayer.

Old-time workers among the Disciples declared this to be the best yet. The quality of the program and the deep spiritual enthusiasm was truly inspiring. The Disciples are earnest Endeavorers. They believe in Christian Endeavor.

The Congregationalists.

An immense throng attended the Congregational Rally at Plymouth Church. Though many additional chairs were brought into the spacious auditorium many were compelled to stand. Indeed, not a few sat on the window sills and the floor. The Rev. Dr. W. T. McElveen, president of the Congregational Endeavor Union presided. The Rev. Francis Von Horn, D. D., who has had pastorates in Illinois, Massachusetts, and Iowa, gave a felicitious word of welcome. A very enjoyable feature of the rally was the forty-minute organ recital given just before the service by Professor Andrews of Oberlin College. Twenty-two speakers delivered addresses, while the presiding officer kept them so well in hand that two hours sufficed for the elaborate program.

Miss Kajiro and Mr. Sawaya, leaders of our work in Japan, Mr. J. M. Ibanez of Ciudad Juarez, Mexico, told us what Christian Endeavor had done in that land. Dr. Ward of Wells College described the culture a Christian Endeavorer ought to possess.

"Old Williston" was represented by Dr. Smith Baker and the Christian Endeavor World by Prof. Amos R. Wells, while Dr. and Mrs. Clark conveyed the greetings of our brothers and sisters in the wide-wide world and all rejoiced that the general secretary was an honored layman of the Pilgrim faith.

Wisconsin, Illinois, California, Massachusetts, Nebraska, Iowa, Connecticut, New York and New Jersey were represented by their presidents, who told us how to organize the young people for definite work. Many valuable hints were given and evidence furnished that Congregational Endeavorers were not idle.

The Friends.

The Friend's Rally was a decided success.

The new Memorial Church not being completed, the Rally was held in the tent. Rev. J. Edgar Williams, pastor of the Seattle church, presided.

The address of welcome was given by Rev. Chas. Replogte of Everett, Wash. Helpful addresses were given by Miss Sarah Ellis, for five years missionary to Tokyo, Japan, and Mr. Bunji Kida of Iberaki, Japan. The chairman then introduced the various delegates and delegations and short responses were given.

Outside of Washington, Oregon had the largest delegation present, and California next.

The Methodists.

The Interdenominational Rally of the Methodist Episcopal and Canadian Methodist Churches was held in the Queen Anne M. E. Church. The church was thronged. Fully fifty ministers were present from both sides of the border.

Rev. E. R. Dille presided. Rev. Wm. H. Leech and Rev. W. T. Randolph, two Seattle pastors, conducted the devotions and Rev. O. H. Magill gave a hearty address of welcome. Mr. Wm. Ivens, a young layman of Winnipeg, Man., spoke on "Pressing Needs and How to Meet Them." It was a bugle call to an advance on mission and evangelistic lines. He was followed by Rev. W. H. Barraclough of New Westminister, B. C., who gave a thoughtful and inspiring address on "Our Young People as a Missionary Force." It was evident that we on this side of the line might learn much from our Canadian brothers about missionary methods and enthusiasm. The two cent a week plan among the Canadian Endeavorers works like a charm, and has greatly increased the young people's offerings.

In the midst of Mr. Barraclough's address, Vice-President Fairbanks came in and was welcomed with the Chatauqua salute.

Mr. William Phillips Hall was introduced as the New Methodist

Episcopal Trustee of the United Society, sharing that honor with Dr. H. K. Carroll. Mr. Hall modestly gave up his turn to the Vice-President.

Rev. Dr. Wilson of Toronto spoke briefly on "Christian Endeavor in Canada, paying a glowing tribute to what it has done in promoting church loyalty and interdenominational fraternity.

Dr. Dille, in introducing Mr. Fairbanks, said: "Our Church is not in politics but to say, as we stand here today, that for President we want such a man as Charles Warren Fairbanks, who stands for the purity of the home, the sanctity of the Sabbath, for the highest temperance ideals, and for civic righteousness, that is not politics; that is patriotism, nay it is religion!

The Vice-President responded warmly to the greeting given him, and then uttered a heart-stirring appeal to Methodist young people to practice all the virtues that make for good citizenship.

At the close of the meeting an informal reception was held and all present met and greeted the honored guest of the hour.

The Episcopalians.

The meeting was held in St. Mark's Church, the Rev. J. P. D. Lloyd Rector. While the attendance was not large it was enthusiastic. Rev. Dr. Tomkins of Philadelphia opened the meeting with prayer. After reading a part of the Fifteenth Chapter of St. John, Dr. Tomkins spoke: He explained the idea and purpose of the Rally and then went on to show what Christian Endeavor was, and what it had done, referring especially to the "Church of England Union" and to the good accomplished in the United States in the Episcopal Church wherever Christian Endeavor was introduced.

The points especially emphasized were:

First, the help in the spiritual youth of the younger members of the church.

Second, the preparation of workers and leaders.

Third, the opportunity for intercessory prayer.

Fourth, the comfort and cheer afforded to the Rector by the young and consecrated helpers.

He urged those present to start societies in their churches, to send to the central office for literature showing what Christian Endeavor has done and can do in the Episcopal Church, and to draw their young friends into this grand union of hearts and hands all over the world.

The Lutherans.

The Lutherans held their Rally in Bethany Presbyterian Church. Rev. Luther DeYoe, D. D., presided. The delegation was unexpectedly large. Dr. DeYoe gave a report of the effort made to form a Lutheran National Christian Endeavor organization. Some eleven hundred Lutheran young people have been gathered into the organization and the work has been placed upon such a footing that it is now possible to keep watch of the societies of Christian Endeavor in the church.

The membership of the union will be rapid.

Addresses were made by Rev. E. H. Delk, D. D., of Philadelphia, and by Rev. R. G. Bannon, D. D., of Williamsport, Penn.

The meeting was one of delightful fellowship and in every way stimulated the blessed Christian Endeavor spirit in the Great Lutheran Church

The Methodist Protestants and United Brethren.

Fellowship and candid expression of the Church Union characterized the Rally, in charge of Rev. J. E. Fout of the United Brethren Church and President J. H. Straughn of the Methodist Protestant Church. The subject of Union was introduced by the first speaker and was continued by the remaining speakers.

"Out of the abundance of the heart the mouth speaketh," being true, there is certainly no question among Endeavorers of both churches as to the desirability of this Union. Revs. Fout, Straughn, Hubbell and Miller of Ohio, Shaffer of Oregon, Van Dyke of Japan and others gave expression to similar convictions. Rev. A. N. Ward, pastor of the Methodist Protestant Church, was present and gave the fifty delegates present a cheery greeting. His new splendid church was not finished, which was a cause of regret.

At four o'clock the entire delegation took the car for the Plymouth Congregational Church to participate in the closing session of that Denominational Rally, but arrived too late, which was a matter of deep regret. Revs. Fout and Straughn were to have presented the greetings from their respective Denominations.

The Presbyterians.

The Presbyterian Rally assumed the proportions of a convention. It was held in the First Presbyterian Church—one of the convention's principal meeting places—and was as crowded as the regular convention session. Mr. Von Ogden Vogt presided. The meeting was world-wide in its scope, for among the principal speakers were Rev. John Pollock of Ireland, Rev. Andrew Beattie of China, Rev. H. W. Fraser, D. D., of Vancouver, B. C., Rev. Edward Marsden of Alaska, besides Mr. Sydney Chipperfield of Saskatchewan, Rev. Lewis S. Hall of Minnesota, Mr. Raymond S. Husted of Colorado, Rev. L. M. Boozer of Oregon, Mr. Edward Tarring of the District of Columbia, Mr. H. G. Lains of St. Paul, Rev. Charles Stelzle of New York and Rev. Ira Landrith, D. D., of Nashville. The addresses were all bright, sharp, witty and to the point. The advance movements in the Presbyterian denomination are now so numerous that it was difficult to find time to speak of many of them. The meeting, however, was of exceptional interest and profit, and our hearts throbbed with denominational loyalty and pride as we learned what was being accomplished in our different fields.

Rev. Edward Marsden told of the work being done by Presbyterians in Alaska. It has resulted in the doing away of many heathen customs. It has also resulted in the lessening of the liquor habit. "And yet," continued Mr. Marsden, "the same ships that bring us our Bibles, our hymn books and our missionaries, also bring us barrels and barrels of whisky and rum to destroy the bodies and souls of our natives. Send us your missionaries, send us your Bibles, send us your hymn books—but, oh, my friends, we don't want your whisky." It was a pathetic plea, which made a deep impression upon his hearers.

The Reformed Church.

Though small in numbers it was full of enthusiasm and profit. Almost all departments of the Church's activity were represented. The devotional exercises were led and the meeting was presided over by the Rev. Benjamin E. Dickhaut, D. D., Pastor of the Harlem Collegiate Church of New York City.

The Rev. Dr. Pockman of New Brunswick, N. J., spoke of the

history of the Church and its educational institutions. Prof. William I. Chamberlain, Ph. D., of Rutgers College, was heard with deep interest in behalf of the Foreign Missionary work of the Church. He was followed by Miss Scudder, who gave a vivid picture of the life of woman in India and the efforts that are being made to uplift her.

The Rev. Mr. Van der Beek of Oak Harbor, Washington, pastor of the most westerly church of the denomination in this country, told of the hopes, the struggles and the encouragements of his particular field. Miss Ricksen of Kentucky, fascinated all with her simple yet interesting account of the efforts that are being made to elevate the mountain whites in Kentucky. Mr. Harry A. Kinports, always full of life and enthusiasm, and who is the newly elected secretary of the Young People's Missionary Work of the denomination, then told of his desires and ambitions for the denomination that has already done so much for the world's evangelization. Mr. Amos R. Wells of the United Society, always bright and stimulating, dropped into the meeting for a few moments and presented the helpful suggestion of a "Denominational Committee" in Christian Endeavor work and then definitely defined its special functions.

The meeting closed with prayer.

The United Evangelical.

Rev. A. A. Winters of Portland, Oregon, presided. There were present representatives from three conferences of the Church—Ohio, Platte River and Oregon. The meeting opened with singing "I'll Go Where You Want Me To Go." Reading of Scripture and prayer followed, after which several addresses were delivered.

Rev. W. S. Harpster, president of the Ohio Union, spoke of the world-wide movement of Christian Endeavor. He also emphasized the evangelistic work, and said the church had made her marked advancement through the power and spirit of evangelism.

Rev. P. A. Layton, of Nebraska, in his pleasing manner spoke of the great opportunity of Christian Endeavor at the opening of the Twentieth Century. Rev. B. S. Shivley, also of Nebraska, gave us a talk on church loyalty and how to inspire our young people with enthusiasm from this convention.

Rev. C. T. Hurd, an active enthusiastic Endeavorer, showed us something of the length and breadth of this movement, and the far-reaching and soul-inspiring work of our young people.

Rev. N. W. Sager, Dallas, Oregon, took up in a most helpful way the missionary side of the young people's work.

Mr. W. E. Critchow moved our hearts to thankfulness as he told what our society had done for him, how it had been to him a training school, and how through this training he had been fitted for a life of service for his Master.

United Presbyterian Rally.

The United Presbyterians met in the New Third Church, the Rev. Wm. H. Freisch, pastor. The program was an informal one, the Rev. R. L. Lanning of Everett presiding and the Rev. H. G. Edgar of Seattle giving the address of welcome. The response and address of the afternoon were given by Rev. W. H. McMillen, D. D. LL. D. of Alleghany, Pa. Mr. Nakuina, president of the Christian Endeavor of Hawaii, told of the work in that country and there were a number of short talks. The best of all was the social hour following, at which lunch was served in the church parlors to about 300 guests. A male quartette added to the pleasure of the hour.

CHAPTER XI.

THY KINGDOM COME.

Tent Williston could not accommodate the throng that desired to hear the two distinguished speakers on Friday night. A half hour before the services thousands of people were turned away. Dr. Francis E. Clark presided, and together with Mr. Guy Withers, of Missouri (who led in the response in the reading of the 24th psalm), and Mr. Wm. Phillips Hall, President of the American Tract Society, led the great throng to the throne of grace.

The two speakers of the evening were opposite: Dr. Francis, of St. Petersburg, short, dark, keen and vivacious; fond of an epigram; quick to make a pun. Vice President Fairbanks, tall, of iron gray hair; a little florid, with a direct, concise, forceful style.

Dr. Francis told of attending a meeting of Russian Jews in Boston. No one knew him but the chairman of the meeting, who asked him to address the gathering. He did so, and on going out heard one Russian Jew ask another: "Who is that little, black, bald headed priest who spoke to us in our own language this evening?"

Dr. Francis insisted that the Christian Endeavor movement was playing an important part in the reconstruction and regeneration of Russia.

Russia of today, he said, looks like the Russia of innumerable yesterdays, but everything except the appearance of things is changed. In the novels of Maxime Gorky, the characters discuss the taking of India from the British, and the driving of the Jews out of Russia. But on the streets and saloons such questions are not being discused by the peasantry of Russia today. Gorky's books are already antiquated. As an illustration of this fact, Dr. Francis told an incident where a charming, well educated young woman showed him an album of portraits. Upon the first page of this album was a picture of a young lady, thrusting a revolver into her lover's hand, and underneath was an inscription, "Prove thyself worthy." The price of her hand in marriage was that her lover be the assassin of some despotic Russian ruler. On the second page of this album was a sketch reproducing the Roman Brutus assassinating Ceasar. On the successive pages were the portraits of over 50 political assassins—men who have

freed that land either by bomb or knife from the despot. Upon the last page of this album was inscribed in the girl's own hand this modification of Longfellow's couplet:

"Lives of great men all remind me
I can make my life sublime."

Of course the revolutionists have gone to excesses, and these excesses have created a reaction, but the creed of a large number of the Russians, even of the better people, is "There is no God, and we need no Czar."

The latter part of Dr. Francis' speech was interrupted somewhat by the hurrahing welcome tendered the approaching Vice President by the crowds without the tent. In a few moments the tall, stalwart Hon. Charles Fairbanks stood upon the platform. The band played and the choir sang; state groups of delegates yelled their state songs or their local slogans; handkerchiefs waived, and every possible method was employed to express the enthusiastic welcome by the great throng to the Vice President.

Dr. Clark in presenting Vice President Fairbanks, said that one of the great glories of our country is that the man who holds an important office must be a man, who, in the estimation of the people, is a good man; that even if nominated by one of the great political parties, a man would have no chance of election if he was not a good man. For many years the nominees for the Presidency and Vice Presidency of the United States have been Christian men.

"It would be easy," Dr. Clark added, "to convert this enthusiastic Endeavor meeting into a great political demonstration, but such a proceeding would not be in accordance with the desires of the honored guest of the evening." He suggested that Vice President Fairbanks be elected as an honorary member of the United Society of Christian Endeavor, and then presented him as the latest accession to our ranks.

When Vice President Fairbanks arose, there was another enthusiastic demonstration. Several times he tried to speak but could not because of the deafening applause. When at last sufficient silence was secured to enable him to proceed, his very first sentence brought forth another round of applause, for he said: "Dr. Clark, I came as a guest, but now I take my place gladly as a member of the household."

He rejoiced in an organization which overlooked all sectarian limits and which aimed to make all mankind everywhere one great, spiritual household. Particularly apt were Vice President Fairbank's allusions to Washington, Lincoln and McKinley.

Some of the newspapers have pictured Vice President Fairbanks as a man of cold demeanor and formal manner, but no man but a warm-hearted man could have delivered the address the ten thousand people rejoiced to hear. In the language of the West, Vice President Fairbanks is a good mixer, and though Republican in politics he is a Democrat in the manner of mingling with men. There is nothing offish about him. He believes in his fellow man, and he believes in God; he believes in the great, enterprising Northwest; and he believes that God has some great purpose to fulfill in the hustling Pacific states.

The 1907 Seattle Convention Committee acted as an escort to the honored guest of the evening, and their entrance into the tent was not unlike a church processional. At the conclusion of the following address the entire audience formed a sort of recessional, cheering Mr. Fairbanks and the sentiments he had uttered every step of the way to the street.

THE VICE-PRESIDENT'S ADDRESS.

"Dr. Clark and fellow members of the Christian Endeavor Society:

I came upon the platform your guest; I take my place now before you a member of the household.

I wish to express the gratification I experience at being commended to your kindly favor by a man whose name was little known a few years ago, but whose name is now known throughout the uttermost parts of the earth.

Dr. Clark, it is given to comparatively few men to impress themselves indelibly upon their times and upon the future. In the last century, yes, even in many centuries before, there has not been produced a man who in the great Christian world has set in operation greater or more beneficial influences than has the one who laid the foundation of the Christian Endeavor society. All honor to him, and all honor to the societies which have sprung into existence at the touch of his genius, his foresight, and his Christian consideration.

This great assemblage is full of significance. It means that the forces which are making for a higher and better civilization are alert and aggressive. I was gratified, sir, to hear you say that there are representatives here not only from all portions of the Republic of the United States but from other lands as well. It is exceedingly gratifying to find gathered here upon the shore of the Pacific, under the banner of the Republic, representatives from all of the flags upon the western continent, and many from beyond the seas. Through the magic touch and inspiration of steam and electricity, nations are being brought closer and closer together. We are brought more and more into fellowship with one another and in all of the storied past. We are brought into such intimate touch with one another that what benefits one civilization in one country benefits in a measure the civilizations of all other countries to the uttermost parts of the earth.

"Our Country!" What a splendid theme that is. I know full well that when we Americans pause to pay tribute to our country we have the kindly regard of those who come from other countries to enjoy our hospitality. For the Republic of the United States has no feeling of envy or unkindness toward any other country upon the face of the earth. Our country bids all other countries to enter the contest for the trophies to be found, not upon the field of battle but in the ways of Christian peace. Our country has the sympathetic good will of all other countries because above and beyond all else it is a Christian country. Our fathers, who laid the foundations of American institutions, walked by Christian faith, and we walk by the lights our fathers raised aloft. Our country is great in material power. A bountiful Providence has scattered his benefactions from sea to sea. No people in the world have had placed in their hands greater natural elements of wealth and power than have the people of the United States. We have been blessed by a bountiful Creator with a wealth of climate unsurpassed, with a wealth of soil that beggars description, with a wealth of mind that no finite intelligence can measure, and above and beyond all we have been blessed by a people drawn from the best bloods of all the nations upon the globe, here making the ideal citizen of the republic, the ideal citizen of the world. While we glory in the manifold evidences of material power, while we cast our eyes abroad and view with gratification the many evidences of industrial and commercial strength, these are not our chief glory, these highways of commerce stretching from ocean to ocean, holding the Pacific and the Atlantic in their iron grasp, these great commercial cities which have risen as by magic, while here and there from East to West and from North to South are countless busy industries, these and all these are not the trophies we most prize. Above and beyond all of them we prize the virtue, the Christian, patriotic intelligence of eighty-five millions of people.

Some time ago, I stood at the Atlantic seaboard with a gentleman who owed allegiance to a foreign flag. A little way off rode a portion of the navy of the United States. This foreign gentleman had come to regard with high favor the country whose hospitality he was enjoying, and as he looked upon this fleet of invincible coursers, he said to me: "You are a great nation, a mighty people; you have won the admiration of the world. You have got a mighty navy, and are able to summon at a moment's notice millions of people to defend the honor and the good name of your country if supreme need should require."

My friends, our chief pride is not in our navy, splendid as it is. Our chief glory is not in the men who have made immortal many battlefields. These are not the chief evidences of our strength. Above and beyond them, and all the commonly recognized evidences of material power, we have the patriotic, intelligent, wise, humane, Christian hearts of eighty-five millions of freemen.

This is a Christian nation. And, sir, this great society, whose foundations you so well laid, will contribute powerfully to the preservation of this nation as a Christian republic.

Here are gathered not only representatives from all states and many countries, but there are gathered here the representatives of the great Christian denominations. After all, no matter to what church we owe our first allegiance, we realize the fact that we are each and all interested in the accomplishment of the same high, beneficent purpose. I regard it as one of the most hopeful signs of the future that the great Christian denominations overlook sectarian denominational lines and fellowship together in a common cause.

Our great leaders in political affairs—and in this country of ours we have no rulers except the people themselves—our great leaders have been men who have had a veneration for the religion of their fathers. It is providential, it seems to me, that in every great exigency which has confronted this people, from their beginning in their crude habitations on the Atlantic seaboard down to the early morning of the twentieth century, have been men of sublime Christian faith.

George Washington, a name which fills the earth, one of the greatest and loftiest characters found in all the recorded history of the past, was a man of sincere Christian faith. Away back in the dark hours of Valley Forge, in that winter which tried the souls of men, he was wont to go out into the forest and invoke Almighty God upon the side of the Continental Army struggling to be free. And when he took the oath of his high office by the undivided judgment of his countrymen, he delivered an inaugural address in which he uttered these significant words:

"No people can be found to acknowledge and adore the Invisible Hand which conducts the affairs of man more than the people of the United States. Every step by which they have advanced to the character of an independent nation seems to have been distinguished by some token of providential agency."

There was here a recognition of divine power in the affairs of the American people by one who is known to history as the father of our country.

When Abraham Lincoln (you do well to applaud that name, for it is sweet and majestic among all the names of human history) stood upon the Eastern portico of our national capital to take the oath of the high office to which he had been called by the divided judgment of his fellow countrymen, when the clouds of national dissolution hung about the horizon, and the lions of war were already speaking in the distance, in that supreme, overmastering exigency Abraham Lincoln uttered these notable words:

"If the Almighty ruler with His eternal truth and justice be on your side of the North or yours of the South, that truth and justice will surely prevail by the justice of this great tribunal of the American people. Intelligence, patriotism, Christianity, and a firm reliance on Him who has never yet forsaken His favored land are still competent to adjust in the best way our present difficulties."

And later, when war again menaced us, another American whose name is a priceless legacy to our country and to every other country beneath the sun, William McKinley, when war was imminent, invoked the Almighty that the cause of our beloved country might triumph, not because of our majesty and power, but because of the justice of our appeal to arms. And in the last sad moments—how long ago they were and yet how brief the time—at Buffalo our great friend (and I speak of him as a friend, for he was a friend and lover of his kind) as he saw this world receding from his vision freighted with all that was most dear to him, he said as a parting benediction which rested upon the nation: "It is God's will; His will, not ours, be done."

We are a peace loving people. Some times we have so loved peace that we have been willing to fight for it; but we have never drawn the sword in an unholy cause. We have never appealed to the sword except commanded by the Christian voice of America.

Our material power and our ability to make war were never more manifest than today. We have no fear of any people beyond the seas, and they need not fear our power; for in our international relations our guiding star shall be justice and righteousness among the nations of the earth. We are throwing, and we propose to throw, the weight of our example and our moral influence in the great debate among the nations, on the side of some means of preserving international fraternity and the settlement of international disputes in the court of reason rather than by fleets and armies upon land and sea. We will never compromise our national honor, and we will never demand that any other country compromise its national honor. We hope to see in God's good time some tribunal established wherein great international questions which might otherwise lead to war may be debated and settled according to the weightier reason. In such an international tribunal, navies and armies will not weigh; only the righteousness of the cause will turn the balance. In that tribunal the greatest and the weakest powers will stand upon a plane of absolute equality.

Not many years ago, before the sun of Christianity had worked its tremendous influence as it has today, disputes between individuals were settled by an appeal to force. No neighbor would now hold the good favor of his fellows who should appeal to force in the settlement of his disagreement with his neighbor. It would be regarded as brutish, as barbarous. I believe, and you believe, that what is brutish and barbarous in the individual is brutish and barbarous in the nation. Wars are, as a rule, due to the selfishness and intrigues of men. As a rule, they are due to the passion of personal aggrandizement on the part of those entrusted with power. Sometimes the "yellow press" has more regard for war than for peace. I have seen, and you have seen, how ruthlessly they undertook to strike down the hand of William McKinley when he was holding war in check a few years ago.

I believe that more than cabinets, more than rulers, and more than all of the civil powers in this world, the great Christian churches are making for international tranquility. And if, any time, there shall be an international court to which the nations may appeal, it will be due in no inconsiderable degree to the influence and power of the great Christian churches in all of the civilized nations of the earth.

I am gratified, Dr. Clark, that this great organization is built upon such broad foundations. I am glad it brings within its hospitable arms all nations of the earth. For such fellowing as we witness here among the peoples of all flags, will lead by a sort of irresistible gravitation to the maintenance of unbroken peace and the establishment of tribunals of justice to which nations may appeal in dire extremity. We look to The Hague tribunal, and to the statesmen there assembled to consider this subject of international arbitration. They have our hopes and our prayers. The task they have is a difficult one, not one to be easily settled. There must necessarily be much and grave debate, much deliberation and consideration. If this conference shall unhappily fail in the accomplishment of its great purpose, I have faith to believe that succeeding conferences will respond to the demand of Christian civilization, and establish a tribunal which will in a great measure render wars impossible in the future.

This Christian Endeavor society is a practical society. That is one of the things I like about it. It takes concern not only of the future, but of the present also. Wherever it is found, it makes for all those things which most distinguish a high order of civilization. It is making better the community, the state, and the country. And above and beyond all else, it is making more glorious and more sublime the homes of our countrymen. The work it has done is great. Before it is a work greater still to be done. The twentieth century upon which we have entered with such splendid promise is in God's providence to be the greatest century since the stars first sang together, a century in which science will flourish as never before, a century in which literature will make splendid advance; and I believe that before the sun of the present century has passed its meridian we shall accomplish the greatest victory in the history of the world, and that will be the triumph of peaceful settlement over war itself.

My friends, all honor to the Christian Endeavor Society of the United States! Yes, all honor to the Christian Endeavor Society throughout the world! I thank you all."

At the Washington Annex, part of the new and splendid hotel which Mr. James A. Moore is building, the convention committee tendered Vice President Fairbanks, the officers and speakers of the convention a reception and banquet. About 150 plates were laid, and after a sumptuous dinner we again had the pleasure of hearing from Mr. Fairbanks. He took advantage at this occasion to express his personal love for Dr. Clark and his faith in the great international society of young people as a solution for the world's great problems.

Senator Samuel Piles, Congressman Jones, James A. Moore, Prof. Wells, General Secretary Wm. Shaw and Mr. Hartman (who for many years was President of the Washington Christian Endeavor Union) and others spoke briefly.

Another pleasing feature of the reception was the presentation by Chairman Barth of the members of the convention committee.

There have been many great sessions of the Seattle convention, but Friday night's session in Tent Williston exceeded them all. Enthusiasm is not dead in the Christian Endeavor ranks, and Christian Endeavor is not a spent force.

FIRST PRESBYTERIAN CHRURCH.

At the First Presbyterian Church on Friday evening an interesting and educative meeting was held.

After prayer and praise Rev. W. H. McMillan, D. D., of Allegheny, Pa., who was chairman of the meeting, introduced the Rev. Andrew Beattie, Ph. D., Presbyterian Missionary, Canton, China, by saying that among the burning questions which interest the American people was that of taking care of the Oriental population that comes to us, and announced that Mr. Beattie would speak on, "Is There a Yellow Peril?" Dr. Beattie said in part:

"A few years ago, a Chinese official was engaged in conversation with a foreign diplomat. The Chinese official turned to the diplomat, and said:, "You are too anxious to wake us up and start us on a new road. But you will regret it, for once we do we will go fast and far— farther than you think, and much faster than you want." That this Chinese official knew what he was talking about has been proven by the rapid changes which have recently taken place in China. China has aroused from her sleep, and the capitols of the nations are anxious, judging from what has been written in the newspapers and magazines; and Europe and the American nation expect the yellow race to revenge itself for the insults it has received at the hands of the white race. Whether or not this result will follow the awakening of China, time alone can tell. It is true, however, that China has aroused from her long sleep, and Western nations (particularly America) should take notice and act accordingly. Whether or not there is to be a yellow peril depends on how the white race treats the yellow race in the future. The young men and young women of China have awakened to a sense of their manhood and womanhood and of their nation's greatness. The whole East has been aroused to the sense of the unjust treatment she has received at the hands of the West, and she is now determined to insist on fair play. No Western or Eastern nation will be permitted to trespass with impunity on the rights of China.

We may speak of China as a heathen nation, but we should not speak of her as an uncivilized people. China is, and has been, great in almost any way you may estimate greatness. She has a past history of which any nation might well be proud. Mr. John Foster has said: "When I see a Chinese gentleman, I have the impulse of standing uncovered in his presence and make a profound bow for their great race cannot be surpassed in literature, in philosophy, in art, and in useful inventions. From China, Japan borrowed her language, her art, and her literature. The Chinese ethical system is second only to that found in the New Testament.

While an industrious, peace-loving people, the annals of no people are more crowded with heroic deeds than those of China. Now, to understand the radical nature of the changes that have taken place, we must remember the educational system that has been in existence in China for centuries. China has conducted civil service examinations for about 3,000 years. This great system of examinations has been the brain and backbone of the nation. It has produced a nation of strong, educated men—the literati of China. While the educated men have been the strength of China, they have also been the conservative element, and prevented all development for hundreds of years. They held China in their grasp, and resisted all change. There was no hope for China until this educated class could be moved. When the war between China and Japan occurred in 1894, China appeared to be as hopelessly chained to her past as Ephraim to his idols. But the war brought a change—it was the beginning of the end. When Japan went to war with China, the Chinese were indignant and insulted from the fact that a little nation like Japan had the audacity to oppose a great nation like China. The Chinese despise the Japanese—they call them monkeys and dwarfs. Probably China had some reason to look down upon the little brown people, for China is greater intellectually, morally, and physically, and they are greater people in history. It was tremendously humiliating then when she suffered defeat at the hands of Japan, and forfeited the Island of Formosa. But now, China was ready to learn. Following the China-Japan war, China suffered her deepest humiliation. The Western nations, assured of China's weakness, began to divide her territory between them. Russia took Port Arthur; England, Wei Hai Wei; Germany, Kaiou Chou; France, Kwang Chau Woan; and the newspapers and magazines were busy discussing how China should be divided up among the nations.

It was at this opportune moment that Chang Chi Tung wrote his great book, "China's Only Hope." His book came as a surprise to conservatives and reformers alike. Chang Chi Tung is a man of profound scholarship and restless activity. He might have been a rich man, but he is comparatively poor. He is a scholar of national reputation, and commanded the respect and admiration of the literati of the whole empire. He began his book by denouncing the greed and stupidity of the officials; he held up the religions to scorn, and demanded a change in the educational system of the country; he suggested that seven temples out of ten be used for schools; that the eight-legged essay be abolished; recommended the organization of a standing army of 300,000 men, and the building of fifty battleships. The old regime was good enough for the past, but times had changed.

The book was put into the hands of the Emperor, who commended it in imperial edict, and began at once to issue edicts calling for reform all along the line. That was in 1898. Some of the old officials appealed to the Empress Dowager to save the country from the ruin which they considered the young Emperor was about to bring upon the nation. The Empress Dowager threw in her lot with the conservatives; put out an edict putting an end to reform; cut off the heads of a few reformers, and the nation seemed to fall back into its old time conservatism. But the spirit of self-preservation had become now a moving power. Patriotism began to stir the people. The government could not or would not do anything—the people must do something to save the country. One of the oldest and greatest nations of the earth was being watched for an opportunity to be divided up among the greedy nations of the world. The troublous events of 1900, which at first appeared to be the dying of the struggle, proved to be but the breaking of the shackles that set the nation free. The Boxer uprising led to the second humiliation of the Chinese nation. Foreign armies marched to Pekin, and took possession of the sacred city. The Empress Dowager and her court were obliged to flee. On her return to Pekin in August, 1901, the Dowager threw herself in with the reformers. She began immediately to issue edicts similar to those she had turned down the Emperor for issuing in 1898. The examinations were changed; modern subjects were added; and schools were ordered in all the provinces.

In 1905, Yuan Chih Kai sent his memorial to the throne to the effect that it was of no use trying to combine the old and new systems of examinations. September 2, 1905, the Empress Dowager issued an edict abolishing the old system of examinations which had been the hope and fear of students for thousands of years. Probably no event in history was more important to the world nor affected so many people as this, for it had been the root of one of China's most cherished institutions. We have no record of a change being made in a nation with so little noise.

No sooner had the edict gone forth than schools began to multiply. In many instances, the idols were gathered out of the temples and thrown into the river or burned by order of the officials, and the buildings turned into schools. Thus China has started on her new road. Last year nine students educated abroad received the Master's degree. This year one hundred students, who have gone through the new schools, received the Master's degree. No better evidence could we have that China will stand by the new order. China, too, is determined to have a modern army. The whole nation is studying war. Schools are full of the military spirit. It is the aim of China to have an army of 1,500,000.

But there are other evidences of China's awakening to the consciousness of her greatness. On every hand there is evidence of a new civilization among the masses. A new life and national spirit are taking place. The women of China are determined to share in the new empire. The women of China have never sunk to the low level which characterizes women of other oriental nations.

Today the women of China have all the elements of noble womanhood. They are demanding and securing schools for the education of women and children. The old practice of foot binding received a death blow by the spirit of the new China.

China is determined to purge the land from the curse of opium, which has been knawing at her vitals. This movement is not simply

FRANK G. SMITH, D.D.
CHICAGO, ILL.
PASTOR WARREN AVE. CONG. CHURCH

W. T. McELVEEN, PH.D.
BOSTON, MASS.

REV. C. H. HUBBELL
COLUMBUS, OHIO
FIELD SEC. OHIO C.E. UNION

REV. B. B. TYLER, D.D.
DENVER, COL.
PASTOR S. BROADWAY CHRISTIAN CHURCH

REV. W. H. BARRACLOUGH, B.A.
NEW WESTMINSTER, B.C.

REV. E. R. DILLE, D.D.
OAKLAND, CAL.
PASTOR FIRST M.E. CHURCH

REV. ALEXANDER FRANCIS, D.D.
ST. PETERSBURG, RUSSIA

REV. JAS. H. STRAUGHN, B.D.
WEST LAFAYETTE, OHIO
PRES. METHODIST PROTESTANT C.E. UNION

REV. ANDREW BEATTIE, PH.D.
CANTON, CHINA
PRESBYTERIAN MISSIONARY

REV. W. H. McMILLAN, D.D.
ALLEGHENY CITY, PENN.
TRUSTEE UNITED PRESBYTERIAN C.E. UNION

REV. H. W. FRASER, D.D.
VANCOUVER, B.C.

MR. J. H. MANSFIELD
NEW HAVEN, CONN.
PRES. CONN. C.E. UNION

a whim of the officials, but is substantially indorsed by the whole Chinese people.

Among the other evidences of China's awakening, there is some semblance of constitutional government; the multiplication of newspapers of improved quality; the introduction of the telephone, the telegraph, and the electric light; the opening of mines, and the building of mills and factories. The whole country is astir with new life.

When the demand for a change came, most of the old officials were opposed to any in the old institutions, but when the Empress's edicts ordered the adoption of the new methods, the officials yielded reluctantly to the demands of the people. It is the people of China who rule, and the people are strong. What China needs is a fair field and no favors. In the present development of China, there is no menace of "The Yellow Peril." But if the West continues its unwise policy toward China by continuing to insult her and threatening to seize her territory, and continue to wrong her with an excessive import duty, then China will be forced into an alliance with Japan against the white race, and the blackest chapters of the world remain to be written.

But the solution of the whole situation in the East is in the hands of the Christian church. Christian thought and Christian teaching have permeated their whole empire. The whole nation has been moved, and lifted into a higher and better atmosphere by the preaching of the gospel. The unnumbered millions of China today are ready to listen to the messenger of peace. The church of Christ has never in all its grand history had such a chance to preach the gospel. China, Japan, and Korea can be all for Christ in this century if all the people who call themselves Christians would rise up and follow the Master. It is in their hands to make the "Yellow Peril" an impossibility."

Dr. Beattie's speech was listened to with attention and closely followed, and at the completion of his speech he was accorded warm applause, especially by a large number of Chinese Christians who were present.

The chairman then introduced the Hon. Oliver W. Stewart, of Chicago, Ill., who spoke on "Our Country: Its Problems and Possibilities." He said:

"Apparent problems of one day are often later shown to be only the passing phenomena incident to government and progress. Seen in right relationship to other things they appear of small consequence Real problems are found in conditions, deeply seated, which must be changed or great loss or disaster be suffered.

The problem of 'greed" and its accompaniment of "graft" presents a serious subject for consideration. The mere fact that some or even many men were actuated by greed would not call for consideration were it not for the effect on the administration of public affairs. It is undeniable that greed has resulted in corruption in government. This has been shown plainly in municipal affairs in all parts of the country. The worst feature connected with its continuance is not that money is misappropriated and the government robbed, but that the final result is the debauching of the public mind and conscience.

It is refreshing to note that all along the line the people are making war on this evil, undaunted by temporary defeat and cheered to victory to attempt greater things. It gives reason for believing that among the possibilities for our country is an honest conduct of public and political affairs, with its fine reflex effect upon all the people.

The legalized saloon presents at once a problem and an evil. Even if we assume that without the protection of the law the saloon would still exist in some form, its protection by the license system presents a serious governmental problem.

I pass by the effect of the saloon on the habits of the people to ask what is and must be the effect of the license system on a government which permits it?

A government cannot sell any kind of protection or support to the liquor traffic without courting ruin for itself and the loss of fine moral fibre in its people. Better far the more or less frequent violation of prohibition, though that need not be, than the accepted pollution and corruption of the government by peace with the saloon for a price, by the license system.

It has been shown on more than one battlefield recently that the people are getting ready for a declaration of independence of the political power of the saloon.

Let us enumerate among our possibilities the coming of the day when our country will give no protection to and accept no revenue from a business which cannot succeed without making drunkards of some of our fellowmen.

Another problem, general in nature and much greater than it first seemed, can be best stated in this question: How may the intelligence and conscience of the people most quickly be brought to a point of contact with the government? or, in other words, how hasten the rule of the people?

An aroused public sentiment amounts to little until it learns how to act, how to get results. It is not so much an increase of power for the people that is needed as a right use of the power they now have. They are learning. Let us be thankful. They are learning.

Among the possibilities of the future will be a citizenship made up of rulers in fact as well as in name.

Granted these changed conditions and our country will be prepared to lead in the establishment of peace among nations—a condition in accord with a Christian civilization."

Mr. Stewart is an orator of the magnetic type, and his masterly address together with its forceful delivery brought forth great applause from the large audience.

After a hymn of praise and prayer the meeting adjourned.

CHAPTER XII

Tent Williston, Saturday Morning, July 13.

TRAINING IN CITIZENSHIP.

The tent never looked brighter than on this glorious morning. After singing several hymns, devotional exercises were conducted by Rev. Dr. Tomkins.

Hon. Nicholas L. Johnson of Batavia, Ill., presided.

Rev. Edwin Heyl Delk, D. D., pastor of St. Matthew's Lutheran Church, Philadelphia, Pa., spoke on "Training the Civic Conscience." His strong, clear voice and his clear reasoning held the large audience closely. He said:

"There are two persistent facts in the constitution of man. He is by nature a religious being and a political being. The one fact expresses itself in a religious association we call the Church and the other in a governmental association we call the State. Neither is an artificial product, or mere compact. Both spring out of human relations and impulse.

The single person or citizen cannot fully express the moral idea. It is only in mutual relation in the State that the individual comes to his true self. There is a civic conscience. After all, however, the State is composed of individuals. It is the training of individuals in the natural relations of the family, the school, the Church, the City that the corporate conscience is made sensitive and robust.

Training in the Family.

The family was the primal unit of political society. From the family as the center and type of organization the State grew by wider and wider additions of families and groups of families. Consider a few of the notes in the true family life.

First of all there is the note of authority. In the parent is vested the sovereignty of the group. Without such authority and the enforcement of parental law the family would end in chaos. The family life is dependent upon subordination and obedience. The child dare not claim too large a place. It is at this point that our American life is weakest. The children too often are made the sole consideration. The disrespect, the disobedience and pampered luxury of many an American home are the greatest menace to our public life. Our problem is to project the family spirit into all other human organizations. If law is respected there, it will be respected in the State. If mutual consideration was learned in the family, then it will go with the boy and girl into social life. If the affections were developed and rightly directed in the home then the nation will enjoy the fruits of sacrificial love. As the homes go so will go the nation.

Training in the School.

The next sphere of activity in which the embryo citizen finds himself is the school and its playground. The head master and teachers stand in the place of the parents. Authority, obedience and discipline continue but the emphasis is largely on the intellectual side. Unfortunately it is still the moral side of the child which still needs the most training. Not only our ignorant immigrant population, but also our American born boys and girls are dangerously educated because the moral and religious education of the child is made secondary to the intellectual. Matthew Arnold said, "Conduct is three-fourths of life." I should make the percentage larger. If this is so, then our whole public school system needs a mighty moral addition to its curriculum.

Through the vital facts of current life, patriotic symbol and civic pageant the whole moral nature of the child may be stirred to higher ideals and resolves. On the playground sane and clear regulations of sports, in examinations absolute honesty and impartiality, and above all the duty of the educated man in politics—these are the desiderata that must be supplied before we dare look for a better civic conscience and integrity in the conduct of government.

Training in the Church.

It is not until the Churchman treats his civic duties with the same seriousness as he does his religious obligations that we dare look for the true City of God of which St. Augustus wrote. Citizenship is a sacred thing. It is largely because we look upon our civic duties as purely secular that much of the indifference and carelessness in public life owes its existence. It is because of the good men who are bad citizens that we find ourselves in the slough of political corruption. "The Kingdom of God" is a political ideal quite as much as a religious ideal of society.

Training Through Political Action.

It is in the midst of life itself that our best training is secured. It is when we come to live our political creed that we are put to the real moral test. The fundamental need in our American life is respect for law. The first step in the training of the civic conscience in the sphere of political action is the strong and solemn determination upon the part of all citizens that the law shall be respected and enforced.

Justice to all individuals and all classes must be our national watchword. The rich man and the poor man must each receive an impartial consideration in our courts. Neither labor unions or corporations must be permitted to rule our land, but what our just and fearless President calls a "square deal" should be meted out to both.

Above all an advancing standard of civic morality must be insisted upon.

"New occasions teach new duties,
Time makes ancient good uncouth."

There should be no toleration of a dual standard of morality. The Ten Commandments cannot be annulled by convention. We have passed into the stage of the Golden Rule in International politics. We must pass on to the Divine Rule in every department of our political life."

Rev. J. A. Francis, D. D., took Dr. Grose's place and spoke on "Our Million of New Neighbors." He spoke of the large exodus of people from Europe and Asia to the United States, and asked what our relations to them must be—what are our duties to them. "St. Paul says that after sin has done its work, God will gather together in one all the fragments and make mankind God's kingdom. We must love these aliens as men, and must recognize our obligations to them. The day laborers are working for us."

Rev. B. B. Tyler, D. D., offered prayer for our country.

General Secretary William Shaw told of the Christian Endeavor Patriot's League, its purpose being the education of young people in the facts of our conditions. They must learn how to live and how to save the lives of others. The league enrolls the young for study in Christian citizenship. The declarations of purpose were passed and the people were urged to read and send in their membership.

(Note—A full outline of the principles of the Patriot's League will be found on page 96 following.)

The third verse of the "Star Spangled Banner" was sung standing.

The Rev. Edward A. Fredenhagen of Topeka, Kas., spoke on "Prison Societies." He urged a remembrance of prisoners, and prayer and work for them. "They can be and are converted," and all who would follow Christ were invited to join the "Prisoners' League of Christian Endeavor."

Mr. George S. Higby, superintendent Floating Work of the California State Union, of Los Angeles, Cal., spoke on "Floating Societies," which he said is a particularly good subject here in Seattle, now becoming a large shipping port, and told wonderfully interesting stories of the good done by Endeavorers among the sailors.

Mr. J. T. Sproull, president New Jersey Christian Endeavor Union, of Arlington, N. J., spoke on "Fresh Air and Philanthropies." He pointed out to the audience, as did the other speakers, the splendid openings and calls for service in this line. "Some children have never seen grass, or milk, or breathed the pure air of seashore or hill."

The huge form and blessed face of the Rev. Ira Landrith. D. D., LL. D., Regent of Belmont College, Nashville, Tenn., came next, and he spoke on "Graft and Grafters." He said:

"The influence of religion, if 'it does anything, ought to be to make bad men good, good men better, and to keep the moral atmosphere wholesome enough to breathe in. The dual duty of the church in this world is to educate in morality and to eradicate immorality. In a word, it ought to provide a generation fit to live and fit to live with. Wanted! More emphasis on both education and eradication! This world is a tenement and we ought to help clean it up during our occupancy so that the next fellow can live in it. Instead of quoting "Cry aloud and spare not," the modern version too often is "Spare aloud and cry not."

What is graft? It is a comprehensive term designed to make robbery respectable and pillagery polite; and grafter is the nicer name which fastidious thieves have assumed because they do not like to be shocked by plain spoken people who call spades spades. There is a danger in not calling evil by its right name.

In a sense any man is a grafter who uses his office or his influence to filch or wrest from other people money which he does not earn by service for the owner's real weal. Food adulteration is an example of graft. In New York city over 52 per cent. of milk samples examined were adulterated, and there is no relief in coffee, which contains anything with a dark brown look and a dark brown taste. Bread is no better in some cities; it has been called the "staff of life," but it is sometimes the "staff of death."

Graft exists in sales and service, as Edward Bok, whom some of you ladies doubtless have heard of, found out when he went to London. It exists in the haunts of loan sharks with their monthly payments, in purchasing agents, and quack doctors. And also, let me say and hurry over it for I know I am on dangerous ground, in patent medicines. It exists in fake mining stocks, in useless new inventions, in Western land investments sometimes. And I sometimes wish that railroads would quit watering their stock and water their right of way instead.

Political graft is our chief concern, such as the ancient system of vote buying, the bribery of legislators and city councils, and there is a modern political graft intrenched in the immunity from prosecution in exchange for votes. Gamblers, lawless saloons and dives flourish by graft—liquor license is in the nature of a graft—and the national government should go out of business. The United States Government has no right licensing what the state forbids. The tax-dodging rich are grafters. "Special interest" representatives are lined up in the same class, all the way from the common council to the somewhat too common United States senate.

But the picture is too dark for this glorious day. There is encouragement in the fact that graft is not a growth of today, and has not sprung up in our generation.

A tribute must be paid to the outspoken daring, the splendid free speech of an independent press. Evil dreads nothing so much as the light, and when you turn publicity on graft it wants to get away. Political issues are growing chiefly moral, because of much preaching and publicity. The people can be depended on when their consciences and their consciousness are aroused. Gov. Hughes of New York says that the most striking result of the insurance investigation is its vindication of the sound moral sense of the people. Statesmen are speaking out for righteousness, the courts are taking a hand, and the deterrent value of sentences is great.

I have the greatest respect for the sincerity as well as for the intelligence of most of our Socialists, but the evil of graft cannot be cured by Socialism if for no other reason than that ideal Socialism would be impossible and possible Socialism is far from ideal.

Our Hadleys, Jeromes and Francis Heneys need help. Their investigations are increasingly easy. The ballot box will help.

I am a party man, but I want to say that ultra-partisanship is responsible for many of the present evils we are talking about. Simply because a bad man is nominated by his party is no reason to support that man. Our popular ideals of politics and politicians are too low. We must purify the stream at its source by regeneration of the life, religious education of the regenerated and of children, and by the complete overthrow of the unscrupulous rich. It will be done. There is no reform wave sweeping over the country. It is a permanent revival of common honesty. And it is not political. No political party can complain, and none dare plead "not guilty."

This profitable session was closed by prayer and a hymn of praise.

FIRST PRESBYTERIAN CHURCH.

The first fifteen minutes were spent in praise and prayer, the latter led by Dr. Bannen, president Pennsylvania Union.

A few introductory remarks were made by the Hon. Oliver W. Stewart of Chicago upon "Civic Consciousness," in which he claimed that the conscience was a monitor that tells right from wrong. The conscience is ever wanting to do right. The civic conscience is ever wanting right citizenship.

The Rev. Dr. Francis of St. Petersburg followed with an address on "Training the Civic Conscience," in which he said in part:

"Nothing is more characteristic of the English than a passion to reform other people than themselves, trusting meanwhile that God will help those who forcibly help some one else. Good citizenship makes right relations with one's fellow citizens. Nowhere is citizenship a harder problem than in America of today. You have now a cosmopolitan population and a complicated life that are not equaled in any land. Never was any people faced with a greater task than that which confronts you now—your population being diverse in race, religion, and divided and subdivided in industrial occupations and interests. A democratic nation is an aggregation of free human beings bound together by common ties, some of which may be called natural ties, and some artificial. The most important artificial ties are those of law, custom, and executive government, but they are not original factors in the cohesion of the people in the same degree as natural ties such as community of race, of language, of religion, and of sentiment or of historical association. Now, owing to the tremendous immigration here from everywhere else, these ties have to be re-created; and to create and maintain them in all sections of your changed and ever changing population is a great social problem. To find a common denominator to solve the problem of your cosmopolitan and complicated life—that is the need of the hour for this nation. Therefore, the Endeavor society proposes to form a patriotic league, whose aim shall be to quicken and train the conscience in each of its members and in the nation at large.

1. We need to be guided by an enlightened conscience in forming social relations in citizenship. Everywhere that men are there is a natural and inevitable clustering and grouping by social grades. Booker Washington, speaking of the relations possible between the white and colored races of America, said that in all things social the races could be as separate as the five fingers, while yet in all things essential to mutual progression, they could be one as the hand.

2. Economic relations in citizenship are seen in the methods

by which individuals co-operate for earning a living, for the mutual satisfaction of their wants, and for the production and distribution of wealth.

Right citizenship in politics involves always the use of political privileges. Now, the ballot is the last absolute vehicle of political expression in the modern democracy. Through it life and all that life can compass are controlled, and, therefore, in a democracy to neglect the ballot is to show criminal indifference to human life.

Right citizenship in politics involves interest and participation in all the responsibilities of national life. In the dawning of this new century, America finds herself like England at once democratic and imperial, inevitably confronted with world conflicts and world politics. You may be of those who regret that you have assumed responsibility in the Philippines and Cuba. But the responsibility is yours; and how grave and responsible it is. The Patriot's League will seek to develop a national conscience."

In conclusion, the speaker urged that "Citizenship Endeavor" to be successful must be Christian Endeavor. Organized Christianity has often proved a devisive force, but by the spirit of Christ—the true religion of Christ—the human as well as the divine harmony is restored and maintained.

The Rev. Dr. Hugh K. Walker of Los Angeles presented the problem of "Enforcement of Law," in which he made the points that in order to accomplish this aim it was necessary to "patiently pick, persistently plod and personally pray" for those who represent us in places of trust and administration. Dr. Walker pointed out the fact that it was comparatively easy to secure the enactment of a law, but hard to maintain its enforcement. To this end, he urged the careful attention on the part of all to these points. He further added: "It was always recognized that bad men made bad citizens; but it was also only too true that good men were often bad citizens. Many good Americans were born outside of their native land. A participation in the civic life of the community was a duty laid upon all, and that we had no more right to neglect politics than religion. By an intelligent, persistent and personal interest in the laws of our land we can secure their enforcement."

Prof. Amos R. Wells presented the new Christian Endeavor Patriot's League which aims to secure good citizenship through a knowledge of the laws of the land.

THE CHRISTIAN ENDEAVOR PATRIOTS' LEAGUE.

At the December meeting of the Executive Committee of the Trustees of the United Society of Christian Endeavor, unanimous and hearty approval was given to a plan which will mean much to our societies and, we hope, to the country and the world.

It is no less than the definite organization of the young people for the growth of patriotic sentiment and training in civic duties.

What is planned is a

HIRAM N. LATHROP
TREASURER UNITED SOCIETY
OF CHRISTIAN ENDEAVOR.

AMOS R. WELLS
EDITORIAL SECY.
U.S.C.E.

PROF. H. B. GROSE
N.Y.

GEO. B. GRAFF
PUBLICATION MANAGER
U.S.C.E.

MR. VON OGDEN VOGT
SECY YOUNG PEOPLES DEPT
PRESBY HOME MISS. SOC.

CHRISTIAN ENDEAVOR PATRIOTS' LEAGUE.

It will be subsidiary to the United Society of Christian Endeavor, in the same way as the Tenth Legion and the Comrades of the Quiet Hour. It will be as practical as the first, as inspiring as the second, as definite as both.

The membership of the Patriots' League will include all Endeavorers and their friends who wish to advance the purpose of the League, and who assent to its platform. It will furnish an ideal method of interesting in the society all young men who are not already interested. Beginning as Christian Endeavor Patriots and taking part in the patriotic meetings of the society, they may be led on to take the definite religious stand of participation in all the activities of the society.

THE PLATFORM

of the League is full, frank and forcible. It is as follows, and this is the document which will be forwarded to applicants, for them to retain as certificates of membership:

The Christian Endeavor Patriots' League is an enrollment of those whose aim is the promotion of civic righteousness and national welfare. It is the purpose of the League to take up courageously the duties of a Christian citizen. Its members will seek a knowledge of public affairs, of the laws, needs, and possibilities of their town, their State, and the United States. They will labor for the election of good and efficient office-holders, for the observance of existing laws, for the adoption of improved laws, for the encouragement and aid of patriots, and the downfall of all enemies of the country. They will seek to promote the cause of temperance and personal purity, the betterment of municipal politics, the improvement of the conditions of labor, the rational use of the Lord's Day for rest and worship. All this they determine to do in the measure of their opportunities and powers, under the guidance and in the strength of Jesus Christ.

This certificate will be sent to anyone who applies for it, twenty-five cents being charged for the certificate and enrollment. There is no reason why young women should not join as well as young men.

To carry on the work, with the large amount of correspondence and superintendence that is involved, it is hoped that each member will make some annual gift, however small, to the treasury of the United Society; but this is not in the least obligatory.

THE THREEFOLD RELATIONSHIP

Will be created by this enrollment. 1. The fundamental one is that of the individual Christian Endeavor Patriot to the United Society of Christian Endeavor. This will be very helpful and inspiring, and will be enjoyed by all patriotic Americans, however isolated they may be. 2. The relation of Christian Endeavor Patriots to one another, which will result, we hope, in the formation of local leagues, for the holding of special monthly patriotic meetings and the accomplishing of local purposes. 3. The relation of Christian Endeavor Patriots to the local societies of Christian Endeavor, the local Christian Endeavor unions, and the State unions. Christian Endeavor Patriots should be especially useful in conducting and aiding all home mission, temperance, and other patriotic meetings of Christian Endeavor societies and unions, and in carrying on State work under the direction of the State citizenship superintendents.

WHAT WILL BE DONE.

The work of the Christian Endeavor Patriots' League will grow with the years. It cannot be foreseen even dimly at the beginning. The possibilities are multifarious and splendid. Here, however, are a few lines of work upon which we may start out immediately:

1. The publication, week by week, in THE CHRISTIAN ENDEAVOR WORLD, of half a column of definite suggestions for Christian Endeavor Patriots. These suggestions will unfold and apply the plans that follow.

2. The further publication in THE CHRISTIAN ENDEAVOR WORLD of many editorials and contributed articles bearing directly on the problems of American citizenship. These have been numerous in the past; they will be even more numerous in the future; and reference will be made to them, and to similar articles in other papers, and to timely books, in the special Patriots' Department of the paper.

3. The publication by the United Society of Christian Endeavor of books, pamphlets, and leaflets most helpful to the work, such as a text-book of American forms of government, programmes of patriotic meetings, and courses of study in civics.

4. The study of American government by individual Patriots and by classes. This should include not only the study of principles in a text-book, but of the practical application of those principles in the State and community where each Patriot lives. For example, a meeting to study your city charter, with your mayor present, or some alderman, ready to explain it and answer questions. Or a meeting to study the judicial system of your city, county, and State, with a lawyer present to tell you about the different kinds of courts, how the judges are elected, and the course a case takes through the grand jury and the courts. Or, a meeting to study the school system of the town, with the school superintendent as your leader. Other meetings may take up the laws for paupers, the temperance laws, the Sabbath-observance laws, the election laws, the town system of water supply and sewage, the care of streets, municipal franchises, municipal ownership, primaries and caucases, party conventions—indeed, before you have gone far in such a series of meetings you will realize how little you have really known about your community and its government; and when you have conducted such meetings for a year, having the aid and instruction of men who are actually in control of affairs, you will be far better informed than the average citizen.

5. Local agitation for better conditions—for the enforcement of laws, the improvement of streets, the abatement of the sign-board nuisance, and other reforms. Tablets may be set up marking historic spots. Local history may be exhumed, presented, and recorded. Village improvement societies may be formed. The field is a wide one, and will open out as you carry on your local studies. First, however, you must inform yourselves thoroughly; then you may act on your information.

6. National campaigns may be conducted, postoffice campaigns, for effecting important ends. This work may begin as soon as we have a single Patriot, and already we have a number enrolled. We are happy to announce the enrollment of President Theodore Roosevelt as the first Honorary Member of the Patriots' League and his hearty sympathy with the plans outlined. Our law-makers do give heed to the written expressions of desire from their constituents. Petitions are effective. Great measures may be introduced in Congress and carried triumphantly through by the pressure of Uncle Sam's mail bags. As indications of what is in mind, take the preservation of Niagara Falls, the creation of forest reserves, national intervention in the Congo,

national laws regarding child labor, a national movement for the formation of a world's legislative assembly. The State citizenship superintendents will be ready to give each Christian Endeavor Patriot the names and addresses of his Senator and Representative. THE CHRISTIAN ENEAVOR WORLD will give full and timely information concerning these great causes, and will suggest how, through brief, individual, respectful letters, each Patriot may become a real factor in national affairs.

7. Much should be done in the way of letters of praise. Righteous causes may be aided by the hearty encouragement of those that further them, quite as much as by the condemnation of those that oppose them. If some statesman who has spoken a word for temperance, or voted for the passage of a reform act, or stood manfully against odds for the sake of right, should receive from different parts of the country a score or a hundred letters of grateful and enthusiastic praise, he would be encouraged beyond measure, and strengthened to work more zealously and powerfully for all good causes in the future. Suggestions for this pleasant and fruitful service will be given the Christian Endeavor Patriots from time to time.

It will be seen that the Patriot's League is to take up positive work, and not merely negative; that its members are not to become hectoring cranks, but helpful, wide-awake, constructive citizens of this great republic.

AND NOW ENROLL!

Some of these enterprises can be entered upon at once and with small numbers. For the greatest efficiency we need the enthusiasm and weight of large numbers. Send on your name, and twenty-five cents, and you will receive your certificate promptly. (If you want to, follow the example of one of the first Christian Endeavor Patriots to enroll and give a dollar for the certificate, instead of twenty-five cents. No one will object!) The address is: George W. Coleman, Superintendent of the Christian Endeavor Patriots' League, Tremont Temple, Boston, Mass.

Think what is involved in this . Think of the possibilities, as faintly outlined. Think of the needs of such a patriotic movement. Think of the pleasure you will get from a connection with it, the wide information, the inspiring stimulus. Do it today.

"Some Contributions of Christian Endeavor to Our Country's Welfare—Prison Work," was then presented by the Hon. C. E. Marks, Salt Lake City, Utah. He stated that 2,000 members of the Christian Endeavor Society were in prisons, converted through the work of members of the society while in prison.

Miss Gibbons spoke of "Floating Societies," especially that portion of the work as carried on in Nagasaki, where so many ships enter the great harbor at that port.

Rev. Mr. Edds, Field Secretary of the New York Union, made a few remarks in regard to the Christian Endeavor Fresh Air Camps. He said that if Christian Endeavor has life, it must go outside of itself and do service in those homes where opportunity offers.

The concluding address was made by Rev. Charles Stelzle, Superintendent Department of Church and Labor, Presbyterian

Board of Home Missions, New York, N. Y., who spoke on "The Laboring Man and the Church of the Carpenter." He said:

"Some day the Church will awake to the fact that the Labor Movement is the most significant movement of modern times. When I speak of the Labor Movement, I do not refer exclusively to the labor unions. There are some people who imagine that if the labor union could be abolished, the labor question would be settled. If every labor union in existence were wiped out today, the labor question would still be present, and, I believe, in a more aggravated form than we have it today. There are forces organized which are comprised in the labor movement. It includes the twenty-five million socialists of the world; it embraces the eight million trades unionists of every land, three million of whom are in the United States and Canada; it includes that movement among the Russian peasants, twenty thousand of whom, last year, suffered martyr's deaths because of their belief in the ideal which somebody had given them; it includes the social movement in Germany, forty per cent of whose entire population are socialists, and who stand today as a great menace before the German Reichstag and the Kaiser; it includes the movements we are hearing about among the people in Italy, in Belgium, in Australia, as well as the social unrest which exists in our own country. This is the era of the common man. When the hour strikes that shall proclaim the victory of the common people, this is the question which will confront us as a Church: "Will they be inspired by a high religious ideal given them by the Church of Jesus Christ, or will they go on to even nobler and better things independent of the Church, because of the consciousness that they have won all in spite of the Church? For win they will. No human power can prevent it, and no divine power will. This, then, is the Labor Movement that confronts the Church of Jesus Christ today.

There is so much religion in the Labor Movement and so much social spirit in the Church, that some day it will become a question as to whether the Church will capture the Labor Movement or whether the Labor Movement will capture the Church.

There are four fundamental facts in this connection to which I desire to call your attention:

First, working people almost universally honor Jesus Christ as their friend and leader, and most of them believe in his divinity. Second, working people are naturally religious, even though their religion is not always expressed in the most orthodox manner. Third, the labor question is fundamentally a moral and a religious problem. History has prophesied it. Our best labor leaders are coming to recognize it. Present reform measures which workingmen are hearing most about today indicate it. Fourth, there has rarely been a time in the history of the Labor Movement when working people have responded more readily to the appeal of the Church than they do today.

For these reasons, the Church is already supreme in the matter of capturing the Labor Movement for Christ. Unfortunately, however, the Church has had too narrow a vision. When most of us think of reaching workingmen, we think of an evangelistic campaign. I believe in evangelistic work; but I desire to say very emphatically that no amount of evangelistic work engaged in for the purpose of reaching the masses can ever take the place of some other things that the Church must do, if it would capture the Labor Movement for Christ. What must the workingmen find in the Church if he is to be attracted to it permanently?

He must find in it an absolute sincerity. Working people will be attracted to the Church when they find in the Church a greater democracy. Furthermore, the Church must preach a clearer social message.

Finally, if the Church is to win working people, they must find in the Church more of the prophetic spirit. Too long have we been boasting of our glorious traditions. The workingman does not care a rap for our traditions. He wants to know what the Church is doing today. The prophet of the people must understand something of the real needs of the people. Rarely does this vision come in the seclusion of the study. More frequently it comes in the labor hall, in the shop, in the tenement, or upon the street. Some day, God will raise up a prophet who shall again win to himself the masses of the people. That day shall reveal whether the Church will capture the Labor Movement or whether the Labor Movement will capture the Church. Much will depend upon whether that prophet comes out of the organized Church or whether, as it happened two thousand years ago, he shall come from the ranks of the common people, a despised Nazarene."

This was followed by prayer and a hymn of praise, after which the meeting adjourned.

CHAPTER XIII.

THE SATURDAY NIGHT SESSIONS.

THE BEAUTIFUL "MESSIAH" AND THE JUBILANT CAMP FIRE.

"THE MESSIAH."

On the evening preceding the opening of the convention, the sacred oratorio "The Messiah" had been given by the Convention chorus for the special benefit of the people of Seattle. It was said that 22,000 people tried to secure seats in the big tent. At any event, thousands were turned away unable to secure admission, and the money which they had paid for tickets was refunded.

On Saturday evening during the convention, the Oratorio was repeated for the benefit of the delegates, and it was fully as great a success as upon the first occasion. There was a chorus of a thousand voices, an orchestra of one hundred pieces, and five soloists of acknowledged ability from some of the leading cities of the United States. The sweetness and tenderness of this beautiful composition floated through the vast convas, coming from one hardly knew whither, like majestic music out of still waters.

It was a most creditable presentation of Handel's masterpiece, and was greatly enjoyed by the thousands of Endeavorers present.

The excellent manner in which the Oratorio was rendered also reflected great credit upon the musical talent of Seattle. Not less praiseworthy was the work of the orchestra, the dignified overture and the exquisite, delicate, pastoral symphony being among the choicest gems of the performance.

THE CAMP FIRE.

At the First Presbyterian church, the second camp-fire to be held in connection with a Christian Endeavor convention was held.

General Secretary Shaw was in charge. He was in his best fettle. That is saying a great deal, for those who know Mr. Shaw realize what a "whirlwind" he can be when he tries. "What is the use of a Christian sitting in a back seat looking better than he really is?" asked Mr. Shaw at the opening of the camp-fire. "Look cheerful. We are here tonight to see how warmed up we can get, and when you leave here you will learn, if you never knew it before, that a religious meeting can be as happy an affair as any other kind of a meeting."

It was the purpose of the meeting to receive messages from as many lands as possible, and Mr. Shaw's definition of a campfire was a place for "roasting" foreign delegates.

The programme was opened with the singing of "At the Cross" by eight Chinese Endeavorers, which was enthusiastically applauded by the large audience present.

Dr. Beattie of China was the first victim selected for the "roasting" process, and he addressed the Chinese present in their native tongue to the effect that by following the Lord Jesus Christ they would be able to overcome the opposition of all those who did not desire their presence in this country. It would help them to resist temptation. Dr. Beattie then addressed the audience in English, and told the affecting story of his leper Christian Endeavor Society, none of whom were Christians seven years ago, but who are now all living good Christian lives and winning souls for Christ in spite of their dread disease.

Dr. Chamberlain began his address in Telugu, and gave a special invitation to those present to attend the Christian Endeavor convention to be held three years hence in Agra, India. Then upon the chairman's insistent request to sing a song in Telugu, he complied. Mr. Shaw's interpretation of the song was: "Me aloney, me aloney; me catchy, me catchy; me happy, me happy." "That is the way," said he, "they solve the matrimonial problem in the Orient; over there they don't have any thin, emaciated young people looking like the last rose of summer, who stop eating when they fall in love." This convulsed the audience, and no one enjoyed the impromptu translation of the Teluga dialect more than Mr. Chamberlain himself.

The next number on the programme was Mr. George B. Graff's excellent exhibition of Christian Endeavor views by means of a stereopticon. Mr. Graff took his audience for a trip around the entire world. There were over one hundred views, all of which were handsomely colored. Each scene that he pictured upon the screen had an inspiring story attached to it, and while Mr. Graff's time was limited to but the indication of these, he did it with consummate skill. The pictures were the means of filling the hearts of those present with renewed zeal for the cause of Christian Endeavor, and with the desire for the placing of the World's Union work upon a substantial and lasting financial basis.

Dr. Clark was called upon to make a few remarks, which he did, showing how the work illustrated by Mr. Graff could be largely increased as soon as the memorial building, for which funds are now being raised, could be built.

The meeting closed with singing by eight Japanese, who sang in their native tongue two gospel hymns. The last number was a male quartette by Japanese singing "Nearer, My God, to Thee." It was a surprise to many of those present, who little realized what beautiful and melodious voices the Japanese have.

Thus closed one of the most entertaining, interesting, and instructive meetings of the great convention.

THE CANADIAN DELEGATES.

CHAPTER XIV.

THE MEN'S MASS MEETING.

A Great Evangelistic Meeting.

There were fully five thousand of them—some thought there were more. At any rate, with the exception of a narrow outer rim the big tent was filled. Business men were there, some of the most prominent in the city—not occupying seats of honor on the platform, but taking their places with the crowd. There were many ministers, of course. One could also see the white glint of the official convention badge in the moving audience. But the great mass were workingmen, residents of Seattle.

As is usual with audiences of this kind, the men were responsive to every appeal of the speakers. The hymns were heartily sung. As Mr. Lathrop read a portion of the Sermon on the Mount there was eager interest on every face.

Mr. Wm. Phillips Hall was the presiding officer. He is an ideal leader for a men's meeting. Immediately he won the audience by his frankness, and by his genial good nature. The crowd at once recognized him as a man's man—and that counts for much with an audience of men.

With a hearty appreciation of what the first speaker represented in the cause of reconciling the church and workingmen, Mr. Hall introduced the Rev. Charles Stelzle, Superintendent of the Presbyterian Department of Church and Labor. The address was an appeal to the intellect. The supremacy of Jesus Christ in the industrial world and in the lives of individual men were discussed, in part, as follows:

"Christianity is not dependent upon the infallibility of the Church. It is not dependent upon the infallibility of the Bible. It is dependent only upon Christ. God revealed Himself to man before there was a Church and before we had a Bible. The Church and the Bible are simply a means to an end and that end is the revelation of God in Christ. Our salvation depends only upon what we think of Jesus. The question which you and I must answer is not: what think ye of this doctrine, that system of theology, that church, that preacher, but what think ye of Christ? Gladstone once said that it is the most important question of the age.

Surely one who could present such wonderful truths as Christ presented must have been unique in his person and in his character. What is it that gives Jesus such marvellous power?

First, his superiority as a teacher. Jesus always spoke with authority. The scribes taught as though they had learned scripture. Christ spoke as though his words were scripture.

He never quoted any other authority. When he used the words:

"As it is written," it was simply to show that prophecy had been fulfilled.

He never argued. He never tried to prove his statements. He simply announced great truths.

He never speculated in theories. He did not deal in non-essentials.

His message never grows old. The world has never yet come up to Christ's teaching. It is just beginning to get a glimpse into the tremendous significance of his words. His religion comes directly from God. Christianity is a result of God seeking man. All other religions are the result of man seeking God. He promises the greatest reward.

Christ's power is growing. The date on every letter and on every legal document is a recognition of Christ's birth. The observance of every Sabbath day is a world-wide acknowledgment of his resurrection. He is today king of the civilised world. He is the court of last appeal. Who appeals to Socrates or Plato to settle the great moral questions of the day? On the other hand, is it not true that if we can get a clear statement of Christ's concerning a matter, the question is forever settled? No one questions his authority or his wisdom.

Is it not a great thing to have such a man as labor's champion? Other men have been put forward as the representatives of labor, but the men who needed their message most of all paid no attention to them. Here is a man to whom everybody will listen—even the oppressors of labor.

Take your stand behind him. Permit him to speak for you. You need never again quote the political economists. Quote Christ. Never has any man more bitterly denounced the oppressor. Ask him to join your labor union. Invite him to sit upon your platform. Take him into your councils. If you do you are sure to win—for Christ is sure to win.

What think ye of Christ? When you say he is merely a social reformer, you know that that does not satisfy. When you declare that he is simply a great teacher, you know that you are evading the issue. You cannot get away from the question. It will follow you to the ends of the earth.

Asked with regard to Shakespeare or any other man, and you could dismiss it with an offhand reply. But asked concerning Christ, and it resolves itself into the most personal of questions: "What shall I do then with Jesus?"

Pilate once asked it. Do you suppose that if he could have looked down the ages and heard, every Sunday morning, millions of men, women and children repeating the words, 'Suffered—crucified—under Pontius Pilate," do you suppose that his answer would have been what it was? You say that your answer does not mean as much as Pilate's. It may not mean so much to the world, but it means as much to you—and to Jesus. Of all men the workingman should give a clear answer to this question. Christ means so much to you and this will be increasingly so."

The Rev. James A. Francis, director of the evangelistic work for the Baptist Church in New York, was next presented by the chairman, amidst the hearty applause of the audience. Mr. Francis had already won the hearts of many in the audience through the noon-day theatre meetings, at which he had been speaking daily since the opening of the convention. With the kind of humor that only men appreciate, and with a pathos that touches their hearts, Mr. Francis captured his listeners as he spoke of what it meant to believe on the Christ, who had been presented by the previous speaker:

What does it mean to be saved? It means at least three things.

First—It means to have every sin that you ever committed, whether of thought, word or deed, absolutely and completely forgiven by Almighty God, and to know it. When a soul comes to Jesus Christ and casts himself or herself on His mercy, then and there God for Christ's sake, takes the whole dark catalogue of that person's sins and casts them into the ocean of His forgetfulness and says: "Your sins and your iniquities I will remember no more." Someone has said: "There is one thing in which all men are alike and that is that they are all different." Well, there is one thing in which there is no difference—"all have sinned." Every sane man that lives knows in his deepest heart that he has sinned against God, and one of the first fundamentals of the gospel is this, that since Jesus Christ died for all men his blood can take away sin to that "whosoever believeth in Him shall receive forgiveness of sins."

Second—The second mighty thing that it means to be saved is that in the same hour that Christ forgives man's sins He does for him something else even grander than that—he puts within him a new and divine life that never was there before. A Christian is not a reformed sinner, he is a man who has been born from above with a heavenly birth and has become a partaker of a divine nature. This new life has two marks. The first is a genius for kindness. Witness yonder jailer of Phillippi. When the two preachers are committed to him with the charge to keep them safely, he thrusts them into the inner prison and made their feet fast in the stocks. That night he was converted. Look now: "He took them the same hour of the night and washed their stripes and set meat before them." Who told him to do that? No one. It is the natural outworking of the new life. No man is truly religious who has not an honest interest in his fellows. The new life has another mark—self-control. It makes a man a king over himself and restores the harmony of the soul, bringing all the passions under the control of the will because the will is under the control of Christ.

Third—To be saved means a new blessed hope beyond this world. A skeptically inclined man once said to John Wesley: "Mr. Wesley, if you knew that tomorrow night at 12 o'clock you were going to die, what would you do?" "Do," said Mr. Wesley, "if I knew that I was to die tomorrow night at 12 o'clock, I'd go to such a place where I'm advertised to preach tomorrow afternoon and I'd preach; then I'd go on to such a place where I've promised to preach tomorrow night and I'd preach again. At the close of the meeting I'd go to my lodging, wherever that might be, and at half past 10 I'd read a chapter in God's word, kneel down and pray to my God, go to bed, go to sleep, and at 12 o'clock I'd wake up in Heaven. That's what I'd do." Why not? Were not all his arrangements for the other life made? Are there not hundreds of men in this presence today who can say with equal truth, "All the arrangements for eternity I ever expect to make are already made." Before Jesus went away he said to his disciples: "I go to prepare a place for you and if I go to prepare a place, I will come again and receive you unto myself, that where I am, there ye may be also." We believe that the Son of God told the truth. The soul who entrusts himself and all his concerns for this life and the other to Jesus Christ has forgiveness for the past, a new life in the present, a blessed and sure hope for the eternal future. God help us to be all of one mind today in believing in His son.

With the audience in a most receptive mood, Mr. Hall began his address. It was an appeal for an immediate and unconditional surrender to Christ. Heart and reason were again stormed, by Scripture, by the narration of personal experience, and by the presentation of the goodness of God to sinful men.

Mr. Hall said in part:

At this moment my thoughts go back to a week ago when, after nearly two days spent in crossing the great plains of Minnesota, North Dakota and Canada, we first came in sight of the Rocky Mountains. Just as the sun was rising we were thrilled with delight and admiration as we suddenly beheld the great snow-capped peaks running from North to South across the horizon. The powerful locomotive labored hard to surmount the great divide. Higher and higher we rose, until, at last, we crossed the divide, and then ran down the glorious Pacific slope to the beautiful country below. Like that journey, this meeting has steadily progressed with rising tide of power and interest, until now we seem to see the great white peaks of God's grace and salvation. We shall soon cross the great divide of Christian decision, and I trust that all will stay on board until we cross it, and cross it with us—that none may be left behind!

You have now listened to two advocates of the claims of our Lord and Savior, Jesus Christ, upon your hearts and lives. Most powerfully, sweetly and effectively have these advocates pled their holy cause. I am now to make the final argument, and close the case. The decision rests with you.

Under the inspiring guidance of the Holy Spirit, Matthew says: "And whosoever shall exalt himself shall be abased; and he that shall humble himself shall be exalted." James says: "Humble yourselves in the sight of the Lord, and He shall lift you up." "For this is good and acceptable in the sight of God our Savior, who will have all men to be saved, and to come unto the knowledge of the truth," says Paul. To humble ourselves that God may exalt us into heavenly places and may grant us salvation, pardon and cleansing from every sinful stain, and deliverance from every form of spiritual and moral bondage, should be our immediate purpose and deed.

Our loved American poet has beautifully written:

> "Lives of great men all remind us
> We can make our lives sublime;
> And, departing, leave behind us
> Footprints on the sands of time;
> Footprints that perhaps another,
> Sailing o'er life's solemn main,
> A forlorn and shipwrecked brother,
> Seeing, may take heart again."

But we have a greater object to follow in life and service than the great men of whom the poet speaks—we have the Son of God, the Prince of Heaven, the Saviour of men as our supreme exemplar, our Saviour and our Guide! We beg you to note that our appeal is, first, a purely unselfish one. We have no other purpose in view than your salvation from sin unto righteousness, and from selfishness unto God.

In the second place, our appeal is made, not in our own name or behalf, but in the peerless name of the only-begotten Son of God; and we appeal to you to sit in judgment upon your sins, and to acknowledge your sole dependence upon Him for your salvation!

Third, our appeal, when responded to, is certain to bring its own reward: "Seek ye first the kingdom of God and His righteousness, and all these things shall be added unto you." Matthew 6:33. These are the words of our divine Lord, and He always makes good His promises! Put His assurance to a practical test here this afternoon, and realize its worth in your own hearts and lives. I can bear personal testimony to the worth of this promise. At a very critical period of my life it was wonderfully made good, and I am sure that our dear Heavenly Father will make it good to you if you will but honor Him by yielding obedience to His commands.

And, in conclusion, I entreat you to note that no man should defer decision in response to this appeal.

"Whom the Lord loveth He chasteneth, and scourgeth every son whom He receiveth." Alas, how true that is of many of us! I well remember the earnest entreaties and agonizing prayer of my dear father, when he pled with me to turn from sinful, worldly ways, and devote myself to the life and service of our Lord. I failed to yield, but was well-nigh heart broken a few days later when news came of that loved father's death, and I realized that I could never, in this life, make response to him in answer to his heart-felt appeal. By the side of his body, cold in death, I finally yielded myself to my Lord. That is what it cost to bring me back to God, but I pray that no such bitter experience may come to you because you fail to yield your heart and life to Jesus Christ.

After further remarks along this line of thought, during which thousands of the great audience were moved to tears, Mr. Hall called upon his hearers for an immediate decision for Christ. After earnestly and tenderly quoting Dr. McIntyre's "Upon the Edge of the Timber Line," he invited those who would decide for Christ to meet the three speakers at the front of the platform. Scores upon scores responded, until over one hundred had yielded to Christ. It was a scene long to be remembered, and, doubtless, caused angels as well as God's children to rejoice.

CHAPTER XV.

THE WOMEN'S MEETING.

The capacity of the First Presbyterian Church was tested to the utmost Sunday afternoon by an audience composed entirely of women, with the single exception of the leader of the chorus and some of the babies, doubtless, who were present in considerable numbers, and who frequently expressed their approval of the proceedings. Chairs were placed on the platform, wherever possible on the floor, with due respect for the fire regulations, and still many were obliged to sit on the floor and many more to stand throughout the service.

"Mother" Clark presided in her usual tactful manner, graciously introducing each speaker in a friendly, easy way that made her feel at home with her audience immediately, and following up each address with a few practical applications that drove the truth straight home to each one present.

After prayer, offered by Mrs. H. N. Lathrop, the topic of the meeting, "Woman's Work for the Kingdom," was opened by Miss M. K. Scudder, of the Arcot Mission, India, who presented the work that women are doing for the Kingdom in India in a most telling fashion by giving to the great audience a Bible reading in the same way that she does each day in India to her native Bible women. She told us that first, as they entered, each woman would salaam and then pull her cloth over her head in token of reverence; then they would engage in silent prayer, and in this the audience imitated them, praying for these Christian Bible women of India. Next came a hymn, of which Miss Scudder sang a portion in Hindu. This was followed by her exposition of the Scripture passage chosen for the day, Deut. 11:22-26.

The women are expected to prepare themselves on four principal points, four T's, the Topic, the principal Truth, the principal Teaching and the Text. The teacher gives out the topic beforehand, and the rest they are expected to discover for themselves, and that, too, without the help of either a commentary or a concordance.

In conclusion, the practical application was always pressed, and each one bidden to tell of the difficulties and hindrances found in her work and how the Lord had helped her to overcome them. In closing, an obect lesson of some sort was usually employed, in this case, concentric circles cut out of paper, built upon two diameters, representing that the limit of our possessions is only the limit we find by the length of the one diameter, obedience and love to God; the other diameter, God's help, being unlimited.

At Mrs. Clark's request, Miss Y. Kajiro, Dean San Yo Girls' School, Okayama, Japan, greeted the audience in Japanese fashion, with a graceful salaam. In beautiful, precise English, she told the story of her life. Brought up by Christian parents, who were converted when she was six years old; taught by her mother to say "Now I lay me" when she went to bed; taught by her own mother in the Sunday school of a church of which her father was pastor—a rare experience for a Japanese girl—no wonder she has developed into the strong Christian leader that she is.

Greatly impressed with the life of Mary Lyon, read in Japanese, she longed to get to Mt. Holyoke for training, a desire at last consummated. She pursued a scientific course there, and has since taught science for 10 years in a girls' school at Okayama, but not only science, but Christ also, for, as she sweetly said, "I am thankful every day that I know Jesus Christ and I want to pass it on."

As Miss Kajiro left to speak at the Japanese rally, the audience gave her the Japanese farewell greeting "Saymara," and bade her take their Christian greetings to her fellow Japanese Christians of this country.

Miss Ida C. Clothier, superintendent of missionary work, Colorado Union, basing her talk on a verse of the old hymn, slightly modified, to make it personal,

> To serve the present age,
> My calling to fulfill,
> O, may it all my powers engage,
> To do my Master's will,

eloquently urged upon her hearers the duty of more knowledge of missions, more giving, more service. She told very impressively the story of a little girl who, on hearing of the little girls who had "no doll at all" finally, after many struggles with her own heart, brought her own cherished rag doll, the ugliest, but the dearest of her flock, and begged to have it sent to the little girl with "no doll at all," asking how many of us are unwilling to give up what is not dear to us at all for those who have no Christ at all.

The story of the electric cross on the church steeple whose light was extinguished when the service began, because it cost so much to keep it burning was also skilfully used to illustrate our unwillingness to pay the price of thoughtlessness, prejudice, lack of interest, self-sacrifice that must be given up if we are to fulfill our calling, and engage all our powers in the Master's service.

Japan was again represented by Miss Sarah Ellis, of Tokyo, who told of her work in a girls' school in that city. One feature of the school she claimed as unique and unknown in the schools of this country, a half hour each week devoted to memorizing Scripture; also on Friday evenings a scripture hunt, when a text is given out, and the girls hunt for it, some of even the younger ones finding them with astonishing rapidity, and, on the other hand, repeating the verses, when the place in Scripture was given. This is very necessary work in Japan, as there is no concordance yet in Japanese.

She spoke earnestly of the vital need of more workers at the present moment in Japan, saying how she longed for twice the strength she had. But just as she went on to say that, she was forced to realize that her strength and her time were limited, Mrs. Clark whispered to her and, realizing that her time was limited in America, too, she closed with a plea for prayer for Japan.

A tender story from Mrs. Clark of the little girl who, amazed at the self-control and gentleness of her newly converted mother, a woman with a terrible temper, said to her, "Mamma, if God is like you, then I love Him," closed this inspiring meeting for women and by women.

MISS MINNIE A. GIBBONS
SEC'Y WASH. STATE C. E. UNION

MISS GRACE M. YOUNG
FAIRHAVEN VT SEC'Y C.E.

MISS ETHEL D. PICKETT
KANSAS CITY MO. SEC'Y C.E. UNION

MISS Y. KAJIRO
OKAYAMA JAPAN

CHAPTER XVI.

THE BOYS' AND GIRLS' MEETING.

The Children's meeting was held at the Plymouth Congregational Church on Sunday afternoon. The church was beautifully decorated with the flags of many nations and fragrant flowers. Over the pulpit was an arch supported on columns of white and green, bearing the word "Welcome." Pendant from its keystone in electric light was the emblem of the society, a white "C" enclosing a crimson "E," but the most beautiful sight was the happy faces of the children who thronged the church, filling every seat in the large audience room.

Dr. Clark opened the service by asking a little girl: "What shall we sing?" and the response was: "Yield not to Temptation," which was heartily sung.

After responsive reading of Scripture, prayer was offered by a Massachusetts delegate and Miss Grace M. Young of Vermont gave an address, which held every child's attention to its close. Her theme was "God's Place for Us in Life." She said:

"For a few minutes I want you to think of some Bible boys. Think of Jacob, and remember all that you can about him; as a boy at home; then about the things that came later in his life. Now think of Joseph; follow him from the time his brothers sold him, all through his life; as a slave in Egypt; as a prisoner, and then as ruler of the land. Now think of Moses; call to your mind all you have learned about him—about his boyhood; then his life out in the wilderness, and later as leader of the children of Israel.

Now for a few minutes forget about these men, and put them on a little shelf away back in your brain until I call for them bye and bye. Last week I saw a house being built. I watched its progress from day to day. I was surprised to see how the work done by one carpenter fitted into the work done by each of the others. What was the first step towards the building of that house? What came first? Yes, a plan. Every building is planned before it is built. I have a friend who writes books, and I was in his library one day, and he said to me, "I am going to write a book. Listen, and I will tell you the plan I have for it," and I found that his plan for his book was as clear as the architect has for his house. I have another friend who is an artist, and she said to me a little while ago, "Oh, I wish you could see the picture that is in my mind. It is a gem, and just as soon as it is a little more clear, I am going to put it on canvas." Still another friend I have—he is a musician, and I found that when he writes a hymn, he picks out note after note, and then puts the chords together according to a plan.

So every house, every book, every picture, every bit of music is planned before it lives. And other things are also planned. How about these dainty gowns the girls are wearing; how about this great convention; how about the beautiful flower gardens I have admired, and how about the world we live in? Do you suppose God made it by guess? No, He had a plan for it. And if all these wonderful things—houses, books, and the world itself are planned, do you not suppose that our lives are planned, too?

Now go to that top shelf in your brain and bring down the thoughts you stored there about Jacob, and Joseph, and Moses. Don't you think that God had a plan for their lives? He surely did, and today he plans the lives of his children as carefully as he did in the time when Joseph was living. You may be sure that God has a plan for your life, and that it is just the finest possible plan that could be made for you? If you will let Him work out that plan, your life will be useful, beautiful, and satisfactory. Some times we resist God's plan, and then our lives are a failure in His sight and are unsatisfactory to us. God's plan for us means, first, that we shall open our hearts and let Jesus come in and live there. So if Jesus lives in your hearts, God's will will be carried in your life, and your life will be built according to the plan which He has in mind for it. So if you would have your life grow from day to day according to the plan that God has in mind for it each day, let Jesus live in you, and do those things that are pleasing to Him."

After singing, Rev. Luther De Yoe, of Philadephia, Pa., gave an address on "Influence" which captured all the children, and when in closing he called for an expression of faith in and acceptance of Jesus Christ, with tear-dimmed eyes and earnest purpose, many responded. He said:

"Boys and girls must become interested in the salvation of boys and girls. There is no one who can help a boy do right as a boy himself. The way to help another be true is not by applying force. You cannot drive or pull another boy to the right. You must win him by your influence. That comes from what you are and what you do. It is seldom that anyone acts alone. It is true each one is responsible for what he does. Yet in so many things we are encouraged or discouraged by others. We would not have done the deed if some other boy or girl had not acted with us. You can help others to be honest and give themselves to Jesus. That is what you must do to make your life count for good. Be careful that what you do shall not injure.

If some of you join the Juniors, others will; if you remain out, others will do the same. If some boy here bravely stands for Jesus this afternoon, some one else will. If you remain away you influence some one else to the same decision."

Dr. Clark then in a few impressive words explained the first part of the pledge, and asked all who desired to repeat it with him to do so, and the response was such as made glad the heart of many who were older in years.

At the close of the service, many of the children gathered about Dr. Clark for a word of help and encouragement. The Master alone can tell what the harvest shall be.

CHAPTER XVII.

THE JAPANESE RALLY.

The Occident Greets the Orient—A Remarkable Gathering.

Perhaps the most remarkable gathering held in connection with the Seattle Convention was the Japanese Rally, held Sunday afternoon in the First Baptist Church.

Nearly two hundred Japanese attended the meeting. There were many women, and if any race-suicide exists among Japanese there was no evidence of it yesterday, for the number of small brown boys and girls and the number of dark-eyed babies was surprising. A score or more Japanese business men were present.

Above the pulpit was draped an American and a Japanese flag, between the two a large green and white Christian Endeavor monogram. It was a bit of Oriental color in an American setting, with climbing vines and flowers that grow in the land of the Mikado standing in tall vases. The audience was distinctively Japanese, though there was a sprinkling of American visitors and four of the speakers during the afternoon were not Japanese.

During the program a chorus of nine Japanese, some of whom have voices that with a little training could win them laurels in any country, sang songs, both in English and in their native tongue. It is an unusual thing to hear "There is Sunshine in My Soul Today," "Rescue the Perishing" and the "Glory Song," that became famous two years ago, sung in Japanese in an American church.

Friendly relations between America and Japan were emphasized again and again during the afternoon. The close friendship between the two nations consequent on Christian Endeavor work was stated by several speakers. Mr. T. Sawaya, field secretary for Japan, significantly referred to the war talk indulged in by American yellow newspapers when he said that sometimes "your press tells things about us that we do not know. ourselves," and applause greeted his sentence and the smile that accompanied it.

Rev. O. Inouye, pastor of the local Japanese Presbyterian mission, presided at the Rally, which began at 2:30 o'clock. Secretary Shaw started the enthusiasm that was manifest all through the Rally by declaring:

"This is one of the memorable meetings of the Twenty-third International Convention. Japan is the first to have a national rally under Endeavor auspices. When you write home I want you to tell your people about this; tell them about the big convention and your part in it.

And when you write home tell your people not to take seriously the statements of what we call yellow newspapers. The people of the United States are glad to have you here, glad to welcome you. We love the Japanese and are going to stand with you in this great land of ours. Our hearts were in sympathy with you in your last war.

We welcome you to Christian Endeavor. It includes all races of men, of every color, and we are glad to know that it is making its influence felt in your country."

Rev. John Pollock, president of the European Christian Endeavor Union, conveyed the greetings of the Old World to Japan in the following words:

Our part of the world not only loves you, but enters into partnership with you. I bring you cordial greetings from the Great Britain of the West to the Japan of the East.

Miss Sarah Ellis of Tokyo, Japan, who has been in Japan for five years, brought "heartfelt greeting from Japan of the East to Japan of the West."

Miss Ellis said:

"The next generation in Japan will be much nearer the light for having felt the spreading influence of Christian Endeavor work in this generation. There are 3,800 Christian Endeavorers in Japan.

I would emphasize that you must be loyal, you Japanese; be loyal here and loyal when you return, if you do return, to the land of your birth."

Dr. R. Perry, formerly a missionary to Japan, and now pastor of the First Lutheran Church, in Denver, Colo., spoke to the Japanese in their own language, dwelling on the value of Christian Endeavor work as a part of their training, and telling them of the society's labors in the United States.

Rev. F. Okazaki of Seattle addressed the Rally briefly on "The Mission of Christian Endeavor in Japan," and Mr. Kinya Okajima responded with an address on "The Work Among the Japanese in the United States."

Miss Y. Kajiro, dean of the San Yo girls' school at Okayama, Japan, made a short speech on the progress of Christian Endeavor and educational work in Japan, growing eloquent with her subject and gaining prolonged applause from her hearers when she told how the society's influence is spreading, and its work for women is becoming known in many far away spots of the empire.

Mr. T. Sawaya, field secretary for Japan, made an address both in Japanese and in English on the progress of the Christian Endeavor work generally, with especial reference to his own country. He said:

"There are two splendid openings for the Endeavor work in Japan today. One is assisting the church in missionary work among people of the other religions, Shintoism and Buddhism, and the other is in developing the Sunday schools. The Christian church is still struggling for existence and has not the strength to do these two things, and when the Endeavorers in Japan found things they could do, the influence of the society began to grow."

Mr. B. Kida, the pastor of a Friends' Church at Ibaragi, Japan, and one of the delegates to the Convention from Japan, gave testimony covering his conversion and what God had done for him.

A chorus of nine Japanese Endeavorers sang between each speech. It was with regret that the time came for the meeting to close, but it set a good model for future Japanese Rallies to follow and also proved a great spiritual blessing to those in attendance.

CHAPTER XVIII.

INTERNATIONAL PEACE AND ARBITRATION.

A Congress of Nations.

The International Peace and Arbitration meeting was held in the spacious Plymouth Congregational Church, which was crowded to its utmost capacity and many failed to gain admittance. Mr. William Shaw, general secretary, presided. Brief devotional exercises were conducted by the pastor of the church, the Rev. F. J. Van Horn, D. D.; a full chorus and soloists contributing to the impressiveness of the service.

The chairman's opening remark struck the keynote for those who followed: "No question is ever settled till it is settled right." There is a sentiment for peace and arbitration in our Christian Endeavor ranks which will one day make itself felt in the community.

The Rev. Andrew Beattie, Ph. D., was introduced as the representative of the oldest nation. "China," he said, "had been largely benefitted by us but also grievously injured. Opium has been forced upon her alongside of the Bible. Christian nations have settled all disputes with China by force. How to kill the largest number of people in the shortest possible time at the smallest possible expense—that, according to the recent Chinese utterance, was what Europe had taught China."

Mr. Bunji Kida stepped upon the platform in Japanese costume. He said that the mind of Christ was to do good to our enemies and to love those who hate us. He spared those who came to arrest Him, and prayed for His enemies on the cross. Nations ought to help one another. How it would draw one nation to another if this principle were acted upon! Christ is among the nations and will yet make all one.

India was well represented by the Rev. W. I. Chamberlain, Ph. D.:

"The progress of a land is not to be measured by the success of any selfish national policy. All power is a trust to be held on behalf of weakness; all wealth for the behoof of those that are poor. We Americans are called to break the alabaster box of service on the feet of humanity. These principles have a peculiar application to India. It has enjoyed the benefits of good government for a century. The new movement shows, as John Morley says, there is a new spirit in India. The natives are rising to national consciousness. This result has come from the truth that has impressed itself on the rulers that the largest education, the deepest ideas, the truest faith found in the Christian faith of England."

For Africa it was the Rev. W. T. Johnson, D. D., who spoke. The National Baptist Foreign Missionary Association of the United States has sixteen missionaries at work in Africa. The Carey Missionary Convention has one missionary in the Congo Free State, one in Liberia and one in Capetown. In South Africa there are twelve tribes consisting of 9,000,000 souls, 42 mission stations, 6 ordained preachers, 48 evangelists and 126 native helpers.

The Rev. John Pollock, president of the European Union, said that Europe was standing armed to the teeth, nevertheless, he did not believe there would be the great European war so confidently predicted. The peace sentiment had grown enormously among the people, not only of Great Britain, but of the continent of Europe. The burden of militaryism was greater than they could bear.

"In Mexico," said the Rev. J. M. Ibanez, "the movement for universal peace has had a cordial reception." The government has sent its peace representatives to the Peace Congress. The cause of this favorable state of affairs is due to the recognition of the immense benefits that have been realized by our country during the period of peace which she has enjoyed, both at home and abroad.

A final word was spoken for the United States by the Rev. E. R. Dille, D. D. The nation has never sought territorial aggrandizement in the East. President Roosevelt has had more than any other to do with the arrangement of the Hague Conference. The United States has had more cases of arbitration than any other nation.

Altogether the meeting was one of the most interesting and inspiring of the Convention.

CHAPTER XIX.

"FATHERHOOD AND BROTHERHOOD."

"No greater themes than those we have tonight, 'The Fatherhood of God and the Brotherhood of Man,' can possibly be considered," were the opening words of the Rev. Smith Baker, D. D., of Portland, Me., who presided at the tent meeting Sunday night. The audience was superb—every seat was filled. An invitation was given to those standing to come up on the platform and occupy the few vacant seats that remained back of the choir. The masterly address by the Rev. Edwin Heyl Delk, D. D., pastor of St. Matthew's Lutheran Church, Philadelphia, Pa., was listened to with wrapt attention. His theme was "The Fatherhood of God."

"It is a gracious compliment to any popular assembly to suggest the presentation of so profound a theme as the "Fatherhood of God." In any serious discussion of the fact three presuppositions must be made. First, we must predicate God's creatorship. In a word, this energy is unitary, causal, and eternal in its nature. Secondly, we must presuppose that this creative power is personal. In a word, personality stands at the loftiest ascent in the constitution of being. We have to deal with a self-conscious, intelligent creator of the universe and mankind. There is a third presupposition which makes up a part of our theistic background for the Fatherhood of God, i. e.: He is a holy being. As over against the immoral note of classical pagan deities and the emptiness of Godbead as declared by Hindu philosophy, we predicate the Hebrew conception of the moral perfection and holiness of God. Postulating these three elemental attributes of creatorship, personality and holiness, we are prepared to consider the Fatherhood of God.

On one ocasion, Philip, voicing the longing of the Apostles, came to Jesus and said, "Lord, show us the Father and it sufficeth us." That is an eternal need of man. The clear revelation of the fact was the supreme mission and work of our Lord. The fact of God's fatherhood is an intellectual, a moral and a religious demand of the human soul. Jesus meets the challenge. He makes the startling, glorious claim, "He that hath seen Me hath seen the Father." This is the central and profoundest revelation and work of Jesus. "No man cometh unto the Father but by me." We may come to Jehovah through Moses. We may come to the "Absolute" through Hegel. It is through Jesus Christ alone among all teachers of religion that we come to the full orbed idea of God's Fatherhood and personally experience the sense of full sonship with a holy Father on earth and in heaven.

Let us rejoice that there were earlier intimations of this idea in Oriental and Occidental religions. The early Hindu thinkers and poets had some dim premonition of an all encompassing force which by reason of its creative relation had some quality of paternity in its constitution. Hindu philosophy repudiates all personality and specific

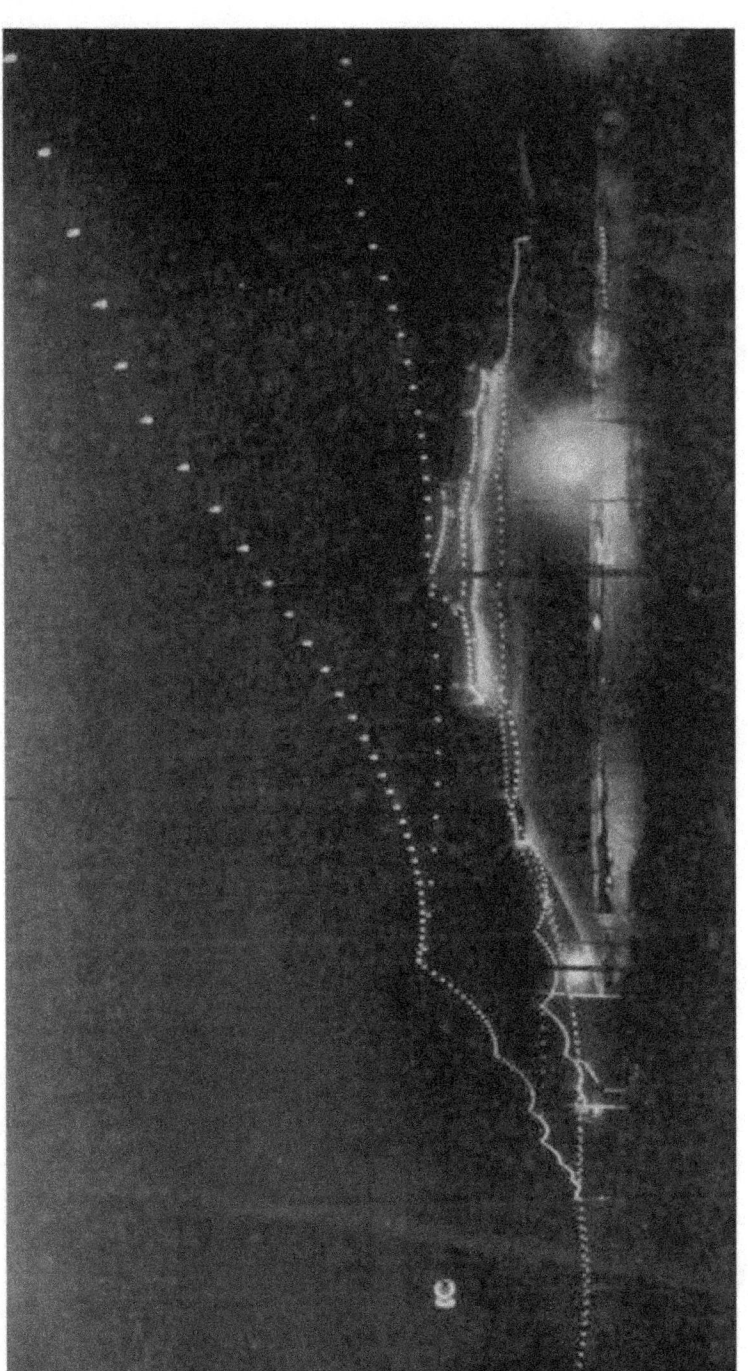

TENT WILLISTON AT NIGHT.

attributes in its conception of the infinite. If there is any real idea of Fatherhood of God in Hindu thought it exists as a dim, poetic haze which hovers about an inscrutable world spirit of which man is a component part. Pantheism has no logical place for the Fatherhood of God.

In Greek and Roman religion there emerges the idea of God's paternity, but it is a fatherhood which commands no moral respect. The Hebrew prophets did attain unto a fuller and truer conception of the Fatherhood of God. Its slow but certain emergence in the history of Israel is one of the glories of her national life. "As a father pitieth his children, so the Lord pitieth them that fear Him." But after all, the fact of God's fatherhood did not come to perfect revelation in Israel. The idea of His fatherhood was applied to the nation rather than to individual Israelites. God was conceived as the Father of the Jewish race. The later prophets conceived Him as the God of the whole race but, as the chosen people, they alone could claim Him as Father; His love and pride and solicitude was for them. The other nations and the individual Hebrew could not claim God as their immediate Father. And further, there was a missing note in Israel's conception of the Fatherhood of God which waited upon the perfect revelation of Jesus Christ. The inner heart of solicitude, mercy and love for the sinful and rebellious child was heard but dimly, if at all, in the teaching of Israel's greatest prophets and poets.

The words and life of Jesus were needed to give truest and fullest expression to the greatest of all revelations concerning the nature of God. The sense of God's fatherhood filled the consciousness and life of our Lord. It was the ground plan on which the Sermon on the Mount was reared. It was the distinctive note in the one prayer He gave for our constant use. It was the controlling idea in the matchless parable which we miscall the "Prodigal Son," but which should be called the Parable of the True Father. Jesus based His teaching of the Universal and personal Fatherhood of God in His essential nature—love. God's fatherhood He made the determinative principle in Christianity.

If God is truly our Father then we possess something of His moral life. His transmited life in creation and redemption makes of us responsible moral beings.

Man's contradiction of God's will and his consequent sin does not annul the initial relation and obligation of parenthood. Punishment for wrong doing is an essential note of true fatherhood. But above and beyond sharp correction is the fact of God's solicitude for and seeking of His lost children. The Good Shepherd giveth His life for the sheep. In some way the lost child must be reached and saved. God redeems through inexpressible sacrifice.

If God is a true Father, then men should be true sons. The first duty of a child is absolute obedience to the Father. There is no doubt but that there is conflict of desire and will between man and God. This very rebellion conditions the expression of His fatherhood. Only the obedient son is the true son.

Obedience must be supplemented by honor. A slave may obey, but only a son truly cherishes the will of a father. "Hallowed be Thy name" is as essential an obligation as "Thy will be done." Private and public worship are the normal flowering of all true reverence for God.

Honor must deepen into love if the full relation of a divine childhood is to be realized. "Thou shalt love the Lord thy God with all thy heart" is the only sufficient power and motive in the Christian life.

Further, love must actualize itself in service. Nothing is more demoralizing than a great and noble passion which is not translated into action. Jesus said: "He that would be greatest among you let him become bond servant of all." Service is sainthood.

To show us the Father was the mission of Jesus. To see the Father in the face of Jesus Christ is to satisfy mind, conscience and heart. Then when perplexity, care, pain and sorrow sweep over our soul we still can press right on to victory and sing:

> "And so beside the silent sea
> I wait the muffled oar;
> No harm from Him can come to me
> On ocean or on shore.
>
> I know not where His islands lift
> Their fronded palms in air;
> I only know I cannot drift
> Beyond His love and care."

Dr. B. B. Tyler, one of the most loved trustees of the United Society, and who, though sixty-seven years of age, still calls himself the youngest member of the board, spoke upon the theme "The Brotherhood of Man."

"About all the religion I have," said Dr. Tyler, "can be expressed in two words, 'Our Father.' This is the soundest of sound creeds. These words, suggesting the brotherhood of man contain more political wisdom than all of the platforms of statesmen that ever lived. When we learn that we are brothers, the strife between labor and capital will be at an end. Christ's religion is chiefly concerned in putting men in right relations with one another. The time will come when all men will regard each other as brothers. They will no longer maltreat and oppress one another but will gladly render every assistance, and give new meaning to life's struggles. When that time comes, all great world questions will be settled by reference to God's creed. I am serving the world better by teaching that all men are brothers than I could by teaching or doing anything else. We English readily believe that we are akin to God. I go beyond this, and say that the red man, the black man and the yellow man is my brother. The Japanese and Chinese are my brothers, for when they give their hearts to Christ, they can all say 'Our Father.'"

Dr. Tyler's remarks on the "Brotherhood of Man" were very heartily applauded, showing the impression that peace and fellowship had already made upon the hearts of the delegates.

In introducing Rev. W. H. P. Faunce, D. D., president of Brown University, Providence, R. I., Dr. Baker said that we had now heard "from the center of the country, which had given us some good things; that we had heard from the West, which had also given us some good things; and now we were to hear from the East, the center of culture and all wisdom."

The theme presented by Dr. Faunce was "The Brotherhood of Nations." He told how in visiting for the first time the University of California a few days ago, he said to himself that he would note the character of the first student he met. He wondered what sort of a young man he would be; would he be one in which he could see the making of a president, or a congressman, a minister, or a lawyer. Lo, it was not a young man at all but a demure Japanese young maiden with her books under her arm and her eyes on the ground. This incident became the text for an appeal for sympathy between the nations on both sides of the Pacific, an appeal which was loudly cheered.

Dr. Faunce pointed out the new force of an international public opinion made possible by our swift means of modern communication—a force making strongly for international brotherhood. He also drew attention to the fact that the athletic contests, which are so popular, are training our young people in the wisdom of heeding the decision of umpires in all disputes, and are leading directly to international arbitration. "Moreover, men are learning the absurdity of war. Duels are no longer tolerated. A man who would fight his neighbor every time he does not believe the same as himself would be considered brutish. What is brutish in an individual is brutish in a nation, and there is no more reason for one nation to go to war with another than there is for an individual to war with his neighbor. Men are discovering the heroism of peace, of careers like Graham Taylor's and Jane Addams.'"

President Faunce's address was scholarly throughout, and was one of the finest and noblest utterances ever heard at a Christian Endeavor convention.

CHAPTER XX.

TWO ENEMIES OF OUR CIVILIZATION.

Life today is filled with reforms. It is a good time to live, for there are questions innumerable to be answered and problems many to be solved.

At the First Presbyterian Church on Sunday evening two enemies of our civilization were analyzed and a remedy prescribed.

The Rev. Dr. Wm. F. Wilson, pastor of the Trinity Methodist Church, Toronto, Ont., and the Rev. Ira Landrith, D. D., Regent of Belmont College, Nashville, Tenn., diagnosed the two great diseases with which modern life is afflicted—"The Saloon Power" and the "Gambling Hydra," and the Hon. Oliver W. Stewart of Chicago wrote the prescription.

Dr. Wilson looks not unlike our American patriot, William Jennings Bryan. Indeed, Dr. Wilson is somewhat of a politician, for at the Methodist Rally he nominated Vice-President Fairbanks for the presidency of the United States.

The great church was crowded. Every available inch of space was occupied. Window sills became seats—aye, many were content to sit upon the floor.

A feature of the service was the splendid singing by the church quartette. Dr. Francis E. Clark presided. He said that three things characterized this convention. First, the spirit of brotherhood; second, the emphasis placed upon good citizenship; and third, evangelistic endeavor.

Dr. Wilson is an orator of the old type, with a splendid voice and expressive gestures. He said:

"Some problems which are common to Canada are common to the United States, but in Canada there is no divorce court, no Sabbath desecration, no negro problem; but in Canada, as in the United States we have the whiskey curse blighting the homes, health and happiness of the people. The saloon protected by law is doomed. It is soon to have its Waterloo. In Canada the temperance sentiment is strong. The Methodists and Episcopalians have paid temperance agents. Local option is a failure. The liquor traffic is humble and begs not to be obliterated, but to be regulated. In Toronto, with its 300,000 people, there is not a saloon, though there are hotels where liquor is sold. The young people are on the firing line with rapid firing guns. Some of the best helpers in the temperance cause are Christian Endeavorers. The saloon would close every church if it could. The church could close every saloon if it would."

Dr. Matthews, pastor of the church, was asked to present his personal friend, Dr. Landrith. He declared that gambling was just plain thievery, and that in America the old commandment "Thou shalt not steal" could be revised to read "Thou shalt not gamble."

Dr. Landrith is droll but caustic—funny, but pointed. He knows how to marshal his words. He picks them out with care, but there is a sting as well as a sentiment to his sentences.

His address was in the main a report of the eradication of the gambling evil in the great state of Tennessee. He said:

"Four years ago that most vile form of gambling, the licensed race track, held full sway in that Southern state, but now our race horses are working in drays. The most pathetic thing was that many women in the South land were gamblers. But one day William Thompson, a Presbyterian minister, was called upon by a widow whose only boy (a newsboy on the railroad) had been taught to gamble by a magnetic villain. William Thompson listened to her story, and then he swore that he would rid the state of that awful evil. Finally enough sentiment was created to enable the people to say to the legislature: If you don't put the race track out of the state, we will put you out of office.

In comparison with the smooth, slick, oily, clever professional gambler, the common thief is a gentleman. And the most insidious professional gambler, the greatest and the most insidious gambling is that run in connection with the race track. If American people knew the truth about race track gambling, how it permeates American life, and honeycombs American virtue: if they knew this for one hour, they would rise in the next hour and sweep all gambling off the face of the earth, from the piccaninny matching pennies, or the newsboy tossing nickels, to the well-dressed, jewel-bedecked women gaming for silver or cut-glass prizes.

If you knew the truth! You can tell the drunkard by his leering eye, the man who stays too long at the cup by his reeling gait, but you cannot tell whether or not that boy with the clean, honest face and bright eye is tempted and falls prey to the insidious temptation to gamble away his own or other people's money."

When Dr. Landrith waxes indignant, there is a peculiar rasp in his voice by which he is enabled to express his contempt for things loathing and despicable. Many times during this graphic recital, he pulled out this particular stop in his vocal organ to express his hatred and what he considers the most insidious and most viscious and most ruinous evil with us today—gambling.

He called himself a Democrat who loved to scratch the dirt out of the Democratic ticket, and regretted to say that he needed to do it very often.

Dr. Stewart served a term in the Illinois legislature. He has traveled all over the land inspiring the people to fight its great wrongs. His subject was "A Nation's Greatest Need."

"A nation's greatest need is not a large standing army, for some other nation may raise a larger one. It is not a great navy, for another nation may build more and better ships; not wealth, for the best things money cannot buy.

A nation's greatest need is a people with patriotic zeal, a right conception of the inter-relation of government and citizen, and lofty ideals for themselves and their country.

By patriotic zeal is not meant merely a fighting spirit. Physical bravery of a certain sort is rather common. By patriotism is meant a holy passion for one's country and a faith in it and its mission. It is not blind to the faults of one's country, but sees them and attempts to correct them.

Of unmeasured value to a country is a citizenship with a proper conception of the interrelation of citizen and government. A government implies a mutual compact among citizens. When one wrongs the government, he wrongs a neighbor. If he cheats the government, he cheats his neighbor. Let this conception become the common one, and tax-dodging and avoidance of jury service and other such deflections from the straight line of public and private duty would become unknown.

Then it would be remembered that the law is the will of the people to be respected and obeyed not because it is right, for it may not be, but because it is the will of the people, and its violation an injury and wrong to our fellow-men.

There is or has been a disposition to violate law and what is even worse, a tendency to smile at the successful evasion of the law by someone who had either the shrewdness or money to enable him to do so. Every thoughtful man believes this constitutes a menace to public safety.

The only thing more dangerous than a public official who violates his oath of office is a people who complacently smile at his crime. There is no greater danger than a people who lack respect for a nation's laws.

It is not sufficient that there be high personal ideals, but high ideals for the country. And with these high ideals there must be coupled a determination to get results in affairs.

All of which is another way of saying that a nation's greatest need is character in its people. A nation is great only in its people. Let them be great in soul, in aspirations, in high ideals, and the nation may submit to or suffer nearly all other limitations and yet be great.

In turn laws and institutions should have as their chief purpose the production of such a people. A law or policy which means the degradation of any of the people is a dagger aimed at the heart of the nation. Most dead nations committed suicide.

Anything which tends to produce higher ideals among the people, purposes truer to humanity in its struggle upward and a greater love for our fellow-men and more anxious desire to serve him, helps to satisfy a nation's greatest need."

CHAPTER XXI.

TWO PRESENT DAY PROBLEMS.

As at other meetings Sunday evening, many were turned away from the First Baptist Church and about a hundred stood during the entire service.

Mr. Von Ogden Vogt, secretary of the World's Union, presided. The first speaker was the Rev. Frank G. Smith, D. D., of Chicago. Everyone seemed to realize the vital nature of his theme, "The Great Black Plague," and listened with intent interest to his timely message on the scourge of pain that follows in the train of sin. He said:

"I am sure I need not tell you tonight that the theme I have is a most delicate and difficult one about which to bring a message that shall be true to the facts as they exist today and at the same time breathe an atmosphere of helpfulness and blessing. I have earnestly prayed that I might bring a message here that would leave no suggestion of a stain even in thought, upon the whitest soul here present and at the same time a message that would inspire us all to keep our own lives absolutely pure, in thought and meditation, as well as word and deed, while we give ourselves upon the one hand to the sweet and beautiful service of guiding the lives of the young into the paths of purity and power, and upon the other to the heroic and helpful service of lifting up the fallen and the unfortunate and helping them to stand upon the heights once more.

Did you ever stop to think that our greatest blessings have in them the possibilities of becoming our worst curse when wrongly used. Take the eye: O what immeasurable, inexpressible blessing rushes into life through the eye, this Soul's window; and yet through that same window, if left unguarded, may come that which damns and blights and ruins. Men may look to see only to sink into defilement and degradation. Many a boy and many a girl has taken the first step in a downward way through the power of a temptation that came through an unguarded eye.

Now I am sure that I am not revealing a secret tonight when I say that there is no earthly joy or blessing that is commensurate with that which lies in the natural attraction of the sexes. Every married man in this audience tonight who is a true husband, and I trust that we all are, knows that when he goes from this great convention and gets home at last, whether his home be north or south, or east or west, whatever continent, whatever clime, whatever language, it is all the same, when he stands again with his arms pressed closely around the wife of his heart, the companion of his joys and sorrows, the sharer of his triumphs and defeats, when he stands there again I say with his arms about her and his lips pressed to her unstained lips, and feels her head resting upon his shoulders and her trusting heart beating against his own, there and then he experiences a thrill of joy, bliss, happiness, deep, transcendent, inexpressible, the like of which no other earthly experience brings. In the most perfect seriousness, I say that every young man in this audience who has found his heart's companion, and assured himself that by and by she is to be his own, knows that in the touch of her hand and in the light of her eye and in the music of her voice there is a rapture, a blessedness, a thrill of joy, that is not found in any other experience of life.

Now in this greatest of all blessings, following the law laid down, lies the possibility of humanity's greatest curse: to misuse this strange, subtle, powerful force, the attraction of sex, to give it free rein and let it roam where it will until love is dethroned and lust wields the scepter, until happiness is destroyed, burned out, and hell rages in the human heart; this is the greatest blight that can fall upon a human life, visiting the fruits of its iniquity upon children's children, even to the third and fourth generation.

Blessedness can only be attained for the individual and the race by confining this attraction in its outworking to one person, knowing that uncontrolled and miscellaneous relationships even though instigated by this subtle power that was intended as the channel of our greatest blessing and happiness, can only end in degradation and ruin for the individual and the race, spiritually. I say knowing this, in His love and mercy, the Father has set up danger signals in the form of physical diseases, the most loathesome and awful in their finality to which the human flesh is heir. And it is these diseases, sweeping like a scorching breath of hell over the face of our fair land today, visiting the awful fruitage upon the guilty and the innocent alike, that constitutes the "Great Black Plague" of our times. One word spells out the cause of all our past reticency and indolence in battling against this great plague, as we have against other perils to human life and happiness, and that word is "Ignorance."

Ignorance as to the prevalency of these diseases. Not long ago a prominent and well known professor, in an address upon this subject, said: "So prevalent are these in our large cities that at least half of the adult male population of all social grades, according to conservative estimates, contract one or both of them." In God's name think of it; that a pure girl in a great city only has an even chance, just one in two, of getting a husband free from the taint of these loathesome diseases.

Ignorance as to the fact of how many who are innocent of any moral wrong have to suffer. The most careful statistics reveal the fact that among women those afflicted number more of our purest and best than of immoral women: the reason for this is readily apparent and should make the blood run cold.

Ignorance of the fact that the most virulent and loathesome of these diseases may reappear in children where the father had congratulated himself that he was healed of his youthful follies. It is authentically stated that 25 per cent of the blindness from birth in this country is directly so traceable. 10,000 persons it is said in our own America are groping their way about in the midnight of blindness tonight for this very reason.

Ignorance of the fact that the most virulent of these diseases may be transmitted in other ways besides inheritance, and that which is more commonly believed to be the only means of transmission. The highest medical authorities today tell us that the worst and most persistent of all these social diseases can be transmitted in the public bath, the public toilet, the public drinking fountain, and even as Judas betrayed his Master, with a kiss; so even can this evil be transmitted with a kiss.

Now, then, we are face to face with the question, what is the remedy? What can we do to purge out this mighty social evil and make our social conditions such that that sweet-faced, pure-souled

MR. JAMES M. ELLIS,
BOISE CITY, IDAHO
PRES. IDAHO C.E. UNION.

REV. A.W. KOKENDOFFER
MEXICO MO.
PRES. MISSOURI C.E. UNION

REV. EDWIN HEYL DELK D.D.
PHILADELPHIA PENN.
ST. MATTHEWS LUTHERAN CHURCH

REV. J.A. FRANCIS,
NEW YORK

REV. R.G. BANNEN, D.D.
WILLIAMSPORT, PENN.
PRES. PENN. C.E. UNION.

BISHOP ALEXANDER WALTERS D.D.
JERSEY CITY, N.J.
TRUSTEE A.M.E. ZION CHURCH C.E. UNION

DEAN HERBERT L. WILLETT, D.D.
CHICAGO ILL.

REV. LUTHER DE YOE, D.D.
PHILADELPHIA, PENN.

J.M. IBANEZ,
C. JUAVEZ, MEXICO.

REV. W.A. SCHIMLEY,
SHENANDOAH, IOWA.
PRES. IOWA C.E. UNION.

EDWARD TARRING
WASH. D.C.
PRES. D.C. C.E. UNION.

REV. J.M. LOWDEN, D.D.
PROVIDENCE R.I.
TRUSTEE FREE BAPTIST C.E. UNION

sister or child of ours will never have one chance in a thousand, aye, in ten thousand, of falling by marriage into the mire and slime of this contagion.

First of all, if we are fathers and mothers, or when we come to be fathers and mothers, be the loving, watchful, sympathetic, trustful companions of our children from the day of their birth to the day of their death. Blessed is that boy and girl who learns from the parent the great secrets and mysteries of life that he needs to know as life unfolds. Blessed is that boy and girl who learns the things he must ultimately find out somewhere, in an atmosphere of purity and tenderness and sympathy and wisdom, at the right time, thus safeguarded from the harm that comes with such knowledge under other circumstances.

Second, let us have a single standard of morality for men and women alike; away with the idea that man should have larger liberty than a woman. He is not a man in the truest and best sense who does not bring to her that same deep purity of life that he demands in her, whom he would call his wife. Leprosy is leprosy, whether it is in the man or the woman, and when the fathers and mothers of this land exercise the same care in safeguarding their daughters against keeping the company of the fallen man or wedding him that they now do, in keeping their sons from marrying a fallen woman, we shall have taken a long step toward the solution of our problem.

Third, we can lend a hand in every possible way in cleaning up the great cesspools of immorality and impurity that we find in all our great cities.

And my fourth and last word, is for all of us. If we would help God to cleanse this dear old world of its iniquities and make it every whit whole, we must keep our own lives pure. Not alone in deed and word, but in thought. Sin always follows a single law: there is first the sinful desire, that is in the heart. No one can see it; we can hide it away. Impure meditations: but if we keep it there and fondle it at last it develops into the sinful purpose, that too, is in the heart. We can hide it away, but if we nurture it at last it breaks out in the overt act of sin and the reputation is blackened and ruined because the character, which is the inner life, had already succumbed. O, young people, keep the heart clean! Keep it with diligence, for out of it are the issues of life. "Blessed are the pure in heart for they shall see God." There is nothing really worth while, but the fight for character in ourselves and in our fellow-men. God help us to go forth from this convention a conquering host on every battlefield where purity and right are struggling against impurity and wrong."

The presence of Dr. McMillan of Pittsburg was a benediction. His plea for the holy keeping of "The Sabbath for Man" was so sweet and so reasonable that it was an education to hear it. It was refining and cultivating. In it he told of the digression from the olden-time Sabbath day of worship to the present Sunday of picnics, larks and social calls. He declared that the Sunday of worship was rapidly passing, and in its place was being substituted the Sunday of vacation. He implored the congregation to return to the earnest, holy, reverential Sabbath day that our parents had observed.

The closing address was fascinating. Nothing is more inspiring than to get into touch with institutions that are transforming and developing whole regions. Such an institution is Whitman College at Walla Walla. President Penrose did not speak of the college except incidentally. He sketched the life stories of four "Heroes of the West," traces of whose influence are found at every turn in the great north coast country. They were all home missionaries. In part, he said:

"Our mild, modern Christianity needs the infusion of the heroic, and the oft times flabby fibre of our virtue needs to be quickened with the blood of Paul and Xavier.

For this reason I take as my text four Western heroes, not heroes of mining camps or the railroad but of the Cross. I take them by preference from the field of home missions, because the romance of the foreign missionary has seemed to outshine that of his brother, no less heroic, in our home land. "Let us save America to save the world."

First, a minister, Rev. Jason Lee. The Methodist church must ever have the glory of sending the first missionary to the Pacific coast. It was a hero's work in 1834 to turn one's back on home and native land, and venture to a remote and unknown wilderness to carry the gospel to a despised and savage people. The Willamette valley of Oregon became his home, where he taught the first school and preached the saving love of Christ.

Second, a layman, Dr. Marcus Whitman. In 1836, Dr. Whitman, in company with Rev. H. H. Spaulding, Mr. W. H. Gray, and most noteworthy, Mrs. Spaulding and Mrs. Whitman—the first white women to reach the Pacific coast—started westward upon his life's work. His story is so well known to every school boy that I will not repeat it here. Have we a nobler hero?

Third, a preacher and teacher, Cushing Eells. He has been called the St. Paul of the Northwest. In 1858 he decided that a Christian college should be planted in this great Northwest, and he thereafter gave his earnings and his prayers to the accomplishment of this end. He lived on diced salmon and water that he might save for it. When he died he left it what little property he had saved.

The fourth was Myron Eells, the first white boy of Oregon to give himself to the Christian ministry. He was a simple, quiet, unassuming man, whose spirit was that of his Master, and whose faithfulness was unto death. He was a scholar, yet his scholarship and scientific work never interfered with his preaching the gospel or kept him at home from exposure to storm and night. He died last January. I have been reading his diary the last week, and will quote a passage from it:

Monday, January 1, 1906—Have traveled 5,838 miles, about the usual amount; horse-back, 2,195; afoot, 296; wagon and buggy, 493; row boat, 335; steamer, 975; cars, 1,540.

None of it was for pleasure or personal ends, but all in the path of duty. But besides his apostolic labors, he was the first living authority upon the language and customs of the Indians of the Northwest, and a voluminous writer upon many historical subjects of the Northwest. You people of the East must judge the West by the kind of lives it has produced. Will you say that the heroic age has passed? And we people of the West must catch the inspiration of these noble men who lived and died for this Northwest, which God has entrusted to us, and see that it shall be redeemed from lower things to the high things of the kingdom of God."

CHAPTER XXII.

TRAINING FOR MISSIONARY SERVICE.

The Appeal of the Nations.

The sky is the roof of one vast family. The world is shrinking. Everybody now lives next door. Never had we a deeper sense of brotherhood as at the present hour. This was manifest at the service held in the First Presbyterian Church on Monday morning.

The Rev. Dr. R. G. Bannen, of Williamsport, Pa., presided, and after a brief prayer and praise service, Dr. Francis of St. Petersburg, Russia, told us of the industrial, moral and religious problems of that empire. The Nihilist prescribed one cure, the Socialist another, but there was only one way under heaven whereby the Russians could be saved, and that was by accepting Christ.

The Rev. Walter H. Brooks, of the Nineteenth Avenue Presbyterian Church, Washington, D. C., told of the deplorable things in Africa:

"Here in America the negro problem is in process of solution, but some aspects of the problem in Africa are darker than they ever were.

The plea of Africa is a cry for the Gospel of Jesus Christ; it is a cry for Christian civilization which gives power and influence, and brings happiness and makes you what you are. Why should we heed this cry? Because Christ died to save Africa and the African as well as people of any other color or nationality—they are our brothers; and therefore, Christ commands you to give the Gospel to Africa; and, furthermore, this nation is indebted to Africa more than to any other nation or people."

The Rev. J. M. Ibanez, of Ciudad, Juarez, Mexico, declared that the history of his land was glorious and attractive. He said:

"Without doubt the ancient history of Mexico presents some striking pictures which awaken admiration for the intellectual culture and development of the arts and sciences in that remote period of our history. Netzahualcoyotl was an inspired poet and a wise legislator.

But what can we say of the religious culture, which is the subject of the greatest importance to us? We must confess, that notwithstanding their intellectual culture, they were pagans; they worshipped many gods, among which, Hnitzilopoxtli, the god of war, was chief. On the altars of this deity human sacrifices were offered. After the victim was laid upon the sacrificial stone, the heart was taken out and offered to the false god. Such was the sad condition, and such the degrading religious influences under which my ancestors were found at the beginning of their written history.

It was in the year 1521, twenty-nine years after the discovery of

America, that the Spaniards, anxious for glory and thirsty for gold, began to plan and to execute those various enterprises which culminated in the conquest of Mexico. After the Spanish conquest, a new era began for the natives, that is to say the Spanish Domination, which continued for three hundred years.

Spain, at the same time that she sent her viceroys to govern the new Spain, took an active interest in the conversion of her subjects to Christianity. In order to accomplish this purpose, many Roman Catholic priests were sent to Mexico to preach the Gospel. It would be very natural to suppose that under such favorable circumstances the propagation of the truth would work a beneficial transformation in the new colony during these three centuries. However, history shows us with terrible eloquence that the religion taught and practiced by the priests from Spain was unworthy the name of Christian.

There is one more point I wish to emphasize and that is, that Mexico, in spite of her culture and progress along various lines and her many Roman Catholic temples, is not a Christian country. She is, to a great extent at least, under the influence of a false religion.

The American Missions are doing a great work, because they are presenting the teachings of Jesus, and the fruit of their labor is seen in the salvation of many souls. But even now 'the harvest is great and the laborers are few." May you all take more interest in my people, and I trust you will continue to help us with money' and your prayers, so that we may be able, very soon, to take Mexico for Christ."

After Dr. Floyd Tomkins had offered a prayer, which was full of compassion for the child race of the world, the Rev. Wm. I. Chamberlain, Ph. D., ex-president of the United Society of Christian Endeavor in India and Ceylon, voiced the appeal of India. He said:

"A new India is being born. Old things are passing away,' but many of the new things that come are not Christian. The hour for service was never so great. 300,000,000 people are crying for the religion of Jesus Christ! Among the men who have given their lives for the cause of Christian India, two of them have tablets, which bear these inscriptions:

Here lies Wm. Carey, wretched, poor, helpless and worn. "On Thy kind arm I fall." The other reads: "Here lies Henry Lawrence, who tried to do his duty."

The religions of India have proven inadequate to meet the demands of morality and failed to give the people what they need, and it is our duty to spread Christ's religion among them that they may become alive to virtue and the exercise of their conscience in the right direction."

Dr. Clark, who left South America in May, spoke for that continent of nations. He said:

"North America knows less about South America than about any other part of the world. It knows more about China and India than about Brazil or Argentine, but the Panama Canal will make a knowledge of our nearest neighbor necessary. You cannot generalize about South America. As every state in the United States has its own problems, so each of the eleven republics of South America has its own individuality and peculiarity. South America has been called the neglected continent, but they are not neglected by God. The great mountains, the immense rivers, the cattle feeding upon the hills, the fertility of her valleys—all tell of His benevolence. Neither has it been neglected by man. Rio Janeiro is the most beautiful city in the world. Its citizens have spent or are spending $50,000,000. to beautify it. It has docks and streets the like of which many American ports might covet. Neither has South America been neglected by the religious socities. Thirty-seven missionary societies are at work. Some are small, but the most of them are splendidly organized and are doing splendid work. The Y. M. C. A. is not strong in South America. There are many independent religious movements. Some great unifying force is necessary. The Christian Endeavor societies of South America promise to be that force."

Mr. Shaw announced that a friend had pledged $250.00 to help in supplying literature for the Christian Endeavor movement in South America; that there was an opportunity and there was a need for just such benefaction.

At the close, Dr. Bannen conducted a brief consecration service. He told of an incident of the San Francisco catastrophe—that how when the people of Los Angeles heard the dreadful news of the earthquake they sent at once two carloads of bread less the San Franciscans might die. We need to send the bread of life to the people about whom we have just heard lest they may perish.

A feature of this consecration service was the many sentence prayers offered by the delegates in the audience and the tender singing of the Christian Endeavor hymn. "I will go where you want me to go, dear Lord."

TENT WILLISTON—MONDAY MORNING.

In some respects the meeting held in Tent Williston on Monday morning was the most interesting and important of the whole Convention. It was presided over by the Rev. B. B. Tyler, D. D., of Denver, Colo., who briefly prefaced the proceedings. The general topic was "Training for Missionary Service at Home and Abroad," and the program consisted mainly of a series of appeals, presented by the representatives of different nationalities.

In the absence of Bishop Walters of New Jersey, the appeal of North America was urged by the Rev. W. T. Johnson, D. D., First African Baptist Church, Richmond, Va. In the course of an impressive address he spoke of the importance of the misisonary training school as part of the equipment of a living church. If the American continent was to be effectively evangelized there must be a fuller development of Christian sympathy for all races. And there must also be a larger exercise of Christian liberality.

Europe was represented by the president of its recently formed Christian Endeavor Union, the Rev. John Pollock of Belfast, Ireland.

"My appeal is not for financial assistance—the United States having liberally contributed in the past for the extension of the movement on the continent of Europe—but for a deepened interest in the work beyond the seas. There are nearly 12,000 registered and unregistered societies in all Europe, the 10,000th British society having been registered in the present year. The European Council is confronted with continental problems, which are difficult of solution, but the solution of them is essential to the very existence of the movement. We ask for the prayers of American Endeavorers that the Council may be guided in dealing with these problems, and devising means for the extension and consolidation of Christian Endeavor in the old homeland, and on the European continent."

The meeting was then led in prayer for the work throughout the world, by the Rev. Dr. Johnson.

Alaska made its appeal through the Rev. Edward Marsden of Saxman. Mr. Marsden is a native Alaskan, and spoke not only for his own people, but for the whole Indian race. He said:

"My people do not require assistance in the sense of nursing. We have no desire to be settled in reservations as is threatened, but to be given a place in the great American nation. We want a fair chance as men. Segregation is at the best a lame solution of a problem that can be more easily solved, and more satisfactorily solved, by education alongside the white man. When an Indian boy comes along be ready to take him by the hand, and you will find that he has in him the makings of a good citizen of the United States. The Gospel is making progress in Alaska, and Christian Endeavor is doing good work there."

It was a statesmanlike utterance, which called forth the hearty applause of the large and sympathetic audience.

Mr. Tatsujiro Sawaya of Okayama presented the appeal for Japan. He rejoiced that there was abundant evidence of a growing friendship between Japan and the nations of the West. He and his fellow Christians realized their responsibility in this transition period in the history of their beloved land. It was today the land of the rising sun, for the sun of righteousness had arisen upon it with healing in his wings. He thanked God for Christian Endeavor, which had a great future before it in Japan. Mr. Sawaya added greatly to the interest of his address by appearing in picturesque native costume, receiving enthusiastic greeting at the opening and applause at the close of his impassioned appeal.

The Rev. Andrew Beattie, Ph. D., of Canton, presented the case for China's millions, one-fourth of the human race:

"The Christian Church has now the grandest opportunity that ever came within her reach. The new China, with its coming importance in the community of nations, is the key to the East. An evangelized China would be a blessing to the world. The educational system of the empire is being re-organized. Missionary enterprise has now a chance to seize strategic points, to train young men and give the Chinese an object lesson in the possibilities of a modern education.

Mission boards ought to strengthen their educational machinery without delay. The character of the Christian Church in China further emphasises the appeal. Their converts have shown that they can be faithful unto death. In a few years the grand opportunity may have passed. It behooves us to act promptly, assured of ultimately securing the victory through Christ."

At this point Mr. H. N. Lathrop, treasurer of the United Society, anounced that the next convention under the auspices of the World's Union would be held in India in 1910. He gave some interesting information regarding it and uttered a strong appeal for organized effort to secure a large attendance.

A solemn consecration service was then held, the motto of which was: "Here am I, send me; or help me to send someone else." The session closed with prayer and the benediction.

CHAPTER XXIII.

CHRISTIAN ENDEAVOR'S OPPORTUNITY.

Dr. Clark presided at the Monday afternoon meeting in Tent Williston. The opening devotional exercise of praise and prayer was led by Rev. Mr. Lee of Seattle. The body of the tent was well filled.

The first address was made by Rev. W. I. Chamberlain, Ph. D., of India, on "The Mission of Christian Endeavor in Foreign Lands."

He pointed out the opportunity of Christian Endeavorers for making living nations out of the dying nations of the world, and indicated something of the wide and fundamental differences that exist in the religious conditions of the home and foreign fields, and the opportunity which this fact offered Christian Endeavorers in the latter. He referred in particular to the opportunity offered for creating a memorial fund and to the further opportunity of personal service in those lands. The missionary motive is the dynamic of the world's best civilization, and the redemptive purpose of God is the impulse of the world's progress. Christian Endeavorers are offered the opportunity of identifying themselves with this divine purpose. He quoted Ambassador Choate's definition of natural greatness as being not wealth and power, but as the nation's contribution to the thought, intellectual happiness, moral energy and spiritual hope and consolation of mankind.

Rev. Smith Baker, D. D., of Portland, Me., spoke with much power on "The Mission of Christian Endeavor in the Home Land."

"Christianity is a supernatural religion. When Christian Endeavor was first founded it was for the purpose of furthering the spiritual and the supernatural among its branches. The importance of the spiritual life cannot be over-stated. It is not a development but a gift of God. The idea of the spiritual life is first and before other things. The object of Christian Endeavor is to endeavor to establish the spiritual life and these other things follow. The Christian life is not in order to be saved. God has saved man. The Christian Endeavor Society is to lead men into a definite, positive, spiritual life. It is to prevent the spirit of the world from taking possession of the church. The real living of the spiritual life is more than a philanthropic or intellectual life.

When some now living were young, it was an unusual thing for young men and women to join the church. Now the Christian Endeavor is a cradle to nourish the young who come into a Christian life. The Christian Endeavor Society also leads many into the certainty of a Christian life. It is not a matter of formal endeavor, but

MISS J. KAJIRO

One of Seattle's Reception Committee

the evidence of experience and life. The boy, in the presence of the arguments of some social sceptic, declares that he knows he loves his mother. So the boy, in the presence of some infidel, whose arguments he cannot meet, asserts that he knows that he loves Jesus.

This is the mission of Christian Endeavor, to lead the young into a positive, definite Christian experience, and these other things will settle themselves. What Christianity needs is not more fun, but more prayer. The mission of Christian Endeavor is also to keep the life of the church warm and tender. One conversion is more than many eloquent sermons. When a boy rises up and says "I love Jesus" it is more than much admonition.

It is not a matter of duty. Duty is not a fundamental Christian law. The Christian has risen to a higher life, because it saved him, and he feels that he must, he cannot help himself. That is what Christian Endeavor has done for the church. It has produced a life of gratitude to God because of what God has done for him. That is the mission of all Christian Endeavorers—to show to the world what it is to be a Christian. This is the object of the Christian Endeavor Society."

Dr. Clark then made a few remarks relative to the Memorial Fund, pointing out the purposes of this fund which, in addition to the erection of our headquarters building, would make it possible for the United Society to lengthen the cords and strengthen the stakes of the kingdom of Christ both at home and abroad. He also mentioned the encouragement that had come from contributions received from many parts of the world. Subscription blanks were distributed calling for $5.00 charter membership in the new Christian Endeavor Builders' Association, and a good beginning was made.

FIRST PRESBYTERIAN CHURCH.

The Presbyterian Church meeting on "Christian Endeavor's Opportunity" was presided over by General Secretary Shaw, whose enthusiasm and brightness were never failing.

After praise and prayer, the chairman introduced Rev. Andrew Beattie, Ph. D., Presbyterian missionary at Canton, China, whose theme was "The Mission of Christian Endeavor in Foreign Lands."

Dr. Beattie, by way of illustrating what the society is doing in all countries, indicated the results of its activities in China, Japan and Korea:

"In my own province, Canton, there is a stronger desire to know the Gospel than had ever been manifested—so much so that at much shorter notice than has been given for this present meeting, yes even at a day's notice—even a larger meeting than the one I am now addressing could be secured in any one of the four churches under my charge. This could not have been accomplished but for Christian Endeavor. In Korea there is one church which, a few years ago, was built with a seating capacity for 1,500. Very soon, in order to prevent overcrowding, it was necessary to restrict one of the services to men and the other to women, and at the service for each sex the church is crowded. A prayer meeting there has a regular attendance of 1,500. Christian Endeavor has accomplished this. Indeed, the churches were originally organized as Endeavor societies and the mission of the societies in the Orient is exactly the same as their mission in the Occident. Young people had had no opportunity for self-expression and service; and so their spiritual life was waning when Christian Endeavor arrived, but soon their life waxed strong again."

Dr. Beattie very strongly impressed upon his audience that there is danger of a crisis on the Pacific coast; that China and Japan would not object to a treaty but they deeply resent the violation of a solemn international agreement. They will judge all Christianity by the attitude on this question of the Christian Church.

Dr. Beattie's address, and especially his concluding appeal, were received with much enthusiasm.

The Rev. Ira Landreth, D. D., LL. D., president of Belmont College, Nashville, Tenn., delivered a stirring address on "The Mission of Christian Endeavor in the Home Land," which he said would be in the future what it had been in the past only more intense. He further said:

"The societies for twenty-six years have stood for loyalty to Christ as Saviour and Lord; have taught intelligent individual loyalty to each Endeavorer's particular church and denomination; have stood for constant insistence on systematic and proportionate giving, and it has also formulated the highest order of Christian citizenship. This society cannot outlive its usefulness so long as children continue to be born and to grow into young men and women. The society has never, during the twenty-six years of its existence, proposed any plan or suggested any principle or undertaken any enterprise which had afterwards proved to have been a mistake. That is the best proof that the leaders of Christian Endeavor were themselves divinely led.

The attitude of Christian Endeavor toward other societies is not that of criticism, but of prayer that some day they may be united in one great convention. Christian Endeavor did not start out to promote church union, but it has done much toward it by bringing the leaders of the different denominations together that they may learn more of one another. Christian Endeavor has been back of many reforms, and will some time be an irresistible force moving against the saloon. The church of the future will be financially supported, because Christian Endeavor has taught the children to give to the Lord, and so long as there is a cradle there will be need of a Christian Endeavor Society. Christian Endeavor is a success wherever the pastor is a success—wherever he plans the work and works the plan. There is no agency that will help us so much in our obligation to generations past and present as the Christian Endeavor movement, if rightly used."

Secretary Shaw then told of the great desire he had, as Treasurer of the United Society, to secure enough money to build the Christian Endeavor building that is so much needed, and that as Secretary his desire for the same object is even greater.

He told of the far greater amounts put into Y. M. C. A. buildings in different places, of the generous contributions from Christian Endeavorers of much poorer lands than ours, of the generosity of the Chinese in wanting to send more than was really right for them to send, and finally urged the Christian Endeavorers of this country to give more liberally toward this reinforcement of all the good work now being done.

Blanks were then distributed for subscriptions to the fund, with the result that the amount now in hand was largely increased.

CHAPTER XXIV.

"THE SCHOOL OF METHODS."

Every morning during the convention, except Sunday, from 8:30 to 9:30, "A School of Methods" was held in the different churches of the city. Here the Endeavorers met to discuss plans of work in which they were especially interested. It gave every one an opportunity to take part in the discussion. That the time was well untilized is evidenced by the fact that in every instance the leaders had difficulty in closing the meeting at the end of the hour. The conferences, for the most part, were held in the large auditoriums of the churches, which were always well filled. Even at the Esperanto conference more than 200 delegates were present. We only have space to give a brief account of each of the conferences.

"CHRISTIAN ENDEAVOR METHODS."

THURSDAY.—Rev. C. H. Hubbell, Columbus, O., leader. Twenty-two states were represented. The relation of the pastor and church to the society were freely discussed with splendid suggestions from both pastors and young people.

"How to Get New Members Into the Society" brought out many helpful comments. One society reported twenty-six young men won as the result of a special campaign. Have a front door committee; a strangers' committee; a smile committee. Occupy the front seats. Have a pastor's helper committee. Train your successors. Canvass the hotels. Advertise your church.

FRIDAY MORNING.—Mr. George B. Graff, Boston, Mass., leader. "How to Get Vital Prayer Meetings." Have variety; change the order of exercises, beginning at the last end first. Change the appearance of the room. Have good live singing. Pray for the meetings all the week; occasionally have a meeting of all prayer.

"The Training of Prayer Meeting Leaders." Train the prayer meeting committee first; they are the silent partners of the leader. Have a meeting for leaders once a week. Teach the leaders how to draw out the thoughts of others.

"Keeping a Consecration Meeting Fresh." Water keeps fresh only when moving. Keep the prayer meeting alive. Make it good. Use new methods. Call the roll in different ways. Advertise. Have a gift meeting, the bringing of your gifts being the response to roll call. Have the names on a blackboard, and check them off as members participate. Have the meetings different—one all prayer, another all hymns, another all testimonies, etc.

"The Use of Christian Endeavor Literature." Reading a Christian Endeavor item caused the building of a church in Columbus, Ohio. Have a Christian Endeavor library—the cost is amazingly small. Adapt and adopt the suggestions of others.

MONDAY MORNING.—Mr. H. N. Lathrop, Boston, Mass., leader. Many different suggestions were given as to the proper relation of the society's expenses to the expenditure for benevolence, the various methods of raising money for each purpose, etc. As to the merits of the home and foreign missionary fields, many thought the money could be divided equally between the two, while others held that foreign missions should have the larger share. All agreed that the best method of giving is systematic and proportionate giving. The tithing of time as well as money was advocated. A "recruiting committee" was suggested under whose charge the new members may be placed for the first year and trained for service. A candle light meeting was suggested where only the leader had a light and the rest unlighted candles, to be lighted only after taking part.

JUNIOR METHODS.

THURSDAY MORNING.—Lillian E. Hayes, of Dunreith, Indiana, leader. The Junior Society is the training school of the church. The Sunday school does not take its place. The Superintendent may be appointed by the church as the Sunday School Superintendent is elected, or let the superintendent be nominated by the children or by the older Christian Endeavor Society. Begin now to train the Juniors to be superintendents. Keep the Juniors busy, and the problem of bad order will be solved. Have the pastor speak with the Juniors frequently. Play with the boys, then you can pray with them. Lead the Juniors, do not pull.

FRIDAY MORNING.—Mrs. Francis E. Clark, of Auburndale, Mass., leader. "The Juniors in the Prayer Meeting." Reverence, worship and instruction advised as three essential elements: Good, hearty singing in the beginning is a good way of smoothing the children down and getting the wriggles out. Help the children to pray by suggesting things to pray for.

"How to Tell a Child the Way to Christ." Send them a letter occasionally, asking such questions as "Did you ever think that you had a naughty heart? Did you ever feel that you want to be forgiven? How did you get mother to forgive you when you did wrong? Will you tell Jesus just as you would your mother what a naughty heart you have, and ask Him to forgive you?"

"The Relation of the Children to the Church." The older members may help the children by sympathy with them, by giving them some work to do; by praying for them and creating a home atmosphere in the church.

SATURDAY.—Mrs. Charles Hutchison, of Toledo, Ohio, leader "How to Secure Superintendents." Have young people in training. Let the pastor secure the one in his church that is best qualified. Form a study class for Junior methods. Have a Junior committee in the Y. P. S. C. E.

"Should We Have an Age Limit?" Use judgment in the matter. Have them come as young as possible just so they will sit quietly. A good time to graduate is when they enter high school.

"What Special Features Have You Introduced Into Your Meetings?" Teaching citizenship. Use a flag drill and salute. Teach loyalty. Read "Coming Americans." Use the Bible spell down, repeating verses until they can remember no more. Read band of mercy stories to the children. Talk in the meeting about the special missionary object for which the Juniors are giving their money.

"What Topics Are Most Helpful?" The topics as now used. A series of topics on the pledge. Lessons on "Pilgrim's Progress."

"How Much Should the Superintendent Talk in the Meeting?" As little as possible. Always teach the lesson. Make the closing prayer.

"How to Bring the Seniors and Juniors Closer Together." Let the seniors visit the Junior society frequently. Finance the Junior society. Appoint one or two seniors each week to visit the Junior meeting. Let the Juniors form one committee of the older society.

"Are Auxiliaries Helpful?" In some societies the Knights of King Arthur and the Girls' Guild have proved very helpful in promoting interest.

"Is it Best to Have Junior Unions?" They are usually found most helpful. If there is none, the superintendent should attend meetings of the senior union.

"Are Mothers' Meetings Helpful?" Usually they are. The mothers should get together at least once a year, and find out what the superintendent is trying to do. The church should look after the Junior society.

MONDAY MORNING.—Mr. Wm. Shaw, of Boston, Mass., leader. The sympathy and help of the mothers very much needed in Junior Societies. New plans for missionary work strenuously advocated. Find out from the missionary boards where the Junior's money can acomplish the most good. New plans for Bible study, for object teaching, for extending the extension of Junior work, and for the greater use of Junior literature were all recommended.

INTERMEDIATE METHODS.

FRIDAY.—Mr. Paul C. Brown, of Los Angeles, Cal., leader. "For What Are We Organized?" Intermediate is the bridge between the Junior and Senior. It is absolutely necessary to make a place for the Juniors in our church life if we expect to keep them.

"Is the Organization of Our Society as Complete as It Should Be?" No; more and better helps should be secured. Use all that can be found, and send helpful suggestions to the United Society for publication in new helps.

"Are Contests Helpful?" In some cases, yes. The general sentiment was that they are liable to lower the spiritual standard, and contesting members might lose sight of the real purpose in their efforts to win—to win through prayer is better. The members gained in a contest should be given something to do, and should be taken into active service.

"Graduation." When intermediates graduate into the senior society, put them at once upon a committee with older members so as to set them to work at once until they become acquainted.

"Other Suggestions." A society of six may do great things if their energies are united. Superintendents should not seem to superintend or manage, but give advice and encouragement where needed. The superintendent has a great field for personal work.

SATURDAY.—Mr. Wm. Shaw, of Boston, Mass., leader. "How to Reach and Train a Larger Number of the Youth of High School Age." Get the right motive and inspiring spirit. Get into friendly, chummy relations with the young people. Have intermediate meetings in the young people's society. Get individuals to get into touch with groups and classes of boys and girls. Include the intermediates as well as the Juniors in the annual union meetings. Publish new literature.

CHRISTIAN CITIZENSHIP.

Hon. Nicholas L. Johnson, of Batavia, Ill., leader. Accounts were given of helpful work being done in Christian citizenship classes. Attention was called to the course of study prepared by the intercollegiate prohibition committee which, with alterations, could be adapted to the needs of almost any society. Do not be discouraged at the small attendance at Christian citizenship meetings. Many young people are waiting for some one to lead. Make one issue at a time the battle cry. A good motto is, "At it, all at it, and always at it." Educate to the point where the people have a mind to work. Grace, grit, and greenbacks are needed in this work. A need of high ideals.

THE EVANGELISTIC CONFERENCE.

THURSDAY.—Rev. James A. Francis, of New York, leader. "What is Evangelism?" It is making Christ known to many for their salvation.

"Who Should Engage in It?" Every Christian man and woman. The New Testament says that all who know Christ ought to go to those who do not know him, and make him personally known.

"What Must the Personal or Society Worker Be?" A soul who truly loves the Christ life.

"What Must Be Known?" God, man, and man's relation to God.

"What is Meant by the Atmosphere of a Meeting?" The sum total of the attitudes and sympathies of the entire company. Every soul present helps or hinders in creating the atmosphere.

TEMPERANCE WORK.

Miss Ida C. Clothier, of Manitou, Colo., leader. Do not neglect pledge signing. Do not take it for granted that all Endeavorers are total abstainers from principal. Have a permanent campaign of pledge signing. The young man who is unwilling to give his word and stand by it is not on the road to business success. Have no party politics in local elections. Vote for clean, temperate men no matter what their politics. Sole dependence should not be placed on the mass meeting for winning votes. Individual persuasion is best. It is possible to get drinking men to vote no license by showing them it is to their best interest. Do not think it is a church matter and go only to the men of the church. Much may be done through the mail. A leaflet with an accompanying letter is of great value. Active, definite work was urged upon all Endeavorers.

MISSIONARY METHODS.

THURSDAY.—"How to Get Good Missionary Committees." By wise selection by executive committee. By appointing as chairman one thoroughly interested in missions. By a training class for missionary leaders. By allowing members of a society to make their own selection of committees by ballot. By asking the pastor's intelligence and judgment as to individuals, and by special prayer in the selection of committee.

"Should Every Endeavor Society Have a Study Class?" It is generally admitted that they should. All admit the need of information. Small classes are desirable. Normal mission study class recommended for the instruction of teachers. Missionary institutes are recommended. Two can form a study class if no more can be secured.

"Text Books." Those now in use and furnished by the United Society and the Young People's Missionary Movement.

"Method." Always have a study assigned in advance in which all should participate. Always have questions asked regarding the chapter under discussion.

"How We Can Better Our Missionary Meetings." By good, live meetings. By missionary study classes. By missionary libraries. By the reading of missionary books. By maps, chalk talks, and other interesting aids. Twelve yearly missionary meetings is commended.

FRIDAY MORNING.—Mr. Von Ogden Vogt, leader. "How to Help the Missionary Boards to Get Hold of Young People." Use all the helps the boards supply, such as the programmes of the monthly missionary meetings, letters from missionary fields issued in printed slips, text books for study classes, leader's manuals for each book, and supplemental studies for Sunday schools. When some one present asked to know how many young people were present who proposed to become missionaries, at least nine arose, and an earnest prayer was offered for a blessing on their lives, and for others who might be won for the same purpose.

PRISON CHRISTIAN ENDEAVOR.

THURSDAY.—Mr. William Shaw, of Boston, Mass., leader. Hon. C. E. Marks, president of the Utah Christian Endeavor Union and father of the legislation establishing the juvenile court in Salt Lake City, described the plan of work, and showed how Christian Endeavor could develop a public sentiment that would demand a reform in our treatment of boys and girls who fall into the hands of the law. Healthful work can also be done in promoting general prison reform, and a more intelligent treatment of the criminal classes.

Rev. E. A. Fredenhagen described the organization of "Leagues of Christian Endeavor" in the prisons, and the helpful services of the society in caring for prisoners after their release, and in trying to establish them as good citizens and securing employment for them. Truant schools, jails, and penitentiaries, as well as state prisons, furnish large fields for service. Every state union should have a superintendent of prison work, and every local union with a prison within its bounds should have a committee on prison work to organize and carry it on.

METHODS OF BIBLE STUDY.

SATURDAY.—Dean Herbert L. Willett, D. D., of Chicago, Ill., leader. The topic was considered under three phases—individual study, group study, and the best helps. The relation of various Bible books to each other and outside literature, not of contemporary character, was outlined. The different versions and translations were indicated. Such methods as the study of the Bible according to historical growth, according to divisions, and according to books for divisional and doctrinal purposes were pointed out. A list of the most important helps was given.

MONDAY MORNING.—Address by Mr. Wm. Phillips Hall, of New York City. "He who would truly possess and be possessed of the great and precious truths of God's whole world, must pursue a right method of acquirement. There are wrong as well as right methods of Bible study. The very first thing that Paul exhorted Timothy to do was to 'Continue thou in the things which thou hast learned.' This is good advice for those who, like Timothy, were in childhood's early days taught to believe and study the Bible as the word of God. We are commanded to study the Bible as the very word of God. We are not asked to dissect and recompile the Bible, but to appropriate and use it. We are to master it that it may master us and enable us to master others for Christ. Rev. Daniel S. Gregory, D. D., Educational Secretary of the American Bible League, recommends the 'natural, constructive, cumulative' method as set forth in Bible League Primer No. 1. It presents an outline view of the Bible as God's revelation of redemption. Rev. James M. Gray, D. D., Dean of the Moody Bible

REV. JOHN POLLOCK
President of the European Christian Endeavor Union and Pastor of St Enoch's Presbyterian Church, Belfast, Ireland.

FOUR RACIAL REPRESENTATIVES
In the rear are Dr. W. T. Johnson of Richmond, Va., and Mr. K. Nakuina of Hawaii. In front are Rev. Edward Marsden, a Tsimpshean Indian of Alaska, and Mr. Tatsujiro Sawaya, field secretary of Japan.

Institute, has written a little book, entitled 'How to Master the English Bible.' It is called the sympathetic method, which, instead of analyzing or taking the Bible apart, puts it together, considering it as a whole. Both of these methods build up a firm faith in the Bible as the word of God. When we desire to become acquainted with a novel, an historical work, or a scientific treatise, we do the most natural thing under the circumstances—we read the book itself; but when we desire to become acquainted with the Bible we do the most unnatural thing under the circumstances—we read other books about the Bible, commentaries, encyclopedias, lesson sheets, in fact, nearly everything we can find upon the subject except the Bible itself. The new methods propose that we become acquainted with the Bible by reading the Bible. The entire Bible should be read. The Old Testament is as necessary as the New. Let me emphasize these points: First, that our study shall be of the individual books of the Bible; second, that such study shall take the form of prayerful reading of the same; third, that each book shall be read and re-read so many times as may be necessary to give us a complete mastery of its contents; fourth, that in all of our study we shall consistently seek to ascertain the bearing of it upon the life and purposes of our Lord; fifth, that such study shall continue from day to day until it becomes a fixed life habit, as necessary to our peace of mind and spiritual prosperity and effectiveness in Christian service as our daily food is necessary to the efficiency of our physical frame and the life of our body."

THE QUIET HOUR CONFERENCE.

MONDAY MORNING.—Miss Ethel D. Pickett, of Kansas City, Mo., leader. Many testified to the great helpfulness of "The Quiet Hour" to the individual and through the individual to the society. It has made personal workers of many. Most of those present found the most helpfulness in the morning hour. Whatever the time of day, be sure that there is a regular time sacred to this hour. Some used the time in meditation and prayer, while others used devotional books to supplement the Bible reading, but all agreed that no book should ever take the place of the Bible in the quiet hour. At the close many of those who were not Comrades of the Quiet Hour wanted literature to give them more information, while at least eight handed in their names to become Comrades at the close of the conference.

THE ESPERANTO CONFERENCE.

SATURDAY.—Mr. Amos R. Wells, of Boston, Mass., leader. As most of those present were ignorant of the international language, Mr. Wells gave an initial lesson illustrating the language in many ways, including a song. The delegates were apt pupils, and readily translated what he gave them. At the close of the meeting, Mr. Ibanez, of Mexico, gave a greeting in Esperanto, which, as Mr. Wells repeated it slowly, was translated sentence by sentence by those present. A new interest was created in the international language.

CHAPTER XXV.

The Noon Evangelistic Meetings.

The place was the Grand Opera House, down close to the business district, the hour twelve to one, the leader a railroad man, opened and closed the meeting as on the drop of the hat. They were held but four days and it was a case of making the most of a fleeting opportunity. Mr. William Phillips Hall, of New York, presided at each meeting. His commanding personality, majestic vigor and large-hearted tenderness pervaded the sessions with a charm that none can describe but which all could feel. His very manner of listening during the address each day compelled everybody else to listen. It was truly a specimen of "eloquent listening." A brass band played for ten minutes in front of the entrance before each service. At the stroke of twelve a hymn, a second hymn, a scripture reading by Mr. Hall, a prayer, another hymn, and at twenty minutes past the hour the address timed to exactly thirty minutes.

Rev. J. A. Francis, general evangelist of the American Baptist Home Mission Society, was the speaker each day. The first address was on "How Jesus Won a Soul"—the story of Sychar's well-side; the second, "Peter's Fall and Restoration;" the third, "The Light of the World," and the fourth, "Can a Man Get Beyond Reach of God's Mercy in This Life?" In view of the fact that four-fifths of the audience were Endeavorers Mr. Francis made his addresses something more than an appeal to those who had never confessed Christ; he made them also truly teaching addresses for those who knew the Lord, that they might know Him and His service better.

Ten minutes of the hour is still left. This Mr. Hall used in such a summing up and such appeals of manly tenderness as are too seldom heard. The number of non-church members present was not large; but some days it seemed as if almost every person who came in a non-professor confessed Christ as Saviour before going out.

The average attendance was about nine hundred. Probably not less than fifty persons publicly confessed Christ during the four meetings. The service on the last day was marked with peculiar solemnity and power. The awful truth was tenderly pressed home that it was perfectly possible for a man to reject or neglect Christ till that attitude became the permanent habit of the soul and then all hope was over. When the invitation was given it was noticed that some persons well past middle life yielded themselves to Christ. The meetings greatly deepened the conviction that in future years this form of service ought to be an integral and very prominent part of every great C. E. Convention.

CHAPTER XXVI.

THE GREAT PURPOSE MEETINGS.

The Closing Meetings of the Convention.

The closing session at Tent Williston was scheduled to begin at 7:30 p. m., but at 6:30 state delegations were present vying with one another in slogans and songs. One state would start a gospel hymn and in a moment the entire throng would unite in it.

Dr. Francis E. Clark presided. At many sessions of the convention we have been favored with the presence of foreign missionaries, but from none did we receive more inspiration than from the Rev. Mr. Irwin of the Laos country. Mr. Irwin led the devotions.

Then followed the endeavor to crowd into two hours the elaborate program planned for the evening. First came the procession of states. The delegations from the various states, provinces, and countries arranged themselves in the great left aisle of the tent, and as Dr. Clark called the name of the state or province, the delegation named marched to the platform, singing either a gospel hymn or state song. Then the leader of the delegation stepped forward upon the platform, announced the state motto, and gave the purpose of their organization for the work of the coming year.

Canada had the largest delegation that ever attended a Christian Endeavor convention. California displayed a great orange flag. The District of Columbia sang "The Star-Spangled Banner." Congressman Johnson was the leader of the Illinois delegation, who sang a "Forward" song. Indiana sang a song patterned after "The King's Business" to the tune of "Maryland." The Iowa delegation declared that their state was the fairest state in all the land. Massachusetts combined with all New England and gave expression to their love for New England and of what New England had been to the nation by a song that had been written on the train by Prof. Wells. Massachusetts' motto was declared to be "Unity in Evangelism." "Onward to St. Paul" was the cry of the Minnesota delegation, and the leader pledged that every Endeavorer in the state would seek to win one soul for Christ between now and the convention of 1909. "Michigan, My Michigan," to the tune of "Maryland," was the song of that water lapped state. Nebraska declared that it was not ashamed of the gospel of Christ, and the Nebraska delegation was apparently not ashamed of itself for it sang of Nebraska as "the land of Bryan, the land of corn," and of themselves as "the finest people ever born."

With the whoop "Who are we? Who are we?" the Empire state delegation marched upon the platform, the leader declaring that when President Roosevelt goes home, he goes to New York. A fair young woman declared that North Carolina had been reorganized during the year with the motto "Look up and lift up."

Yelling like a band of Indians, the North Dakota delegation advanced, but on arrival at the platform sobered down sufficiently to declare that it was not by might or by power, but by the spirit of God that it hoped to prevail.

"Help save Ohio to help save the world," a new song composed for the occasion, was sung by the Ohio delegation, whose leader announced that that state was the mother of presidents, and that she gave to Christian Endeavor such men as John Willis Baer and Amos R. Wells.

When Dr. Smith, president of the Oklahoma Christian Endeavor Union, declared that the forty-sixth star of the Union would not be stained by the saloon evil, Dr. M. A. Matthews, of the First Presbyterian church, Seattle, threw his puritan hat in the air and yelled his delight, and of course the audience responded. Dr. Clark said he wished we had a whole hour to yell for Oklahoma.

Little Dr. Lowden was little Rhode Island's representative.

Only one delegate was present from South Dakota, but that delegate reminded us that one properly energized can put thousands to flight.

Tennessee, the state that has banished the race track and the saloon, headed by the inimitable Dr. Landrith, announced as its intention, "Tennessee for Christ."

The Washington delegation was so large that it could not be accommodated upon the platform.

Wisconsin vied with Wyoming in declaring its love for Christ and the church.

The most enthusiastic delegation, however, was that from Japan. About 40 men and a dozen young women waived their red-balled flags, sang their enthusiastic song, and yelled their "banzai" for Endeavorers and for Dr. Clark.

Dr. Beattie spoke for China; Dr. Chamberlain for India; Dr. Francis for Russia; Dr. Pollock for Scotland, Ireland, Wales and Europe.

Dr. Clark read letters or cablegrams from India, France, Costa Rico, Queensland, Italy, South Australia, Gilbert Islands,

The Marshall Islands, Madagascar, Hungary, South Africa, China, South America, Iceland, Trinidad, Germany, New South Wales, Victoria, and other lands.

Mr. F. Edgar Barth, chairman of the Seattle Committee of 1907, was then presented, and he in turn presented the many members of that committee to the audience, each member being enthusiastically cheered. Mr. Barth stated that the committee wished in some way to express its affection for and admiration of Dr. and Mrs. Clark, so that they had made a miner's pan of silver, upon the face of which Mount Rainier was engraved, and on the back the names of the committee.

Dr. Ira Landrith, of Nashville, Tenn., presented resolutions of thanks felicitously, expressing the gratitude of the delegates to all who had contributed in any way to their physical enjoyment and moral enrichment.

Then followed an unheard of wonder. Nine preachers and one layman spoke each for just one minute, in a series of earnest talks to Christian workers:

To Ministers—Rev. Smith Baker, D. D., Portland, Me.
To Sunday School Workers—Rev. W. T. McElveen, Ph. D., Boston, Mass.
To Junior and Intermediate Workers—Rev. J. E. Fout, Toledo, Ohio.
To the Choir—Rev. John Pollock, Belfast, Ireland.
To Active Members—Bishop B. F. Lee, D. D., Wilberforce, O.
To Union Officers—Rev. Frank G. Smith, D. D., Chicago, Ill.
To Tenth Legioners—Rev. John M. Lowden, D. D., Providence, R. I.
To Comrades of the Quiet Hour—Rev. Floyd W. Tomkins, S. T. D., Philadelphia, Pa.

Mr. William Phillips Hall, of New York, N. Y., who rendered such splendid service in the daily evangelistic services at the Grand Opera House, urged all to engage in evangelistic services.

After a few earnest words from our beloved leader and the repetition by the great throng of the threefold benediction, Dr. Clark pronounced the twenty-third International Christian Endeavor convention adjourned.

THE FIRST PRESBYTERIAN CHURCH.

A novel, impressive, and inspiring meeting was that held at the closing session of the Convention in the First Presbyterian church. Multi-colored banners and bannerettes, upon which were inscribed the names of the various states, added beauty to the decorative effect of the edifice.

Long before the opening of the meeting, delegations came pouring in, and on their entrance to the church would either sing their state song or a sacred anthem, one state seeming to vie with another as to which possessed the greatest volume and enthusiasm.

General Secretary William Shaw presided, and prefaced the opening of the programme with the request that no state yells be given—simply the state song or anthem. He further requested that the leaders and standard-bearers only mount the platform, the rest of the delegations to rise as their state was called, and that one minute would be allowed for remarks from each state leader. After singing "Onward, Christian Soldiers," prayer was offered by the Rev. Inuyi, pastor of the Japanese church of Seattle.

Following the prayer the leaders and standard-bearers of the various delegations marched up the left aisle of the large church, and as they filed up the aisle with their banners waving, they presented a sight long to be remembered.

"We are from Kansas," was the cry of the first leader. "We are after the saloon and gambling." The delegation sang their state song.

The lone delegation from Arkansas was next to come forward, saying, "Our banner speaks for itself." He announced as their motto "Arkansas for Christ." He also stated they had a state song, but as he was the only delegate he did not wish to sing a solo.

Idaho's leader announced that they had no banner, but would have one at St. Paul. Their motto is "A Christian Endeavor in every valley; a Junior society in every church." The delegation sang their state song, "Idaho," receiving applause.

Hawaii's lone representative was treated with tremendous applause, and he introduced himself as coming from the lone star of the Pacific and their motto as "Forward." A song in his native tongue was well received.

Colorado's representative stated that their purpose is "Just work." The delegation sang "Colorado for Christ."

Dr. Bannen, as Pennsylvania's leader, stated that the banner with them was given to Dr. Clark by India, and given by him to their state for increase in societies. He gave as their purpose "That in this great arch of Christian fellowship and service, the Keystone dare not weaken." The state delegation sang "God Will Take Care of You, He will."

Oregon's representative was next to advance, and he stated their state had the largest delegation outside of Washington at the convention. After expressing their motto, the delegation sang an appropriate song.

Connecticut said he represented the first local union and the first state Christian Endeavor Union organized. He gave as their motto, "Our boys and girls for Jesus Christ." This was followed by their state song.

A fair young lady represented New Hampshire. She stated their watchword is "Re-organization."

Vermont's leader stated that though their state was very small, still it afforded the leaders an opportunity to come in contact with and become personally acquainted with some worker in every society. Vermont and New Hampshire then united in singing the hymn composed by Mr. Wells.

Missouri's delegate announced that while the Missouri river divided the state in the center, her Christian interests are not divided. After expressing their motto, the delegation sang, "Will There Be Any Stars in My Crown?"

"Utah for Christ," was declared to be the motto for Utah, and their chief object "To save the boys and girls of our state."

Alabama's delegate stated that while he was a bannerless man, he was not from a bannerless state. Their purpose is "Increase and Betterment."

"I am proud to appear before you as an American Indian," was the announcement made from the Indians' leader, and he received an ovation. He stated that even to this day people seem to think they could not trust an Indian, as he had noticed some of the children here run away at his approach, which reminded him that we were going back to the days of Columbus. He wished to impress upon all that Christ's gospel spirit is among the Indians. He also said that it was a common belief that an Indian likes his fire-water, but they have 400 temperance people out of six churches on the reservation from which he came. He was sorry that tobacco was not also included in temperance, as it was harmful to the body as well as liquor. On the reservation they train their children not to smoke. In 1492 Columbus landed and found Indians smoking. He called them savages. "On the 10th day of July, 1907, myself and comrades landed in Seattle, and found the white people smoking. It made me think they must be savages." Three Indians, composing the delegation, then sang in their native tongue, "When the Roll Is Called Up Yonder, I'll be There."

"We come from the land of the mosquito—that little insect that gets in its work quickly and yet makes itself felt, and when he has anything to do he does it singing," was the cry of the New Jersey leader. Their object is "Larger work in dividual societies, and for bringing into a church that has no society, a Christian Endeavor society."

West Virginia's announced motto was "Look unto the hills from whence cometh our help." The delegation sang "The West Virginia Hills."

Montana's representative announced "Service" as their watchword, and their motto as being "Montana for Christ through personal work." The delegation sang "That Will Be Glory for Me," in which the entire audience was invited to join.

"We are not ashamed of Nevada. All of Nevada's delegation is on the platform," said the leader of that state, and then stated that more men than women attended the Christian Endeavor meetings in Nevada—in fact, the proportion was about 16 to 1.

The representative from Texas then came forward, saying, "Last, but, I hope, not least." He stated that sixty days ago the legislature of Texas had passed a bill making gambling a felony. Their motto is, "Texas for Christ."

The Chairman then remarked that such a meeting as this could not have been held twenty-five years ago, and that the intelligent and enthusiastic remarks made by the various delegates was due to twenty-five years of Christian Endeavor training. He then spoke briefly on the Christian Endeavor headquarters building, asking the delegates to go back to their societies and gather some bricks and stones for the erection of that building.

After a hymn of praise, the following charges were given:

To Ministers—Rev. W. T. Johnson, D. D., Richmond, Va., who gave as his charge the fifth chapter of Peter and I. Timothy, 4th to 16th verses.

To Sunday School Workers—Rev. B. B. Tyler, D. D., Denver, Colo. Dr. Tyler said: "I charge you before God and the Lord Jesus Christ that you engage in this work—give yourself, soul, body, and spirit to it. Study the book from Genesis to the last word of Revelations.

SUNDAY SERVICE IN COUNTY JAIL.

Study your boys; study your girls; study your men; study your women that they may be brought into fellowship with Jesus Christ."

To Junior and Intermediate Workers—Rev. Luther DeYoe, D. D., Philadelphia Pa., who urged that no one desert his post; to teach the children that they are missionaries; but above all "Remember the children."

To the Choir—Rev. James L. Hill, D. D., Salem, Mass., who stated that such songs as the "Marseillaise," the "Watch on the Rhine," etc., were born in a burst of passion, but that it was only the redeemed and blood-washed who could sing the song of Christ, and that it was in the power of all to sing this song and have a new heart and a new hope.

To Active Members—Rev. Henry F. Cope, Chicago, Ill., who said: "I charge you, returning to your homes, your fields, church, societies and schools, to give continual expression to the impressions you have received at this convention."

To Union Officers—Rev. Claude E. Hill, Mobile, Ala., who said: "My words to union officers are these: Remember that your position stands not alone for honor, but for service; second, that you are the leader of an army, the efficiency of which depends upon your own fidelity and courage; third, that Christian Endeavor means infinitely more than big conventions, speeches and addresses."

To Tenth Legioners—Rev. E. R. Dille, D. D., Oakland, Cal., whose charge was: "As you have put up a standard, rally to it. Be like the colored soldier who ran ahead of the ranks with the flag into the hands of the enemy, and when the lieutenant ordered him to bring back the flag, said: 'No, bring the men up to the flag.'"

To Comrades of the Quiet Hour—Rev. Edwin Heyl Delk, D. D. Philadelphia, Pa., who said that the Quiet Hour in communion with God was the secret of a Christian life.

After a few moments of silent prayer, "God Be With You 'Till We Meet Again" was sung, followed by the threefold benediction by all.

With the words "God grant that the influence of this convention may just begin," Secretary Shaw declared the twenty-third annual convention adjourned.

CHAPTER XXVII.

GLEANINGS BY THE WAYSIDE.

"A man needs to do good, not merely to be good."—Rev. Ira D. Landrith.

* * * * *

It was said that over one hundred pulpits in Seattle were occupied Sunday by visiting clergymen.

* * * * *

There were an unusual number of state presidents present—for the most part young men—and a splendid set they were.

* * * * *

The weather was ideal. "We have never had such weather" was the universal comment. Sunshiny, but cool and pleasant.

* * * * *

A Nez Percz Indian aroused great enthusiasm when he told about the Indian Christian Endeavor Societies in Washington numbering 360 members.

* * * * *

Said Rev. Alexander Francis: "I have met Dr. Clark in Australia, Africa, Russia and the United States, and the man that I know I shall meet in heaven is Dr. Clark."

* * * * *

The most popular delegate, next to Dr. Clark, was the Rev. John Pollock, of Belfast, Ireland, who, with his insignia of office about his neck, was always an interesting figure.

* * * * *

It was voted by the convention to send a cablegram to The Hague assuring the American representatives of the sympathy of three million Endeavorers in their efforts to promote peace and arbitration.

* * * * *

During the convention, our former Secretary, George M. Ward, D. D., was called to his home in the East by the sudden death of his father. By vote of the Convention a telegram of sympathy was sent to Dr. Ward in his unexpected sorrow.

* * * * *

By far the most popular delegation at the Purpose Meeting Monday night, if the cheers of the audience are any indication, was the band of thirty Japanese who waved their flags and gave their "Banzai," in which the audience heartily joined.

* * * * *

On Sunday, a band of Christian Endeavorers under the direction of Rev. Edward A. Fredenhagen, held four prison services—two in the city lock-up and two in the County jail. Forty-nine prisoners responded to the call to accept Jesus as their Lord and Savior.

* * * * *

The entire roof of the Hotel Lincoln, where the trustees and speakers of the Convention were entertained, is a beautiful garden of flowers. Three of the four pictures showing Vice-President Fairbanks that are found in this volume were taken on the roof-garden of The Lincoln.

* * * * *

At the close of one of the sessions the Convention Committee endeavored to take all visiting delegates for a ride about the city in automobiles. They found this almost a hurculean task but by making several trips this unexpected but much appreciated courtesy was accomplished. One of our illustrations shows the procession of automobiles decorated for the occasion.

* * * * *

It is safe to say that never have the churches of Seattle been so filled as on Sunday morning, July 15.

Long before the hour of opening, the streets were thronged with bright-faced and badge-bedecked Endeavorers wending their way to their various denominational places of worship. "Standing room only" was the universal rule.

* * * * *

Sunday evening from 6:15 to 7.15 Christian Endeavor prayer meetings were held in the various churches of the city. The leaders of these meetings were active Endeavorers from other parts of the country. The meetings were excellently attended. The general subject was "Laborers together with God," and many testimonials as to the value of the convention were given by the visiting delegates.

* * * * *

The excursion on Puget Sound given to the Vice-President and to the officers and trustees Saturday afternoon was an occasion never to be forgotten. All can echo the sentiments of Mr. Shaw, when he said: "I had the best time of my life." The dipping of the colors and the vice-presidential salute at the Navy Yard were formalities of great interest to the two hundred Endeavorers aboard.

* * * * *

Rev. John Pollock, president of the European Christian Endeavor Union, is pastor of what is considered the largest church in the world—St. Enoch's Presbyterian of Belfast, Ireland. There are one thousand families in his parish, and considerably more than three times that many individual members. It took Dr. Pollock seventeen days' continuous traveling to reach Seattle from his distant home.

* * * * *

Of the many toasts given at the banquet to Vice-President Fairbanks and to the officers and trustees of the United Society, none were more apropos than the turn that Prof. Wells gave to a couplet from Whittier:
"A green leaf to 'our own Fair banks'
The memory of a friend."

* * * * *

Tent Endeavor was not seated, but was placed within a few feet of Tent Williston for the Convention conveniences—registration booths, committee headquarters, etc. Around the great center pole was the literature tables of the United Society, in charge of Mr. Walter S. Mee, manager of the Chicago office. Around the sides were restaurants, lunch counters, information booths, press headquarters, etc. Certainly these departments of a Christian Endeavor Convention never had such comfortable and commanding quarters before.

* * * * *

Edward Marsden, the full-blooded Tsimpshean Indian from Alaska, thrilled his audience as he plead with the Christian Endeavorers to aid him and his people in securing from the United States government what they believe to be only intelligent dealing and Christian justice. When he sat down, after making perhaps the most remarkable speech of a whole series of remarkable speeches, a storm of cheers burst forth that could not be quieted until he had made his acknowledgements. Dr. Tyler, the presiding officer, said: "He had heard of another Indian somewhere, pleading with great men of this country for justice to his people, but his speech, for eloquence, could not compare with this."

* * * * *

Said a local paper the day after the Convention closed:
"So far as the City of Seattle is concerned, it welcomed the Christian Endeavor Society with open-handed good will, and will regret its departure. Not often has it been the city's fortune to entertain so many bright and brainy men and women from all parts of the world; it has been an exceptional and grateful privilege, and one which Seattle will remember.

"The delegates and visitors attracted hither by the Convention will carry to all parts of the world messages of good cheer and noble import; a plea for social purity, right living, cleaner morals, and a prayer for the peace of the world. The work of the Society will leave a profound impress upon the city of Seattle; citizens of this city will not be unmindful of the debt they owe these earnest men and women, and they can show their appreciation in no more enduring fashion than by walking in the Light, and living for the Truth, acording to the faith of the city's departing guests."

* * * * *

The Seattle papers gave most excellent reports of the Convention proceedings. This was especially true of the Post-Intelligencer, which gave several pages each day to the meetings.

In a leading editorial, this paper had the following to say regarding the Christian Endeavorers:

"No organization has played a more important part in movements in behalf of the moral uplift in the world than the Christian Endeavor Society. Its good work is written large in the world's history, and the field of its usefulness is constantly widening. Reports submitted by the officers of the organization plainly tell the colossal character of the work carried on by this band of earnest and worthy men and women.

"The society's record is inspiring. With so much good achieved, it is no desperate hazard to say that the half is not yet told. Seattle is fortunate to entertain men and women who have wrought so enduringly in the world's affairs."

* * * * *

SEATTLE DECORATIONS.

From the ragged little newsboy with a bit of faded green and white ribbon in his coat lapel to the tops of the tallest skyscrapers, all Seattle greeted the delegates with the silent nod of its emblem. The big buildings in the downtown part of the city vied with each other in displaying their charms, set off with a dress of green and white. Here and there some more ambitious structure had donned a garland of "Old Glory" for this occasion and looked disdainfully at its more retiring brothers and sisters. Many were the devices used to let the visitors know that the city welcomed them to her midst. Electric signs with green bulbs having a white background of the letters C. E., flags with those letters upon them, and streamers of green and white bunting waved high above the passing throng.

Second Avenue was a sort of green and white garden in which the red and blue roses of the flag, rose brightly into the summer sunlight.

From Yesler Way, with but a few undecorated spaces here and there, clear to Union Street, there was a lane of C. E. color. On First Avenue much the same picture was to be seen. Green and white streamers with the flag flying from windows and from poles on the top of buildings rendered this artery another place to attract the eye. Stores and other places of business, catching the holiday air from their more lofty neighbors bloomed out in color, too, while the caps and badges and the smiling faces of the reception committee and delegates put a pleasing finish on the whole picture.

* * * * *

SEATTLE'S GENEROSITY.

Never have the delegates or the people of a city been more generous than at Seattle. At the close of Mr. Graff's stereopticon trip around the Christian Endeavor world Saturday night, Mr. Douglass of the Douglass Light Company of Seattle stepped forward and asked him if a stereopticon and accessories would be acceptable to him. Upon being answered in the affirmative, Mr. Douglass replied that he was now building a stereopticon for the Interior Department of the United States Government, and that he would be pleased to present the United Society with one of the same kind. The offer was accepted with most hearty thanks.

The delegates without exception were greatly interested in promoting the Quarter Century Memorial Fund and many dollars were added to this fund by the delegates. Just before leaving Seattle a very substantial pledge to this Building Fund wah made to Mr. Shaw by three of Seattle's leading business men.

CHAPTER XXVIII.

Greetings From Many Lands.

To the Officers and Delegates of the Twenty-third International Christian Endeavor Convention, Seattle, Wash.

Dear Fellow Endeavorers:
Again do your companions in Endeavor from the Land of the Trident send hearty greetings in the Name of Christ.

We congratulate you upon your noble achievements in the past, upon the hopeful and contagious enthusiasm which, we are confident, marks your present gathering and upon the imperial plans for extending the Kingdom of God which are becoming more clearly apprehended and more fully adopted by you. The World-plan of our King, the Christ, of all imperial plans known, is the farthest from being fulfilled. He awaits a loyal, devoted army of larger dimensions. Pentecostal fires are being kindled. Many hearts owning His sway are burning with strange longings and a powerful purpose.

Slumbering nations, aroused, are more willing than ever to arise. Even India, prisoner of the Past, is entertaining ideas which are in sharp contrast to those possessed by her forefathers.

Young India has been captivated by the wide-awake spirit of Japan, but we know that the Spirit of God can revolutionize this land.

We rejoice in the belief that Christian Endeavor is one of His chosen agencies for the accomplishing of this. It is being acknowledged as such more widely than ever. Its strength and also its opportunities are increasing. The pressure of God's command has been constant, but the call of India's millions is growing louder and more urgent. "The battle is the Lord's," therefore defeat is impossible.

The Endeavorers of India rejoice that the World's Christian Endeavor officers have decided that the next World's Convention shall be "India 1910." That will be the first Endeavor Convention of its kind to he held on a mission field. It will be, God willing, a great missionary gathering. Not yet have Endeavorers had such an opportunity as that will be to study first hand the successes, failures, needs and possibilities of Christ's campaign—or better, preliminary preparations for the conflict.

The Convention will not be as large in numbers as many with which India is familiar. Nor are India's great "melas" devoid of enthusiasm—but they are utterly lacking in any controlling altruistic motive and unacquainted with that overpowering divine purpose which thrusts forth men and women to help those who know no victory in life or death. Will not hundreds of you plan to visit India then and get a glimpse of the unequal conflict?

India's preparations for 1910 began last February and she expects to receive you in one of the most interesting cities of this most interesting country. Will you not all plan and pray that the World's Convention in 1910 may be unusual, not only in personelle, but also in power?

"The battle is the Lord's"—"In His name we conquer."

In behalf of the United Society of Christian Endeavor in India, Burma and Ceylon.
Yours fraternally
A. G. McGAW,
President.

GREETINGS FROM FRANCE:

"Only they would that we should remember the poor; the same which I also was forward to do." Gal. 2:10.

"For we know the grace of our Lord Jesus Christ, that, though He was rich, yet for your sakes He became poor, that ye through His poverty might be rich." 2 Cor. 8:9.

* * * * *

To the International Christian Endeavor Convention, Seattle, Washington, U. S. A.

COSTA RICA Union sends greeting, and prays that the presence of The Holy Spirit, the great Inspirer and Guide may he abundantly realized by you through all your exercises and that this may be a season of rich blessing to you. May your efforts for "Christ and the Church," hitherto so signally blessed by God, be yet more abundantly owned of Him in the further extension of the work, so that the time may not be far distant when "Christian Endeavor around the World" shall be an accomplished fact.
STEPHEN WITT, President.
E. A. PITT, Secretary.

* * * * *

GREETING FROM QUEENSLAND:

I Thessalonians, 3:12, 13: "And the Lord make you to increase and abound in love one toward another, and toward all men even as we do toward you. To the end He may establish your hearts unblameable in holiness before God, even our Father at the coming of our Lord Jesus Christ with all His saints."

And we send it with all love and wishes for a good convention in every sense.

The cable word will be "Bunyip."
MR. WILLIAM MORRISON,
South Brisbane, Queensland.

* * * * *

GREETING FROM ITALY:

To the Twenty-third International Christian Endeavor Convention. Dear Fellow Endeavorers:

We are sure that among the testimonies of fraternal solidarity which reach you in this solemn circumstance, from every nation under Heaven, the words of the Italian Endeavorers will not be least welcome.

We are few but faithful to the banner which bears this device: "For Christ and for the Church." What will not God do in the world by means of our Society! Certainly more than we dare foresee or hope. Let us have faith and expect great things.

When springs comes, one cannot say at once what will be the harvest, but we have a sure hope and the abundant blessing is the pledge of it.

The Christian Endeavor has brought into the world a blossoming of faith, zeal, enthusiasm, brotherliness, co-operation in Christian work; what will be the harvest if not a worldwide revival, the maturity of the time for the coming of Christ. May this be your clearest vision in your Convention, in which so many will unite in praises which shall sound like the voice of many waters.

The Italian Endeavorers in whose heart the same faith, the same enthusiasm and the same ideals burn, congratulate you and unite with you in the prayer that you may receive such a blessing that there will not be room to contain it.

For the Italian Union of the Christian Endeavor,

REV. GIUSEPPE SERVI, Secretary.

* * * * *

GREETING FROM SOUTH AUSTRALIA:

Numbers 14:14: "They have heard (i. e., we in South Australia have heard) that Thou Lord art among this people and that Thou Lord art seen face to face and that Thy cloud standeth over them and that Thou goest before them."

Our exhortation is: "Be mighty in that Lord and in the power of His strength." Eph. 4:10.

* * * * *

GREETING FROM THE MARSHALL ISLANDS:

The Endeavorers of the Gilbert and Marshall Islands send heartiest greetings.

REV. C. F. RIFE,
Jaluit, Marshall Islands.

* * * * *

GREETING FROM MADAGASCAR:

I Cor. 15:58: "Therefore, my beloved brethren, be ye steadfast, unmovable, always abounding in the work of the Lord, forasmuch as ye know that your labour is not in vain in the Lord."

Or in their own language:

Koa amin izany, ry vaholahy malalako, dia miorena tsara, aza miova, avy mahafi be mandrakariva amin ny asan ny Tompo, satria fantahareo fa tsy foana tsy akovy ny fikelezanareo aina ao amin ny Tompo."

* * * * *

GREETING FROM HUNGARY. (Cable):

Hungarian Christian Endeavorers greet enthusiastically their American brethren. Our land is also a land of liberty, therefore, many of our compatriots do not wish to be pledged. But we know that to be pledged sincerely to follow Jesus Christ is the true liberty. We have many difficulties; therefore we ask you to pray for us and to come to us to help us. We wish you good success.

A. SZABO,
President Hungarian Christian Endeavor Union.

* * * * *

GREETINGS FROM SOUTH AFRICA:

To Endeavorers Assembled in Convention at Seattle, 1907.

Dear Fellow Endeavorers:

The members of the Executive, and the Endeavorers of the South African Christian Endeavor Union desire to send you heartiest greetings in the name of our common Lord and Master on the occasion of the Twenty-third International Christian Endeavor Convention.

We have not your numbers, and some of the associations which make for enthusiasm and power of demonstration on your side, but as Endeavorers, we have received good and are seeking to communicate it to others.

Remembering that Christian Endeavor came to us from your land, we turn our eyes and thoughts in your direction, with a look of grati-

THE AUTOMOBILE RIDE.

THE BOYS' BAND FROM THE STATE INDUSTRIAL SCHOOL.

tude, but also in expectation of again catching some of that inspiration which your great gatherings are wont to enkindle all round the world.

We pray that the Divine blessing may rest upon you in richest measure, and that the fountain of Christian Endeavor may ever continue to flow rich and strong and pure at its source and we will thankfully drink as it flows on past us to others.

With heartiest wishes that Seattle 1907 may be the "best yet,"
Sincerely yours,
MILDRED CLEGHORN, Secretary.

* * * * *

GREETINGS FROM CHINA:

The Chinese National Christian Endeavor Union, composed of three hundred and ninety Christian Endeavor Societies with a membership of twenty thousand Chinese, sends warmest greetings to the International Christian Endeavor Convention meeting at Seattle.

"God bless you richly. Be fruitful and multiply."

* * * * *

GREETING FROM SPAIN:

"And I heard the voice of the Lord, saying, Whom shall I send, and who will go for us? Then said I, Here am I; send me." Isa. 6:8.

* * * * *

GREETING FROM SOUTH AMERICA:

The South American Christian Endeavor Union, which was installed April 29, at the closing session of the Brazilian and South American Convention by our beloved founder and president, Rev. Dr. Francis E. Clark, sends its first message to the International Convention at Seattle, using the words of Our Lord Jesus Christ, as found in John 17:21:

"That they all may be one; as thou, Father, art in me, and I in Thee, that they also may be one in us; that the world may believe that Thou hast sent me."

All the Christian Endeavor brethren and sisters of the South American continent join in this demonstration of fellowship to the Endeavorers of the Northern continent of America.

ELIEZER DOS SANCTOS SARAIVA,
General Secretary of the South American
Christian Endeavor Union.

* * * * *

GREETINGS FROM BRAZIL:

The Brazilian Endeavorers feel themselves in earnest with the inspiring presence and words of the dear President of the World's Christian Endeavor Union, Rev. Dr. Francis E. Clark, and greet the International Convention at Seattle with the Apostle Paul's words to the Ephesians:

"One Lord, one faith, one baptism, one God and Father of all, who is above all, and through all, and in you all." Eph. 4:5, 6.

ELIEZER DOS SANCTOS SARAIVA,
General Secretary of the Brazilian
Christian Endeavor Union.

GREETINGS FROM ICELAND:

Iceland sends greetings. "They have seen thy goings, O God, even the goings of my God, my King in the sanctuary. The singers went before, the players on instruments followed after. Among them were the damsels playing with timbrels. Bless ye God in the congregations, even the Lord from the fountain of Israel." Psalms 68:24, 26.

* * * * *

GREETINGS FROM TRINIDAD:

Greetings from Trinidad. We cannot give our hands but our hearts are with you. "Grace be with you, mercy and peace from God the Father, and from the Lord Jesus Christ, the son of the Father in truth and love. II John 3.

* * * * *

GREETINGS FROM RUSSIA:

Russia cables, "God with us."

* * * * *

GREETINGS FROM GERMANY:

Germany sends greetings and in the cabled word "Deepening," assures us that the work is deepening and strengthening all along the line.

* * * * *

GREETINGS FROM VICTORIA, AUSTRALIA:

Victoria Union, Australia, sends greetings. We thank God for Christian Endeavor. We rejoice in its hope. We pray that from this Convention may radiate influences which shall bless the world.

* * * * *

GREETINGS FROM MONTREAL, CANADA:

The Societies of St. Matthew's Presbyterian Church extend greetings from the metropolis of Canada, accompanied with the prayer that God may continue to bless the movement that has equipped so many young people for battle under the banner of the Cross.

* * * * *

GREETINGS FROM TOPEKA, KANSAS. (Local Union):

Greetings from Topeka. "The Lord bless thee and keep thee; the Lord make His face shine upon thee, and be gracious unto thee. The Lord lift up His countenance upon thee, and give thee peace. Numbers 6:34, 36.

* * * * *

GREETINGS FROM THE EPWORTH LEAGUE:

Greetings from San Francisco Epworth League Alliance.

A. NELSON, President.

* * * * *

GREETINGS FROM CALIFORNIA:

Alameda County Christian Endeavorers send greetings. John 20:31.

ELLIS E. WOOD, President.

* * * * *

GREETINGS FROM DENMARK:

Denmark regrets that she is not able to have any representative present at the Convention, but sends her greetings and best wishes for the promotion of the cause of Christian Endeavor and asks to be read as her response at the Roll Call, Rev. 5:9, 10.

On behalf of Denmark's Societies of Christian Endeavor,

ANNA SWANSEN, Cor. Secretary,
Copenhagen.

OFFICERS
OF THE UNITED SOCIETY OF CHRISTIAN ENDEAVOR.

Office:
TREMONT TEMPLE, Boston, Mass., U. S. A.

President:
REV. FRANCIS E. CLARK, D. D. LL. D,. Boston Mass.

General Secretary:
MR. WILLIAM SHAW, Boston, Mass.

Editorial Secretary:
PROFESSOR AMOS R. WELLS, Boston, Mass.

Treasurer:
MR. HIRAM N. LATHROP, Boston, Mass.

Publication Manager:
MR. GEORGE B. GRAFF, Boston, Mass.

Denominational Trustees:
President John Willis Baer, LL. D., Los Angeles, Cal.
Rev. W. C. Bitting, D. D., St. Louis, Mo.
Rev. Nehemiah Boynton, D. D., Brooklyn, N. Y.
Rev. Ralph W. Brokaw, D. D., Utica, N. Y.
President C. I. Brown, Findlay, Ohio.
Rev. David James Burrell, D. D., New York, N. Y.
Hon. S. B. Capen, LL. D., Boston, Mass.
Rev. H. K. Carroll, D D., LL. D., New York, N. Y.
Mr. George A. Chace, Fall River, Mass.
Rev. J. Wilbur Chapman, D. D., Winona Lake, Ind.
Rev. Francis E. Clark, D. D., LL. D., Boston, Mass.
Rev. A. C. Crews, Toronto, Ontario.
Rev. W. J. Darby, D. D., Evansville, Ind.
Bishop Samuel Fallows, D. D., LL. D., Chicago, Ill.
Rev. J. H. Garrison, LL. D., St. Louis, Mo.
Rev Alexander Gilroy, Toronto, Ontario.
Rev. Howard B. Grose, D. D., New York, N. Y.
Rev. N. B. Grubb, D. D., Philadelphia, Penn.
Mr. William Phillips Hall, New York, N. Y.
Rev. A. W. Halsey, D. D., New York, N. Y.
Rev. P. S. Henson, D. D., Boston, Mass.

Rev. James L. Hill, D. D., Salem, Mass.
Professor James Lewis Howe, Lexington, Va.
Rev. Wayland Hoyt, D. D., Philadelphia, Penn.
Rev. E. Humphries, D. D., Fall River, Mass.
Rev. W. T. Johnson, D. D., Richmond, Va.
Rev. Gilby C. Kelly, D. D., Lynchburg, Va.
President Henry Churchill King, D. D., Oberlin, Ohio.
Rev. Ira Landrith, D. D., Nashville, Tenn.
Bishop B. F. Lee, D. D., Wilberforce, Ohio.
Rev. J. M. Lowden, D. D., Providence, R. I.
Rev. Cleland B. McAfee, D. D., Brooklyn, N. Y.
Rev. W. H. McMillan, D. D., Allegheny City, Penn.
Rev. Samuel McNaugher, Boston, Mass.
Rev. Rufus W. Miller, D. D., Philadelphia, Penn.
Rev. Charles B. Newman, D. D., Indianapolis, Ind.
Rev. William Patterson, D. D., Philadelphia, Penn.
Rev. Allan B. Philputt, D. D., Indianapolis, Ind.
Rev. F. D. Power, D. D., Washington, D. C.
Rev. Robert E. Pretlow, Brooklyn, N. Y.
Rev. M. Rhodes, D. D., St. Louis, Mo.
Archdeacon J. B. Richardson, London, Ontario.
Mr. William Shaw, Boston, Mass.
Rev. H. F. Shupe, D. D., Dayton, Ohio.
Rev. Wilton Merle Smith, D. D., New York, N. Y.
President George B. Stewart, D. D., Auburn, N. Y.
President James H. Straughn, West Lafayette, Ohio.
Rev. U. F. Swengel, Lewiston, Penn.
Rev. Floyd W. Tomkins, S. T. D., Philadelphia, Penn.
Rev. J. Z. Tyler, D. D., Cleveland, Ohio.
Rev. W. H. Vogler, D. D., Easton, Penn.
Rev. Hugh K. Walker, D. D., Los Angeles, Cal.
Bishop Alexander Walters, D. D., Jersey City, N. J.
Dean H. L. Willett, D. D., Chicago, Ill.
Rev. W. F. Wilson, D. D., Toronto, Ontario.
Rev. C. F. Yoder, Ashland, Ohio.
Together with the President of State, Territorial and Provincial Unions.

INDEX

THEMES OF ADDRESSES

	Page.
Advantages of an Interdenominational Society	57
Affiliated Groups, Clubs and Classes	64
Africa	119, 131
Alaska	134
Around the Christian Endeavor World	103
Brotherhood of Man	122
Brotherhood of Nations	122
Building the Bridge	42
Can a Man Get Beyond the Reach of God's Mercy	146
China	118, 134
Christian Endeavor a World's Organization	61
Christian Endeavor, an Evangelistic Agency	65
Christian Endeavor and Church Union	58
Christian Endeavor and Church Union on Mission Fields	60
Christian Endeavor Fresh Air Camps	99
Christian Endeavor Patriots' League	96
Christian Endeavor—Spirit, not Letter	65
Civic Consciousness	95
Country and Rural Societies	48
Democracy of Christian Endeavor, The	64
Enforcement of Law	96
Europe	119, 133
Fatherhood of God	120
Floating Societies	93, 99
Four Heroes of the West	130
Fresh Air and Philanthropies	93
Gambling Hydra, The	124
Graft and Grafters	93
God's Place for us in Life	113
Great Black Plague	127
How Jesus Won a Soul	145
How the Parents Can Help	34
Ideal Society, The	68
India	118, 132
Influence	114

	Page.
International Brotherhood of the World's Christian Endeavor Union	61
Is There a Yellow Peril	86
Japan	118, 134
Laboring Man and the Church of the Carpenter, The	100
Light of the World, The	146
Memorial Service	63
Mexico	119, 131
Mission of Christian Endeavor in Foreign Lands, The	136, 137
Mission of Christian Endeavor In the Home Land, The	136, 138
Mission of Christian Endeavor in Japan	116
Nation's Greatest Need, A	125
Need of the Day — Trained Christians	32
North America	133
Our Country	82
Our Country: Its Problems and Possibilities	89
Our Millions of New Neighbors	92
Our Unions	46
Pastor's Part in the Training Process, The	36
Peter's Fall and Restoration	146
Practical Plans for Unions to Do	48
Prison Societies	93
Prison Work	99
Right Use of Helps, The	40
Russia	131
Sabbath for Man, The	129
Saloon Power, The	124
Shall Our Unions be Christian Endeavor or General	46
Some Contributions of Christian Endeavor to our Country's Welfare	99
South America	132
Training for Missionary Service at Home and Abroad	133
Training in Expression	37
Training in Giving	39
Training in Prayer—Public and Private	38
Training in Service	40

INDEX

Training the Body 50, 53
Training the Civic Conscience. 91, 95
Training the Children 33
Training the Mind 51, 54
Training the Soul 52, 55
Training the Youth 33
Union Conferences — Their Value and Helpfulness 48
Union Departments and Committees 47
Union Finances 47
Union Programs—How to Prepare Them 48
United States 119
What Can Boys and Girls Do for Christ 42
Woman's Work for the Kingdom 110
Work Among the Japanese in the United States 116
World-Wide Training School in Expression, in Service, and in Fellowship, A 19

RALLIES, CONFERENCES, ETC.

Denominational Rallies
Baptists 74
Christian Disciples 75
Congregationalists 75
Friends 76
Methodists 76
Episcopalian 77
Lutherans 77
Methodist Protestant 78
United Brethren 78
Presbyterians 78
Reformed Church 78
United Evangelical 79
United Presbyterian 79
School of Methods
Christian Endeavor 140
Junior Methods 141
Intermediate Methods 142
Christian Citizenship 142
Evangelistic 143
Temperance Work 143
Missionary 143
Prison Endeavor 144
Bible Study 144
Quiet Hour 145
Esperanto 145

CONVENTION FEATURES

Addresses of Welcome. 14, 15, 16, 24
Banquet, The 155
Automobile Ride 154
Cablegram to the Hague 154
Camp Fire, The 102

Christian Endeavor Prayer Meetings. The 155
Convention Conveniences 155
Convention Shaking Hands.... 17
Dialogue on Memorial Building 49
General Secretary's Report... 26
Glacier Station Prayer Service 12
Greeting from President Roosevelt 16
Hotel Lincoln 155
Illecillewaet Glacier, The..... 11
Installation of Officers........ 17
Japanese Rally, The......... 115
Lake Louise 11
Memorial Fund 137, 138
Memorial Services for Rev C. E. Eberman 10
"Messiah," The 102
Photograph of Assembly taken 23
Poems
"The River of Ice".......... 11
"The Christian Endeavor Pen" 18
"O Golden Day," 31
"The Lost Black Sheep".... 74
Prison Services 154
Response to Addresses of Welcome 25
Seattle's Decorations 156
Seattle's Generosity 157
Seattle Newspapers 156
Steamboat Excursion 155
Sunday at Banff 9
Sunday Services 154-155
Seattle's Welcome 13
Trip Across the Continent.... 9
Weather, The 154

GREETINGS

From India 158
From France 159
From Costa Rico 159
From Queensland 159
From Italy 159
From South Australia......... 160
From Marshall Islands 160
From Madagascar 160
From Hungary 160
From South Africa 160
From China 161
From Spain 161
From South America 161
From Brazil 161
From Iceland 162
From Trinidad 162
From Russia 162
From Germany 162

INDEX

From Victoria, Australia...... 162
From Canada 162
From Denmark 162
From Kansas Local Union 162
From Epworth League 162
From California 162

PERSONNEL

Arnett, Bishop 63
Baker, Smith...36, 76, 120, 136, 150
Bannen, R. G..33, 77, 95, 131, 133, 151
Barraclough, W. H..........34, 76
Barth, F. Edgar............15, 150
Beattie Andrew ....
........78, 86, 103, 118, 134, 137
Boozer, L. M................ 78
Brooks, Walter H...........74, 131
Brown, Paul C................ 142
Carroll, H. K................ 77
Cepherly, Walter K. 48
Chapman, A L................ 75
Chamberlain, William I......
........60, 78, 103, 118, 132, 136
Chipperfield, Sydney 78
Clark, Francis E.............
14, 17, 19, 33, 61, 76, 80, 81, 103
113, 124, 132, 137, 148
Clark, Mrs. Francis E........
.............33, 76, 110, 112, 141
Clothier, Ida C. 111, 143
Cope, Henry F............... 153
Critchow, W. E. 79
Delk, Edwin Heyl..77, 91, 120, 153
De Yoe, Luther.........77, 114, 152
Dickhaut, Benjamin E........ 78
Dickinson, Charles A. 34, 55, 63
Dille, E. R.........37, 76, 119, 153
Edds, Field Secretary........48, 99
Edgar, H. G. 79
Ellis, Miss Sarah 76, 112, 116
Fairbanks, Charles W........
.............74, 77, 80, 81, 82, 86
Faunce, W. H. P. 122
Francis, Alexander..80, 95, 131, 154
Francis, James A............
..........75, 92, 106, 143, 146
Frazer, H. W. 38, 78
Fredenhagen, Edward A....93, 144
Freisch, Wm. H.............. 79
Fout, J. E. 78, 150
Garfield, James R............ 45
Gibbons, Miss Minnie A. 99
Graff, George B...34, 40, 55, 103, 140
Hall, Lewis S. 64, 78
Hall, William Phillips........
.....65, 76, 105, 108, 144, 146, 150
Hamlin, Teunis S............ 63
Harpster, W. S. 35, 79

Hayes, Lilian E. 141
Higby, George S.............. 93
Hill, Claude E. 75, 153
Hill, James L.........24, 37, 57, 153
Hubbell, C. H. 47, 78, 140
Hurd, C. T. 79
Husted, Raymond S. 78
Hutchison, Mrs. Charles...... 141
Ibanez, J. M. 76, 119, 131, 145
Inouye, O. 115
Ivens, William 76
Johnson, Nicholas L. 142
Johnson, W. T................
........57, 74, 119, 133, 134, 152
Judah, Mrs. W. B. 42
Kajiro, Miss J. 76, 111, 116
Kida, Bunji 76, 117, 118
Kinports, Harry A............ 79
Kokendoffer, A. W............ 75
Lains, H. G. 78
Landrith, Ira ....
.........50, 78, 93, 124, 138, 150
Lanning, R. L. 79
Lathrop, Hiram N. ....
..........16, 17, 74, 105, 135, 141
Lathrop, Mrs. H. N........... 110
Layton, P. A. 79
Lee, Bishop B. F. 150
Leech, William H. 76
Lloyd, J. P. D............... 77
Lowden, J. M. 39, 74, 149, 150
McElveen, William T..42, 50, 76, 150
McMillan, W. H...... 79, 86, 129
Magill, O. H. ....●...... 76
Mansfield, J. H. 48
Marks, C. E. 99, 144
Marsden, Edward 78, 134, 155
Matthews, M. A.....15, 23, 124, 149
Mead, Gov. Albert E. 14, 25
Moore, H. C. 24
Moore, James A. 86
Moore, M. A. 75
Moore, Mayor Wm. H. 15
Nakuina, Moses K........... 79
Okajimi, Kinya 116
Okazaki, F. 116
Penrose, Stephen B. L. 130
Perry, R. 116
Pickett, Ethel D. 145
Piles, Samuel 86
Pockman, P. T. 32, 78
Pollock, Rev. John...........
16, 40, 50, 78, 115, 119, 133, 150,
154, 155
Randolph, W. T. 76
Reeves, Carl H... 24
Replogte, Charles 76
Roosevelt, President Theodore 16

INDEX

Sager, N. W. 79
Sawaya, Tatsujiro..76, 115, 116, 134
Scudder, Miss M. K. 110
Shaw, William ....
  17, 27, 35, 46, 49, 86, 93, 102, 115,
  118, 137, 142, 144, 151, 153
Smith, Frank G. 55, 127, 150
Smith, O. L. 53, 75
Sproull, J. T. 93
Stelzle, Charles 50, 78, 99, 105
Stewart, Oliver W. 89, 95, 125
Straughn, J. H. 65, 78
Tarring, Edward 47, 78
Thomson, R. H.............15, 24
Tomkins, Floyd W............
  ...17, 52, 61, 63, 77, 91, 132, 150

Twort, W. J................... 74
Tyler, B. B...58, 75, 93, 122, 133, 152
Van Horn, Francis 76, 118
Vogt, Von Ogden, 46, 64, 78, 127, 152
Ward, A. N................... 78
Ward, George M....24, 54, 76, 154
Walker, Hugh K. 53, 64, 96
Warren, W. A. 75
Wells, Amos R. ....
  17, 48, 49, 68, 76, 79, 86, 96, 145
Williams, J. Edgar 76
Willett, Herbert L. 51, 75, 144
Wilson, William F. ....!...77, 124
Winters, A. A. 79
Withers, Guy M. 40, 75
Young, Grace M. 113

www.ingramcontent.com/pod-product-compliance
Lightning Source LLC
Chambersburg PA
CBHW031346040426
42444CB00005B/207